WRITERS IN CONVERSATION

7	PADDY ASHDOWN
31	ANTONY BEEVOR
53	LOUIS DE BERNIÈRES
69	KENNETH CLARKE
95	J P DONLEAVY
111	RICHARD FLANAGAN
131	DAVID GROSSMAN
155	RICHARD HOLMES
177	KAZUO ISHIGURO
197	PENELOPE LIVELY
217	DAVID LODGE
235	RUTH RENDELL
251	KAMILA SHAMSIE
271	JON SNOW
293	REBECCA STOTT
313	D J TAYLOR
331	ROSE TREMAIN
349	STEPHEN WESTABY

WRITERS IN CONVERSATION
WITH CHRISTOPHER BIGSBY
VOLUME VII

PADDY ASHDOWN

Paddy Ashdown was born in New Delhi in 1941 but raised in Northern Ireland. He served in the Royal Marines and joined the Special Boat Service. He joined the Liberal Party in 1975 and in 1988 became leader of the newly formed Liberal Democrats, a position he held for eleven years. He was subsequently knighted and in 2001 became a life peer. The following year he became High Representative for Bosnia and Herzegovina. He is the author of books about the Second World War including *The Cruel Victory* and *A Brilliant Little Operation*, as well as an autobiography, *A Fortunate Life*.

This interview was recorded at UEA on 19 October, 2016.

BIGSBY: You were born in India and were there until the age of five. Is it right that in that time you began to pick up Hindi?

ASHDOWN: Yes, my dad was in the Indian army. My family actually went out to India in 1805 as soldier adventurers. My father went into the Indian army and ended up as a colonel, although he was most unlike a colonel in almost every way. My mum was down on the plains of India waiting for him to come back, very worried because he came out sick from the jungle. I was left to be brought up by the family servants in the Punjab and they were Muslims, of course, and so I was brought up to the rhythm of Islam and could speak Hindi better than English when I came home. Sadly, all that has gone, although when I learned Malay later on, oddly enough something had clicked in the back of my head. I have this theory that if you are going to learn languages you have channels in your brain that are opened up when you are young.

BIGSBY: Then why did you only get two-and-a-half percent in French?

ASHDOWN: Why did I get only two-and-a-half percent for O Level French? Because I was taught so bloody badly by teachers.

BIGSBY: When I was reading your autobiography, it said of your brother, 'but he died'. But there were three other children who died, weren't there?

ASHDOWN: I am the eldest of seven and, yes, four of my siblings are dead now and it made a real mark on my life. My father's business went bust. He left me behind at the age of eighteen and sailed out of Belfast Lock with my then five brothers and sisters and I didn't see them again. I saw my parents very little between then and when they died. So, I was left behind. This business of bereavement, or separation, has made a very profound impact on my life and the result is that when my kids get ill I just go to pieces completely.

I was four and he was two when my brother Richard died of a tropical disease of some sort. I suppose we would know what it was these days but in those days they didn't. Then my brother Robert died of leukaemia. We were living in Northern Ireland and I am pretty sure he got caught in the winds that blew from Windscale when it burned down. This was when I was fighting a little war in Borneo. Then one of my sisters, twin sisters, was killed in a car accident. She was a nurse in Melbourne. And then, about eighteen months ago, my second brother died, so death and separation have been a tender part of my life.

BIGSBY: You mentioned Northern Ireland and at the age of five you went back with the family because they came from Northern Ireland, your mother a protestant, your father sort-of a Catholic.
ASHDOWN: Yes, a lapsed Catholic, but a Catholic, yes.

BIGSBY: So, between the age of five and eleven you were raised in…
ASHDOWN: A very strong Protestant area.

BIGSBY: Did you have the Orange marches?
ASHDOWN: Absolutely.

BIGSBY: Did you take part in them?
ASHDOWN: No. My grandfather, who was the auctioneer of the little Northern Irish town in County Down called Rathfriland, hated the Orange Lodge, and went out of his way to rescue Catholic families during the Troubles of 1917 and 1918. I hated the Orange Lodge myself so, indeed, did my father. When I went to my first prep-school in Donaghadee at the age of five to six they said, 'Are you a Protestant or are you a Catholic?' and I said, 'I am not sure.' So, I went back and asked my dad, 'Am I a Protestant or a Catholic?' and he said, 'Go back and tell them you are a Muslim.' So, I went back and said, 'I am a Muslim,' and they went, 'But are you a Protestant Muslim or are you a Catholic Muslim?' So, it was all part of my upbringing. I remember the massacre of Muslims and Hindus during the Partition riots when we were leaving India, and it was there in Northern Ireland. It was there in Bosnia. It was there in Northern Ireland when I went back as a soldier, this bizarre, extraordinary, terrifying, phenomenon that people who live next door to each other, who take their kids to school and behave

like decent human beings and neighbours, at one fell, change. Something dreadful happens which tears down that flimsy veil that separates us from the brutes and then the following day, in the name of some bloody, blasted, ridiculous religion or other, they do indescribable things to each other. And once that veil is torn down it takes decades to put back. That has always puzzled me.

BIGSBY: You were sent to school in England.
ASHDOWN: I was.

BIGSBY: So, there was another separation from your family.
ASHDOWN: There was.

BIGSBY: Was it a happy experience, or not?
ASHDOWN: I was bullied a lot and had to fight but, in the end, it was all right, though it wasn't comfortable at the age of eleven for reasons you can imagine. Paddy, by the way, is not my real name. Jeremy John Durham is my real name, but they called me Paddy and it was a nickname that stuck, and I thought it fitted me rather better than Jeremy.

BIGSBY: Didn't you have a report claiming that you were excessively Irish?
ASHDOWN: Yes, I did have that, and I probably was excessively Irish. It was not quite as bad as a report I got from my commanding officer in the commandos who wrote two reports on me; one was, 'Lieutenant Ashdown's men would follow him anywhere, but chiefly out of curiosity.' The second – he was from a frustrated cavalry officer who bred horses – said, 'I would hesitate to breed from this officer.'

I wasn't very good at school, in truth. I was a late developer, which is one of the reasons I hate the idea of grammar schools. I think you need an education system that always gives people a second chance. But frankly I largely wasted my time at school. I would have wasted even more if I had gone to university. I wasted it on rugby and athletics and the girls of the local high school. I had a jolly good time and then, at the age of sixteen, a remarkable friend of mine said, 'Tell you what, Paddy, come to the Poetry Society.' I said, 'The Poetry Society?' but I went along out of respect for him and it literally changed my life. A man called John Eyre, very left wing, introduced me to poetry and to literature and I have been absolutely passionate about that for the rest of my life. He literally changed my life. I had lunch with him in later years with some of his old pupils, all distinguished people like Michael Brunson, the television presenter, ambassadors aplenty, captains of industry, and he knew all of them very well. He knew the parts they had played in the school play. He had never had enough confidence in me to make me anything more than a wordless soldier in *Macbeth* or a monk in *The Ascent of F6*, and he came up to me, looked me in the eye – I was leader of the Lib Dems by then – and he said, 'Ah, yes, Ashdown. You surprised me.' So obviously I didn't make much of an impression on him, but he made a lot on me.

BIGSBY: While you were at school, your father came on rather harder times so that to stay on meant that you needed a scholarship and that scholarship was going to lead you, fairly quickly, into the military.

ASHDOWN: Yes.

BIGSBY: So, you joined the Marines and served in Borneo, hence learning Malay.

ASHDOWN: But do you know why I learned Malay? I was a bachelor then and having got two and a half percent in French I thought, alright, I am going to learn this language, and it is quite an easy language to learn because it is sort of Tarzan English. If you want to say a plural you just say the word twice, so Orang is man and men is Orang Orang, which is quite easy to learn. I discovered that in Malay there was one word which meant 'let's take off our clothes and tell dirty stories', and I thought, goodness me, any language that has that in one word is well worthwhile learning. Unfortunately, I never discovered it, but I learned the language in the process.

BIGSBY: And you learned Chinese as well. In fact, you have a whole array of languages.

ASHDOWN: Yes, some people ask me how many languages I speak, and the answer is I have forgotten six. I can do French better now. So, yes, I am jolly good at languages. I learned Malay, then I learned Dusunic, and then I went off to learn Chinese. Chinese is a monosyllabic language. It is a matter of tone, the sound of a word. So, this leaves an almost inexhaustible capacity for pornographic pun, which the Chinese adore – and they especially adore it when a foreigner, trying to say something polite in Chinese, ends up saying something absolutely disgusting. So here I am sitting round the table with my Chinese language school teacher, my fellow pupils and the whole alumni from the Chinese language school and at one of those moments of silence in conversation that always accompanies conversational catastrophe, I said to my Chinese teacher, a Peking-educated convent-educated lady – at least I thought I said – 'Have you ever flown in an aircraft?' and I got the tones wrong and asked her whether by any chance she had ever sat on a flying penis. And the entire audience, the entire table, collapsed rolling on the floor, so I don't want you to think I was particularly good at all of this.

BIGSBY: I read your account of life in the Marines, fighting your way through forests and wading through mud with creatures all over you. I couldn't quite see what the appeal of this was.

ASHDOWN: Not much, is the answer. It is just what comes along with soldiering. The appeal, without wishing to sound too self-righteous or heroic, because it really wasn't, is very simple. You are nineteen or twenty years old and, in my case, in charge of thirty marines in the middle of a little war and these are men who you admire very much. You are in charge through an accident of birth. Certainly, when I got into the Special Boat Service, with those who are better men than you are, and your job is to command them, you don't want to let them down. You do what is necessary. People think that soldiers die for their country. I don't think many people do. I think you die for the man next door. You die for your mates. That is why you do what needs to be done, and politicians might just like to remind themselves of that once in a while.

BIGSBY: You mention the Special Boat Service and that involved, among other things, being dropped by parachute into the sea to be picked up by a submarine that was submerged at the time. Then, when on an operation, you had to get out of the submarine while it was underwater, get to the surface, swim with your equipment, three miles or more and then, later, swim back out.

ASHDOWN: Not the same night. Two or three nights later, I am glad to say.

BIGSBY: But it is dark. The submarine is not on the surface. It is under the water and you have to have the faith that when you reach a given place that submarine will be there. And if it is not…

ASHDOWN: You go back to the beach.

BIGSBY: Another three plus miles back. Can you just explain the mechanism for getting out of a submarine while it is under water?

ASHDOWN: You put on a breathing set. They lock you out through the conning tower and you wait there. You pop to the surface and then swim ashore and do your job. When you come back, if you are in canoes, the submarine surfaces alongside you. If you are sitting underwater you hear the thrum in your ears which tells you it is coming. It then switches the navigation lights on and you catch it like a London bus as it goes by. Then you lock back in again because you have got a diving set on. We always used to call that the 'Jesus Christ moment' which is, 'thank God it's arrived'. So that was the job we did. It is remarkable what anybody can do in the company of their mates when they are trained up as a team and using high technology. It doesn't require courage. Some of it I loved. I loved the diving bit, but I never liked parachuting at all. It struck me as being deeply irrational to throw yourself out of a perfectly serviceable aircraft on the basis that the thing on your back actually has a parachute in it and not a collection of old socks that somebody had inadvertently left there.

BIGSBY: You subsequently served in Northern Ireland when the Troubles were under way. You were there during that phase when British troops went in to protect the Catholics. But it deteriorated and there you were, from a Protestant mother with a sort-of Catholic father. Did that put you in a particularly strange place?

ASHDOWN: Yes, it did. I had known this was coming from the age of eleven. I knew that the way the Catholic minority were treated in Belfast – denied jobs, denied their human rights – would mean that trouble was coming. I remember having dreams about it and talking to myself about it. So it didn't come as a surprise to me but when it came, I was struck by the way the fact of violence places a carapace over people's true personalities so that the people you thought you knew became different people. The other thing which shocked me and made me think was that I had been doing peacekeeping operations in Aden, and the Persian Gulf, and I suddenly realised that everybody else in the units we were with were treating my fellow citizens in Northern Ireland in the same way as they had a colonial population. I suddenly realised the shock and horror of that and so at this stage I decided that I had done enough soldiering.

BIGSBY: You joined MI6. I have had to look at quite a lot of FBI files and was dismayed by the low level of information in them. A lot of it consisted of open information, newspaper cuttings, domestic and foreign gossip from cocktail parties and stuff like that.

ASHDOWN: I am not going to answer this question, you do realise that?

BIGSBY: I haven't finished yet.
ASHDOWN: I don't care how you ask it.

BIGSBY: On a spectrum from dead drops and safe houses to boring paperwork, where would you have located yourself?
ASHDOWN: I am not going to tell you.

BIGSBY: Now isn't that strange, because the biggest secret of the war was Ultra. Churchill insisted nobody should speak of it and that things should be destroyed. Twenty, thirty years on it was all out in the open.

ASHDOWN: Yes, but you are dealing with human beings here, human sources, and you do not give details of that because you could be threatening the lives of people who are still alive. But I will tell you this story. When I joined this particular organisation, whose building was at 100 Westminster Bridge Road – they have moved now to somewhere much bigger, further down the river – we weren't allowed to say who we were. We were told that the Russians could be watching so if we were entering this building we had to sneak along and dart in. We weren't actually told to wear beards or anything like that, but we had to look not too obtrusive going to work every morning at nine o'clock. So, I remember making determined attempts to see if I could obey this order until I got on the bus, the 159 that I still catch in every morning to the Houses of Parliament, and the bus driver shouted, 'Lambeth North. All spies alight here.' So I thought it was probably worthwhile giving that pretence up for a bit.

BIGSBY: You were attached to the embassy – well, more than attached to the embassy, in Geneva.
ASHDOWN: UK Mission to the UN, doing the day job.

BIGSBY: Then you threw it up for politics and for a party that wasn't actually thriving very much at the time. Why on earth did you do that?
ASHDOWN: I had a day job to do and then I had another job in the UN. I was speaking Chinese at the time so that I was useful because we were re-establishing relations with China. I absolutely adored the job, but this was 1974, the time of the three-day week, and I was representing our country, which was widely regarded as 'the sick man of Europe' and I just couldn't bear it. My wife had a lovely house on the side of Lake Geneva. We could go skiing and walking. We had a boat and lived the diplomatic life, which was a very interesting life, but in the end we both said, 'Are we really going to spend our life like this or are we going to try and do something?' It sounds awfully self-congratulatory but that was the reason why I just felt that I couldn't do other than try and go into politics. We were talking about who runs Britain: is it the trade unions or us? So, we did it because we felt it was right and it

was a very, very, very, very, very stupid and irresponsible decision, though I didn't see that at the time. I wanted to go into politics in my own home town, in Yeovil. I didn't believe in living somewhere else and being an absentee MP, but I didn't even bother to check. In fact, the Liberals had come third and, what is more, the Tories had been in power since 1910. They didn't count their majorities, they weighed them. And I had two children and a wife with no means of support and when I got there the Tories did everything they could to make sure I didn't get a job. So, we were out of work for nine months, and then again for a year when I lost my job in the Thatcher recession. It took me eight years to win the seat. So, so it was the most stupid decision. Some might say 'brave', though I think stupid is a better word. But it was also the best.

BIGSBY: I seem to remember you asking the average age of the constituents and the answer.

ASHDOWN: When I arrived in Yeovil I wasn't actually selected as the prospective parliamentary candidate. I wasn't elected, or anything like that. Nobody else was foolish enough to put their name forward. My party leader had just been arrested for conspiracy to murder and was standing trial in the Old Bailey and we were at six percent in the Polls or less. I managed to get it lower than that when I was leader of the party, and I remember turning up to the great massed ranks of the Yeovil Liberal membership and it numbered eight and the average age was deceased.

BIGSBY: You did eventually get elected at the age of forty-two, at the same time as Tony Blair, and you got on extraordinarily well with him in the early years.

ASHDOWN: Like me, he was somebody from outside politics in that he was not born to the Labour Party. He was a bit of an outsider, as I was for the Lib Dems. We both had the same idea that it seems irrational that people of the centre left, who believe broadly the same things, shouldn't work together. So, we did. We thought it was also very dangerous for our country to see an eternal Conservative government. I thought he was capable of being a great prime minister. So did Roy Jenkins, and we believed that we could put together a coalition government. I still think we could have done and it would have been a much better government had it not been for the constitutional mechanism of the Downing Street removal van which means that you have to make decisions in the aftermath of an election, dog tired and with the bloodstream swilling with testosterone. I thought he was actually a good prime minister right up to the time of the Iraq war. Most of the things he did, particularly Kosovo, where I worked very closely with him, most of the things he did with Sierra Leone, were good. I think his catastrophic error – and I remember talking to him about it – was that he spent the whole of the first term trying to win a second rather than doing things he could have done then but couldn't do later. I thought that was a failure. So, yes, we worked very closely together. We were friends, but note the past tense. I haven't seen him for a long time. I find it very difficult to come to terms with the way he has behaved since being prime minster. I remember saying to him one day, when I was very cross with him because he had ditched Roy Jenkins's commission for a reform of the electoral system, which was the big thing we could have done, 'I think that the ten-year retrospective on John Major will be better than the ten-year retrospective on Tony Blair.' That has turned out to be true. Major wasn't such a good prime minster, but he is greatly loved now, and Blair is not.

BIGSBY: I think he is a little like Lyndon Johnson, whose reputation was destroyed by a war but in other respects was impressive.

ASHDOWN: You are quite right. He set out to do three things and did none of them in the end. He set out to try to realign politics, to see if we could create a centre-left coalition that would make much more sense of our politics, to narrow the gap between the rich and the poor, and to make sure this country was firmly anchored irredeemably in the European future, none of which he accomplished. But he achieved a great deal, particularly on the social front. Paradoxically, probably his greatest achievement will be something that he didn't actually believe in, constitutional change. He never believed in that, never believed in handing over power to others, so that the devolution of power to Scotland and Wales, the use of PR in European elections, were real achievements.

BIGSBY: You, of course, became the leader of a party for eleven years. That is a very unusual distinction.

ASHDOWN: Yes, it is. What I find completely irresistible is if somebody comes up to me and says, 'You can't do that Paddy. It is impossible.' Then I just have to do it. So, I was told it was impossible to win the seat in Yeovil. It took us a long time, but we did in the end. I was told it is impossible to recover the SDP-Liberal alliance and so I am the only political leader in Britain who has presided over a political party represented in the polls by an asterisk, denoting that it had no detectable support anywhere in the land, and rebuilt.

BIGSBY: I would like to turn to some of your books. You have talked about the Special Boat Service and you have written about one of its most famous exploits and those who took part in it. These are those known as the Cockleshell Heroes. That was a very strange venture, with more than a touch of amateurism about it.

ASHDOWN: You bet.

BIGSBY: And absolute derring-do because they had to paddle boats ninety or a hundred miles up the river to Bordeaux to blow up ships. But disasters began quite early. They lost the first people before they had even got into the estuary of the river.

ASHDOWN: I wrote it for the seventieth anniversary, but it was a remarkable episode. They lost eight out of the ten men but that was not great when thousands were dying overnight in the London Blitz. It was a brave attempt. It certainly shocked the Germans and gave great stimulus to the Resistance in the area, but it didn't achieve anything at all militarily.

BIGSBY: Their target was to blow up some ships, but it turned out that the ships were empty, and the river was fairly low so that he ships hardly sank and could be repaired within weeks. But, somewhat bizarrely, they weren't the only people trying to blow those ships up.

ASHDOWN: They weren't because while Combined Operations, situated just opposite No 10 Downing Street in Richmond House, had sent Herbert Hasler and his nine marines about two miles away, in Baker Street, SOE [Special Operations Executive] already had a team of British agents on the ground ready to do the job. In fact, they were going to plant their charges on the same ships when they were full. When they started to blow up by themselves they couldn't work out why. The reason was that the commandos had arrived the night before and Combined Operations and SOE never told each other what they were doing.

BIGSBY: And it is possible that if there had been co-ordination, there might have been some who survived.

ASHDOWN: Absolutely, and not just that but the raid would have worked because they would have caught the ships when they were full. That would have created much greater damage. If only they had worked together it would have worked.

BIGSBY: But it might have saved those who were trying to escape.

ASHDOWN: There is absolutely no doubt it would have done because, as I discovered, there were escape routes already in place. They could literally have walked a hundred metres from the quayside and they would have plugged into a British escape route which would have spirited them over the Pyrenées and home. So, it wasted eight young lives; the Commander, Blondie Hasler, plus one of the Marines, got back over the Pyrenées.

BIGSBY: And you met him.

ASHDOWN: When I was in the SBS I got on a train one day and there was a grumpy old man sitting in the corner. He said, 'Are you going to Poole?' and I said, 'It is none of your business.' And he said, 'Well, are you going to the SBS?' I said, 'Look, you are not entitled to know this information.' When you dig a hole for yourself you then dig it deeper and deeper because when I got out the other end one of my men asked, 'So, what was he like?' I said, 'Who?' He said, 'Blondie Hasler. You were in the carriage with him.' I had been so offensive to him by mistake.

BIGSBY: Most people probably know of this raid from the book or the film, *The Cockleshell Heroes*.
ASHDOWN: The film was wonderful. It inspired me, but it just happened not to be the truth. It is a Hollywood version of it.

BIGSBY: In *The Cruel Victory*, you write about the French Resistance, D-Day and the battle in the Vercors. Can you just explain what the Vercors is?
ASHDOWN: The Vercors is above Grenoble. It is a great isolated plateau with three-thousand-foot cliffs on most sides. Vertiginous roads go up it and this was seen as a fortress that could be captured when D-Day came. The idea was that at the moment of liberation, parachutists would land there behind the German lines and four thousand French Resistance would gather on the mountain tops in this extraordinarily enclosed place. But all the promises that were made to them by De Gaulle and others, that they would have reinforcements parachuted to them and heavy weapons, were betrayed. They were supported by English secret agents who were dropped – including a remarkable man called Frances Cammaerts, and a woman I am deeply in love with called Christine Granville, who was a Pole, the Countess Skarbek. Then the Germans assembled fifteen thousand men, with tanks, aircraft and heavy weapons, and assaulted the plateau. There followed a massacre which in the Nuremburg Trials was second only to Oradour-sur-Glane. Lots of people were killed. It is a tragic story of great heroism, heroism on the ground amongst the young maquisards and unbelievable stupidity at the top. It is dedicated to 'the boy in the white shirt' because literally they left home in their white shirts and died defending the Vercors with Sten guns against tanks. When I was in the SBS we used to have a saying, 'Big thumbs on little maps. That's the way to kill the chaps.' The politicians back there say, 'Jolly good idea if we take this piece here', but they don't realise what war is actually like at the

front line, and the consequence of that can be extremely unpleasant. There are lots of characters in the book, and some remarkably brave ones, but some profound stupid idiots – and in war, stupid idiots kill young men and that is the bottom line.

One of my passions as a politician is that I want to see for myself what is going on and so when the Bosnian war started I went out there in order to see what it was like on the ground. It is a habit of politicians: a) to take decisions without having had any experience of anything else but politics and b) to take those decisions from a long way away which in war time leads to the sacrifice of young men. The Vercors was a very good example of people planning things back in London and Paris which they should have known wouldn't work and people on the ground paying the price.

BIGSBY: They, did, though, play a major role in D-Day.
ASHDOWN: They did, because they probably tied about fifteen thousand German troops down in the South of France waiting for a southern invasion rather than reinforcing the Normandy beaches.

BIGSBY: Your new book is called *A Game of Spies*, and the sub-title is important. It is *The Secret Agent, the Traitor and the Nazi*.
ASHDOWN: These are three men who flittered across my vision when I wrote the *Cockleshell Heroes* book. The secret agent is Roger Landes, a radio operator, a young Frenchman, five feet four, the son of a French jeweller, a Jew – which of course made it slightly more difficult for him. His unique capacity was to be able to vanish into the crowd. He was somebody you just didn't notice and that was why he was, I think, the greatest secret agent dropped into France. The second man was utterly focused, utterly ruthless. He kills far more people than the Gestapo officer – indeed, the Gestapo officer kills no-one. I discovered the memoirs of Friedrich Dohse, the Gestapo officer, the only ones ever written during the war. I already knew enough about the third character, the betrayer. He was the son of a French admiral, a man called André Glandclément: aristocratic, very right-wing,

tall, handsome, striking, impressive, but needy and very, very weak psychologically. He is put in charge of the Resistance. What is betrayal? Betrayal is somebody who betrays their country for another. He always thought he was acting in the best interests of France, that he was still a patriot, but he was a very foolish man, absolute putty in the hands of the Gestapo officer. And here is the counter-intuitive thing – the Gestapo officer is the nicest man in the book. He never tortured anybody, though he didn't mind if others did. He never shot anybody. He took them out to dinner to persuade them. I have been interrogated so I know what it is like. The modern interrogator understands the psychology of the person he is interrogating and uses their psychology to persuade them to cooperate. He captures Glandclément, caught by a double agent, and brings him from Paris to Bordeaux. He has been very badly treated by the Gestapo in Paris, so now he takes him out of his cell and says, 'Come upstairs and sit in front of my fire.' He sits him down and they have a chat.

They talk about politics and his life. What he is doing is assessing the man's psychology, discovering his weaknesses. Then he turns him, and he turns him at first to do a very small thing: to reveal some weapons that have been dropped by the British. Then he draws him in and draws him in and draws him in, so then Roger Landes is betrayed but escapes. The others are all captured or flee. Most of them are shot. Landes gets back to London by travelling over the Pyrenées. He wants to go back but is refused because he is now a blown agent but then they are so desperate to create a resistance organisation in Bordeaux, it having been destroyed by Dohse, that they drop him back in again not thinking he will survive. He manages to raise five thousand men and liberates Bordeaux, Dohse meanwhile escaping. However, when Landes meets De Gaulle the day after the liberation, De Gaulle says, 'you have got twenty-four hours to leave France', because for political reasons he wishes to obliterate all memory of the British-led French Resistance, what the British did to lead the French Resistance. Landes then lives a miserable life having had his best years by the age of twenty-eight. Dohse goes back, is tried, but one of the Resistance agents he had sent to Mittelbau-Dora, a death camp, turns up and startles the court in 1952, when he is on trial for war crimes, saying, 'You were an honourable man. You kept your word. I wish we had had good people on our side like you.' He then goes back to Schleswig-Holstein and spends his life as a wine merchant shipping in wine from Bordeaux – where else?

BIGSBY: Dohse is probably the most fascinating figure in the book, not least because he was fairly low ranking.

ASHDOWN: He was a sergeant and then a sort-of warrant officer and when Berlin said 'no' he just went ahead and did it. He took some incredible risks – including planning, if things went bad, to defect to the British.

BIGSBY: In fact, he ended up almost running a group of the Maquis himself. He was in charge of them and yet they were the Resistance.

ASHDOWN: They were the Resistance and he gave them back their weapons, but not the plastic explosive or hand grenades, and said, 'Okay, we will leave you alone because here's the proposition.' His proposition to the French to betray their country in 1943 was, 'We are going to lose this war.' You would get shot for that if you were a German Officer in 1943. 'After the war,' he said, 'the real threat to Europe will not be the Germans, it will be the Russians from the east. We will need to have a united Europe built on a Franco-German axis, so why not join with us now?'

BIGSBY: The Germans were very successful in rounding up resistance networks. They closed down two of the biggest: Prospero and Scientist.

ASHDOWN: They were very brave people who were dropped in by SOE but boy were they an amateur bunch and very, very snobby, very public school. When Roger Landes was trained, he was trained along with nine others, all of them from public schools, all tall, magnificent. The only one who looked like a Frenchman and sounded like a Frenchman was Roger Landes, so it is not surprising that the rest of them got captured. They were picked up very quickly and so, yes, they were incredibly snobbish and very amateur but better towards the end.

BIGSBY: You point out that the radio operators were sent in all using identical suitcases.

ASHDOWN: All the agents were parachuted in with identical false cardboard suitcases and the same pyjamas, which the Gestapo quite quickly spotted. This is what the head of SOE, Maurice Buckmaster, wrote about Roger Landes in his final report at the end of the war, a comment which portrays all that sense of superiority and snobbishness for which SOE was famous. He wrote of the man who had served him so well, won an MC and bar, wore the ribbon of the commandeur de la légion d'honneur and was arguably one of the most successful agents SOE ever sent into France: 'As a man he was not awfully attractive, and I think his friends are on the whole most unpleasing. I wish he would not wear exotic uniforms, but thank God he doesn't wear much scent like the other Frenchies, but if you want a brave man for a lost venture, choose Roger Landes.'

BIGSBY: The traitor was assassinated but did they always assassinate the right people?

ASHDOWN: No. Bordeaux was known as the most collaboratiist city in France. These guys were selling each other for cases of wine. One was selling downed RAF and US pilots passing through his hands on the escape route at ten thousand pounds a shot to the Gestapo. It is an appalling story of betrayal with everybody fighting each other. Landes was living in a snake pit, a viper's nest, but he was utterly dedicated to succeeding and utterly dedicated to protecting his men, so it was sufficient for him to order an assassination – or, indeed, in one case, assassinate somebody himself, if there was a suspicion. That was enough.

BIGSBY: And there was a broadcast on the BBC congratulating him.

ASHDOWN: There was a broadcast which said, 'You

did jolly well.' If he was going to do his job it was enough that there was a strong degree of suspicion for him to say. 'This man must be killed.' He killed far more men than the Gestapo officer.

BIGSBY: You end the book by explaining what happened to many of the principal players. A number of them ended up in concentration camps where they were hanged – shot in one case, put living into an oven.
ASHDOWN: Three women, yes.

BIGSBY: But what strikes me is the disregard with which Landes in particular was treated. This man, who had done such brave things, been so important to the country, ended up being dominated by his father and largely ignored by the British. The only times things looked up were when he went back to Bordeaux and met these old friends from the war.
ASHDOWN: The point is that we were awash with heroes in 1946, 1947, and yes, they did rather ignore them. To us, it is a great thing because we live such cotton-wool lives that we can't imagine what it must have been like for an ordinary person to face these existential problems day by day. Yes, his was a terribly sad life. At the age of twenty-eight this man controlled the whole of the south-west of France. He decided who lived, who died. He decided what happened. He liberated the great city of Bordeaux largely by himself and his maquisard, then he becomes nothing. He becomes a little travelling jeweller hawking a suitcase full of artificial jewels, costume jewellery, around London, being beaten up by the local gangs, disrespected by his father, living in penury. The other thing is that he – and I think it is the habit of the double agent – lived two lives. Inside his house it's ninety percent or one hundred percent France. He speaks French. Outside, he tries to pretend to be an Englishman. It is a very sad story at the end. He was an amazing man, but I don't think he was a nice man. If someone were to ask me who I would rather have dinner with, I would have chosen the Gestapo officer every time, but he was an extraordinarily successful double agent.

BIGSBY: Why are we so obsessed with the Second World War? Why are you?

ASHDOWN: Why the Second World War? Because the records are still there, because you can touch the tail of history before it vanishes down the black hole. I am also fascinated by moral and existential problems. I am fascinated by the question of betrayal. I have recently come across this extraordinary story which has been well documented but never put together. In 1937 a very extraordinary man of immense moral courage came across to Britain. His name was Carl Goerdeler. He was the Mayor of Leipzig and went to warn the British about the true nature of Hitler, to warn them that we had to take a strong line. He came back along with lots of others, including all Hitler's generals. They warned us in 1938 that he was going to attack the Sudetenland. They told us that they would mount a coup just before he attacked, and they had that coup in place. Five thousand troops were ready to arrest Hitler in the Chancellery, but an hour before the coup was to be launched, Chamberlain pops up and says, 'let's have Munich', which of course gave him Sudetenland without firing a shot. Then these people, led by Admiral Wilhelm Canaris, head of the Abwehr, run a secret organisation which, throughout the war, passes us priceless military information: the date of Barbarossa, the fact that Hitler is going to attack France, when he is going to attack, the fact that it is going to be through the Ardennes, the whole battle plan for Kursk. This is passed to us from inside German Intelligence, with the head of German Intelligence behind it, through two spy rings, one operating to London and Washington, through an extraordinary woman called Halina Szymaska in Bern, who may have been Canaris's mistress, and the other through the famous Lucy ring, which was thought to be run by the Russians but in fact was information supplied by the Germans. These group of people, all of whom died terrible deaths after the 20 July 1944 bomb plot, consistently not only sought to remove Hitler, to warn us of Hitler, to kill Hitler but also passed information which cost the lives of thousands and thousands of German soldiers because they believed that to allow Hitler to win the war would be a calamity from which Germany would be besmirched for a hundred years. They knew what was going on with the Jews and the Poles. They took the decision to oppose him. They gave us that information consistently down the line. They betrayed their country but is it really treachery? Were they in fact acting from some vastly superior moral purpose recognising that the long-term interests of their country, and certainly of humanity, meant that Hitler shouldn't win?

BIGSBY: How have you gone about it? Are there archives?

ASHDOWN: There are archives bloody everywhere. That's the problem. And this time I can't use the French archives, I am going to have to look at the archives in Switzerland, which are in German, and I don't do very good German. I am going to have to look at some archives in Russia because we are talking about one of the principal Russian spy rings, part of the Red Orchestra, one of Russia's great intelligence coups. Nobody has ever connected the fact that this was actually information coming from inside the Abwehr, passed by Abwehr networks through into Switzerland and then handed over to an agent who then transmitted the battle plan the great battle of Kursk, which was the turning point on the eastern front, the largest tank battle of the entire war in which the Germans were fantastically defeated. That information actually reached Moscow from the Abwehr, sent through to Bern, carried by the spy ring Lucy, which didn't know they were getting it from the Germans. It was in Moscow before the German commanders and the front line had it for the battle of Kursk. They were all ready for it when it happened. It will take me a long time to put this together. I have only just connected certain bits of it that make the story stand up and I don't know what to call it. I thought I might call it *The Missed Peace and the Flawed Victory*, because they were prepared to give in on the western front and hand us over the whole of the western European nations, shift all German troops to the eastern front, protect the eastern front from Russian occupation of Poland and we missed the opportunity completely because we refused to believe them. Isn't that a shame? And they were people of extraordinary moral courage who stuck with it right through the war. We think about why we won the war. We won it because of Churchill's magnificent leadership and we won it because of our force of arms. No doubt we won it because of Ultra. But, actually, we also won it in some measure because many Germans took active steps, for which they paid with their lives, to ensure that Hitler didn't win, and I think that story now needs to be told.

BIGSBY: When will we be seeing that?
ASHDOWN: It will take me at least eighteen months to research so maybe in two years or three years' time, I guess.

ANTONY BEEVOR

Antony Beevor was born in 1946 and attended the Royal Military Academy at Sandhurst. He was commissioned in the 11th Hussars in 1967, resigning in 1970. He was knighted in 2017. He began his publishing carer as a novelist but swiftly moved to non-fiction, his first such being a study of the Spanish Civil War. Since then he has published a series of major studies of the Second World War, including *Stalingrad, Berlin: The Downfall, D-Day: The Battle for Normandy, Ardennes 1944: Hitler's Last Gamble* and The Second World War.

This interview was recorded on the 12 October, 2016.

BIGSBY: It is now seventy years plus since the Second World War. There are very few people alive who experienced it. So why does it remain such a fascinating topic to readers?

BEEVOR: There are a number of reasons. One of course is that it has basically formed the world we live in today. Many of the problems that we face in the world come from the Second World War. In the Middle East, the formation of the state of Israel was largely a result of the Second World War. In the Far East, the hatred between China and Japan is still as intense as ever which is entirely based on the war. So, we need to understand it from that point of view. But I think there is another reason why it has such a grip on the imagination of novelists and film makers, and that is the very simple one of moral choice. Moral choice is the essence of all human drama and the Second World War had it more than probably any other period in history. How far could you go to put your own family at risk, in those countries that were occupied, by sheltering somebody who was being searched for by the Germans or by the occupying force? I think it affected everybody's lives in that particular way, so from that point of view I think it has a far greater grip than almost anything else.

BIGSBY: And does that same logic apply to you? Is that what interested you?

BEEVOR: Yes, I think it is, and a need to understand. The reason for doing the big fat book, which came out at twelve hundred pages in the Finnish translation, was that I needed to understand how the whole thing fitted together, how the different theatres of war, whether the Pacific or the Eastern Front or the Western Front, affected each other. In previous books, I had focussed on different aspects of the war – different campaigns or battles – but I really needed to understand how it all came together, and I must say it was quite an eye opener at times, a very useful exercise.

BIGSBY: How did you go about it? The war lasted six years and was fought on five continents, so how did you form a narrative out of all those disparate events?

BEEVOR: To begin with, I was actually quite complacent. Then I started to panic. But you can't really go and sob on your editors' shoulder because you don't want them to panic too as they will think, 'my God, he will never finish the book.' But if you keep your nerve you should be alright. The vital thing, of course, is to get your skeletal structure and if you have got your skeletal structure then gradually it will all start to fit together. One of the best pieces of advice, for novelists as well as for historians, is 'don't write until you are ready,' and especially get the beginning right. Once you have got the beginning right then everything else will more or less follow. Ernest Hemingway and Gabriel Garcia Marquez said 'spend three months on that first paragraph and all the rest will follow'. That may be a slight exaggeration, but they are basically right. You have got to get that beginning right because otherwise you will keep coming back, trying to re-write it, and you will never relax, you will never have, if you like, the confidence of tone of voice and rhythm.

For me, the most wonderful thing of all was to come across this extraordinary story of a Korean soldier who had been forced into the Japanese Army against his will at the age of seventeen, or eighteen. He was then captured by the Russians at Khalkhin Gol, then captured by the Germans and forced into the German army, and finally captured by the Americans in Normandy. He died in Illinois in 1993. It gripped me because my father, who had been with SOE in Italy, told me a story which had always astonished me as a child: that they had captured a soldier in German uniform who looked very foreign and nobody could understand where he came from. Eventually, there was a chaplain with one of the British regiments who had served in India and he tried various Indian dialects and then had an idea and he spoke to him with a few words of Tibetan. The man collapsed in tears. It was the first time he had heard any words of his own language since he had been captured by the Russians, forced into Russian uniform and then been captured by the Germans and forced into service without actually knowing what he was fighting for, what he was doing. For me, then, the story of the Korean was terribly important because it showed the global reach of the whole of the war at the same time as it showed how basically the vast majority of people had no control over their own fate.

BIGSBY: Yes, the essence of war is that it is a massive public event that invades the lives of individuals and indeed one of your strategies is not merely to describe strategies and tactics in a military sense but to drill down into individual incidents in individual lives.

BEEVOR: You need to show what it was like for ordinary soldiers and civilians caught up in this particular horror because there was a period when, I think particularly in the 1980s, oral history became very popular and I never find that entirely satisfying because it lacks context. The vital thing is to integrate history from above with history from below because that is really the only way of showing the effect of the decisions of Stalin or Hitler on ordinary people's lives, people literally being crushed between the two. I was struck by this, for example, when researching *Stalingrad*. It was a battle in which Russian snipers were ordered to shoot down Russian children who had been bribed by German Infantrymen with crusts of bread to fill their water bottles in the Volga because they were so thirsty. It was the children who had been caught, and orphans. There were over a thousand of them still alive who had literally been living off berries and roots and bits of bread which they might have been given by either the German or the Russian soldiers at the end of that battle. That gives you an idea of what some people went through.

BIGSBY: Archives have always been central to you and you went into the Russian archives when they had only just been opened?

BEEVOR: I was phenomenally lucky on timing. We first made our application to the Ministry of Defence in 1994 and I didn't think there was going to be a chance. Then suddenly Rudolf Pikoya, who was the Minister of the Archives under Yeltsin, ordered the Russian Army to open up their archives. They didn't really know what to do because their idea was that foreigners were spies and, as far as they were concerned, secret documents which concerned the Second World War were still secret. It was quite funny because we had to go and negotiate at the Ministry of Defence and with a fairly bluff character who said, 'We have a simple rule in our archives: you tell us the subject, we choose the files.' There was no point in trying to say, 'hang on, that is not quite how it works in other archives.' It was their rules and you couldn't do anything about it, so I said, 'I'm interested in the Battle of Stalingrad. That is what I have been writing about. To give you an example of the sort of material I would love to see, in the German archives the most interesting reports, or the most revealing ones, were by outsiders, by doctors attached to the German army or by priests'. Roar of laughter from the Russian saying, 'no priests in the Red Army.' So, I said, 'No, but what about the political department reports?' and that actually was where the real gold was. But it was the *Berlin* book which was the one which, if you like, 'did for me' as far as Russia was concerned. I was very lucky again there because the window of opportunity was basically from 1995 to 2000. We had just finished the research in the Russian archives when the barrier came down but then when the book came out in 2002 the Russian Ambassador in London, Grigory Karasin, basically accused me of lies, slander and blasphemy against the Red Army. He is now Deputy Foreign Minister under Sergey Lavrov and, three years ago, I remember Catherine Merridale and I were in Estonia at a literary festival and it was while I was on the stage with this Estonian Professor who was interviewing me that she suddenly said, 'by the way, you know that Sergey Shoygu Law went through?' Interestingly, Shoygu, when he was Minister for Extraordinary Situations – wouldn't you like to have that as a title? – wanted to put through this law saying that anybody who criticised the Red Army in the Second World War is liable for up to five years imprisonment. It didn't go through at the time, but he said that the crime was tantamount to Holocaust denial, which I thought was quite an interesting comparison, to put it mildly. Then, suddenly, we heard that the law had gone through so that technically both Catherine and I were guilty. In fact only yesterday the Minister of Culture said that anybody who undermines any of the myths of the Second World

War is guilty. There is a new film which has just come out in Russia, paid for by Putin, by the Kremlin, called *Panfilov's 28 Men*. It is about a supposedly heroic incident in the defence of Moscow, but this was totally made up by a Soviet Journalist and Sergei Mironenko, who is the head of the Russian State Archive, has now been sacked because he said a few months ago that it was totally untrue, the incident never took place. But the point is they have now made a film of it and anybody who undermines that film has been described as 'filthy scum' for touching any of the myths. The myths are sacred.

BIGSBY: And the archives have been adjusted accordingly?

BEEVOR: Funnily enough, last October the Russian Army announced that they had formed a special unit of soldiers, apparently trained in sociology and history, and I can't remember what else, 'to go into the archives to correct the falsifications of history by historians such as Beevor.' So, a curious compliment in a way I suppose but it basically means that they are removing the documents.

BIGSBY: When did the Second World War begin? The problem, surely, is that there is almost infinite regress. Did it start with the Spanish Civil War or maybe the First World War or maybe the Franco-Prussian war? The same thing is true of biography. Do you start with the birth of the subject, their parents, their grandparents, the wider context? You begin your book not on this continent. Why?

BEEVOR: On the Manchuria Mongolian border. Yes, absolutely.

BIGSBY: If not unknown, that aspect of the war is little known.

BEEVOR: Unfortunately, it is too little known because we do not really know the influence of the Sino-Japanese war and a whole lot of other things in the course of the Second World War. This wasn't a very large battle, at Khalkhin Gol, what the Japanese called Nomonhan, but it was actually Marshal Zhukov, or in those days General Zhukov's, first victory. I say it wasn't very large, but there were about fifty thousand involved on each side which was nothing in comparison to some of the titanic clashes we saw later but it was a very influential battle because this was in August 1939, i.e. before the invasion of Poland, which most people set as the start of the Second World War. It was a very influential battle because the Japanese got such a bloody nose that they decided that any plans for invading Siberia, which they had gone into in great detail, were out of the question. They realised that the Red Army was not as weak as many had suspected after the Stalin's purges. Zhukov had basically led them into a trap and was very effective in that particular way. So that is why the Japanese decided to attack south, against the Americans and the British and Dutch colonies, rather than attack Siberia. That is what saved Stalin in 1941.

BIGSBY: One thing I didn't realise was that of the sixty million lives that were lost in the Second World War, twenty million were lost in China.

BEEVOR: Certainly, getting on that way. The figures on China are terribly difficult. I think it is probably boiling down closer to fifteen million but there are some Chinese historians who claim forty million, rather as Russian historians try to claim forty million Russian dead on the basis of birth predictions if everybody else had not been killed already. We reckon nowadays that about twenty-four million Russians were killed, nine million military and the rest civilian. But actually, in terms of the loss of population, Poland was higher. It lost a quarter of its population and in Belorussia it was far higher. It was simply terrifying.

BIGSBY: It seems silly to talk about extremes of violence in war because war is about extremes of violence but, forgetting Europe for the moment, the violence of the Japanese in China is chilling.

BEEVOR: It was not just violence, it was cruelty, real sadism. The so-called Rape of Nanking or Nanjing involved appalling torture. Funnily enough, there was a wonderful German in there who actually saved lots of people by hiding them in the International Zone at considerable risk to himself. He asks himself in his diary, 'why is it that the Japanese here are trying to be so sophisticated, trying to emulate the British Empire in so many ways, and yet they are behaving worse than Genghis Khan?' He was trying to understand and I, too, was fascinated by it, and of course you have got no answer when you have a very ancient culture like Japan. In the Russo-Japanese war, they treated their defeated enemy with a certain amount of grace, but this was no longer the case. They treated their enemy as sub-humans.

BIGSBY: There was a contempt for other races, other countries.
BEEVOR: Yes, it was deliberately racist.

BIGSBY: While in Europe, the Eastern Front was chilling in terms of violence and something more.
BEEVOR: Dehumanisation.

BIGSBY: The Slavs were regarded as an inferior race.
BEEVOR: Yes, and what I found very, very striking – it took me a bit of time, I am afraid to say, to realise this – was that there was a form of self-fulfilling prophecy within the Nazi mind-set. If you treat the Slavs or the Jews as below animals by throwing bread over the wire so that they have to fight amongst themselves because they are starving they can be seen as behaving like animals. So, you are a proving your own racial theory in that way. There was a deliberate element to this total humiliation of their prisoners in that particular way and the diabolical genius of Goebbels, of course, was to realise that hatred wasn't enough. It was necessary to combine hatred with fear. It was almost as if one was the explosive and the other was the detonator and that was how they managed to achieve such murderous intent in ordinary soldiers and many who had never been anti-Semitic before. Some of the worst perpetrators in the Holocaust had never been anti-Semitic beforehand but this is I think one of the chilling aspects of the whole thing. 'When,' people ask, 'will there be a third world war?' I think the answer is 'it's when you start seeing the de-personalisation or the de-humanisation of particular groups, then that is the time to start worrying'.

BIGSBY: There is a detail about life on the Eastern front which stopped me in my tracks. The Germans didn't have the kind of boots they needed but they couldn't get them off the dead bodies because they were frozen, so they cut the legs off in order to get them. For all the grand strategies, the movements of armies across vast tracks of land, it is such details that really bring it home. There is another detail, different but equally compelling. You describe Himmler watching the killing squads at work and deciding that he wants to make it more humane. Not, it turns out, for the victims, but their murderers.

BEEVOR: Not for the victims. Himmler was horrified that so many in the SS Einsatzgruppen were resorting to alcohol and were having nervous breakdowns because of being splattered with brains and blood every time when they were shooting people in the back of the head. That was one of the reasons why the industrialisation of the Holocaust took place. It shifted from what Vasily Grossman called 'the Shoah by bullets' to 'the Shoah by gas'.

BIGSBY: And you point out that the *Einsatzgruppen*, the killing squads, and the Wannsee Conference, which set up The Final Solution, were full of people with doctorates?

BEEVOR: Yes.

BIGSBY: Before the war Germany was thought of as a cultural centre of Europe. Students from America would go and do their doctorates in Berlin. Germans, it appeared, were lovers of art, lovers of culture, and I think we all have a tendency to feel that culture is an antidote to this brutalism but in fact it became its handmaiden during the war.

BEEVOR: I think that is absolutely true. This was always the question: 'How could the country of Goethe and Schiller have perpetrated such crimes?' You can't blame Goethe or Schiller, there is no doubt about that, but your point is absolutely right, and I don't think anybody can argue the fact that you can have art which is also turned into a form of propaganda. A lot of art in history has been propaganda, whether it is the heroic portraits of kings or so forth, but then what we were struggling to see was the idealised Aryan, both male and female in terms of body, so anything which was different to that was somehow dubious or despicable in some form. There was tremendous conditioning. Art, of course, should provoke thought but it can also be a conditioner.

BIGSBY: The epitome of that was in the concentration camps where you had a men's orchestra and a women's orchestra in Auschwitz-Birkenau.
BEEVOR: But that was much more to calm the prisoners when they arrived.

BIGSBY: Yes, but it was also to entertain the officers. Tears would come to their eyes as beautiful music was played by these people who could go into the gas chamber at any moment and whose job was to play while people did go into the gas chamber.
BEEVOR: Yes.

BIGSBY: We have talked about the Slavs and the de-humanisation of them and the Jews, but in both Hitler and Stalin you had people who had the same level of disregard for their own troops?
BEEVOR: Yes.

BIGSBY: That is quite startling.
BEEVOR: Hitler kept on arguing, 'there can be no glory without deaths.' Quite often he was thrilled at the casualty rates, even amongst his own personal bodyguard. Stalin took it to a completely different level. One has to remember that with Operation Mars, just before the great counter-attack, as a diversion Stalin sacrificed two hundred and sixty thousand men in a diversionary attack where the details of it were passed deliberately to the Germans beforehand so that they did not move troops down to the south. I think that that must be the most appalling sacrifice in military history, to have sacrificed that number of men. They weren't given any artillery support. They were just sent again and again into the killing zones.
BIGSBY: When you read books about the Second World War, or watch documentaries, there are very often

assertions that a particular event was the turning point, the thing that shortened the war by six months, twelve months, two years. It was decided in the North Atlantic, by the battle of Stalingrad, by Ultra. Is that fanciful thinking?

BEEVOR: Yes. 'Did Ultra shorten the war'? In films you get that awful weasel thing at the end: 'certain scenes have been changed for dramatic purpose.' My wife will never accompany me to a war film – not that I really go to very many – because she knows I will be grinding my teeth all the way through in frustration. I think one of the great dangers is that the vast majority of the population get their so-called historical knowledge from fiction.

BIGSBY: David Lodge has quoted you as saying that you don't like the biographical novel, even suggesting that the real bits should be in a different font.

BEEVOR: This was in a lecture at the Royal Society of Literature. I thought, let's really stir this one up. I was just saying that there are some wonderful works of historical fiction, but that the danger comes when novelists put thoughts and words into the mouths of real historical characters. I hugely enjoyed Hilary Mantell's *Wolf Hall,* but I was very uneasy about it, purely from the point of view that one doesn't know what comes from verifiable historical sources, what has been invented, what is pure speculation.

BIGSBY: In the post-Brexit referendum world we have seen attacks on Poles, one murdered, others beaten up. I wonder whether there is a lack of awareness of the role the Poles played during the war.

BEEVOR: A total lack of awareness, I am afraid.

BIGSBY: Ten percent of those in the Battle of Britain were Polish and they gave us Ultra. They smuggled out one of the major weapons that the Germans had, and they had a very large Resistance movement and, as you say in your book, suffered tremendously.

BEEVOR: Yes. We have had a very large Polish community in this country ever since the Second World War and we shamefully betrayed the Poles I think, not that there was much we could do. When it came to

Yalta, Churchill was let down by Roosevelt who was not prepared to support the Poles and of course the Poles did feel totally betrayed. The most shameful thing of all I am afraid was Attlee's government when they refused to allow the Poles to take part in the Victory procession for fear of upsetting the Soviets. The British, the Canadians, the New Zealanders all failed to capture Monte Casino but the Poles, suffering appalling losses, took it.

BIGSBY: The Poles will also play a significant part in your next book.

BEEVOR: Yes. This is going to be about Arnhem. I know I have said this before, but it really will be my last book on the Second World War.

BIGSBY: You have said it many times.

BEEVOR: Oh dear, how embarrassing, but in this particular case General Sosabowski had obtained from the British the agreement that all the Polish troops and forces, of which there were considerable numbers, would be under British command but that the Independent Polish Parachute Brigade would be held back for use in Poland for its liberation. It was a fantasy because in those days the aircraft couldn't even fly all the way to Poland with a full load of parachutists and come back but there was tremendous bitterness because this had been a promise, but the Polish Parachute Brigade was involved at Arnhem when their fellow Poles were still fighting in Warsaw in the uprising against the Germans.

BIGSBY: And that was the time when one of our spies, that is to say one of their spies, was smuggling Ultra secrets to Stalin: John Cairncross.

BEEVOR: Yes.

BIGSBY: How significant was that because they were our ally and we were not sharing with them?

BEEVOR: He was doing it as an ally and we were not sharing it, that is absolutely true. At one stage Churchill did want to start sharing it with Stalin but the idea was immediately sat on, not that one can sit on the Prime Minister quite so easily. He was persuaded against it purely because we knew that the Russian radio code systems had been broken by the Germans so that if we had passed information to the Russians the Germans then might be able to work backwards and realise what had happened. That was another reason why De Gaulle was so unhappy because he, too, wasn't trusted purely because we knew that the French radio codes were so easy to break that the Germans would find out immediately.

BIGSBY: Let me turn to your most recent book, *Ardennes*. I note that you don't call it *The Battle of the Bulge*?

BEEVOR: That is very much an American term. In fact, I had to fight a rear-guard battle, which I lost, with my American publishers who insisted on putting it in the sub-title, but I was damned if I was going to have it as the main title.

BIGSBY: You don't actually start this book with that battle, but you start with a brutal battle in a forest. Why did you begin there?

BEEVOR: The Hürtgen Forest was probably one of the nastiest bits of fighting, certainly on the Western Front. There was also real savagery in the Ardennes battle where you had both sides killing prisoners in a way which was truly shocking. The SS started it and the Americans certainly didn't hang back but the fighting in the forest was awful. There was a badly wounded American soldier and the Germans put an explosive charge under him and just left him there. If he moved it would blow up. He survived for three days and three nights and still had just enough strength to warn those who discovered him that there was this bomb liable to go off if they moved him.

BIGSBY: And they developed this terribly ingenious way of killing people because in a forest the lines of fire are liable to be obstructed.

BEEVOR: But if you have tree bursts…

BIGSBY: Which meant that it sent splinters flying down onto those below.

BEEVOR: Imagine what a naval battle would have been like in the eighteenth century. Most of the casualties were from splinters.

BIGSBY: It is amazing the ingenuity fostered by war.

BEEVOR: It is terrifying. War is the greatest accelerant of social change and technological change.

BIGSBY: The depressing fact is that war is a natural condition. There have been few times in history when there has been universal peace.

BEEVOR: Since the Second World War there has only been one year where there hasn't been a war.

BIGSBY: So, in that sense it would seem a default position of human kind?

BEEVOR: It has been argued that far fewer people are killed, proportionately, nowadays by war or violence than in previous centuries, but in the Second World War you would have thought that war was one of the greatest killers of all.

BIGSBY: With sixty million dead. Back to the Ardennes. There is a new book by a German…

BEEVOR: Yes, Norman Ohler [*Blitzed: Drugs in Nazi Germany*].

BIGSBY: He details Hitler's drug-taking which intensified precisely at this period, 1944 to 1945. Do you find that convincing when it comes to explaining something of the Ardennes offensive?

BEEVOR: Yes, I do. It was a brilliant bit of research on his part. This was somebody who was a novelist but proved himself a brilliant researcher, though he was being helped by Hans Mommsen the great German historian to a certain degree. He almost acted as supervisor while Ohler was doing all of this. Ian Kershaw has quite rightly said that this opens a major window into an area which we should have perhaps thought of before. Ohler went through all of the notes of Theodor Morell, Hitler's rather spooky doctor, to analyse what he had been giving him. Here, it turns out, is Hitler, the great vegetarian, getting essence of pig's liver injected into him.

Yet a key part of German propaganda was that Hitler lived such a pure life. He was also getting cocaine and methamphetamine. All these things were being pumped into him. Because of the effect of the botched July plot, Morell was giving him lots of stuff. He was an absolute junkie. The interesting thing is that what Norman has discovered is that in 1945 you start to see Hitler suffering from cold turkey because the aerial bombing has knocked out the factories which were making his favourite drugs of choice. Of course, methamphetamine, labelled as Pervitin, which was far more powerful than Benzedrine, was being given to the German army. Thirty-five million tablets were dished out for the invasion of France in 1940. That is why the Germans managed to dash to the Channel coast. They didn't need sleep. Most of them were probably juddering by the end of it.

BIGSBY: If we put that aside, what was Hitler's objective in the Ardennes? What did he believe he could achieve?

BEEVOR: His Generals were appalled. While he was suffering from jaundice in the *Wolfsschanze* [Wolf's Lair] in East Prussia, he suddenly had this vision. He was sick of the idea of German power being crushed little by little between the Soviet Union and the allied armies in the west, so he wanted to go for a great big gamble. I am sure this was being accelerated because he had this tremendous euphoria when he was being injected with Eukodal, a form of heroin. So, he would have these moments of euphoria where he had this vision that if they launched a sudden surprise attack coming through the Eifel, which was on the German side of the border from the Ardennes, through the Ardennes, across the River Meuse, they could swing north, charge all the way to Brussels and Antwerp and cut off the British and the Canadians in the north on the sea. He then had this fantasy that that would force them into a Dunkirk-style evacuation which would mean the collapse of the alliance. All the Generals were horrified, even Josef Dietrich the SS Commander of the 6th Panzer Army. Field Marshall Von Rundstedt was appalled when he heard that the Americans were referring to it as the 'Rundstedt offensive.' He was deeply offended by that because he thought the whole operational plan was absolute madness. The big mistake that the allies made was to think that the July 20th plot meant that the German army was collapsing, disintegrating and that this was August 1918 all over again. The war was all going to be over in a matter of weeks.

BIGSBY: But we had Ultra?
BEEVOR: Yes, but the trouble is that Ultra was only good when they were using their radios, but they were on radio silence, so nothing was coming through. Also, we got complacent thinking we always knew what was going to happen because we had Ultra. Actually, the Germans were quite clever with their use of diversions. They set up fake headquarters with radio signals going out, so we didn't realise that these two Panzer armies had been concealed in the Eifel. But the real mistake was to believe that because of the bomb plot carried out by German Officers that meant the whole regime was collapsing. It meant the absolute opposite. Because it failed the Nazis now had total control and nobody could ever dare to contradict Hitler.

By the way, in 1944 the British decided to cancel Operation Foxley, the plan to assassinate Hitler, because Hitler was becoming so crazy they knew that they would win the war more rapidly with him in command rather than without him. Medanwhile, Stalin cancelled Soviet plans to assassinate Hitler using a former boxing champion who had been smuggled into Germany, because he was afraid that if Hitler was killed then the western allies might make a deal with a successor government and allow the whole of the *Wehrmacht* to concentrate itself against the Soviet Union.

BIGSBY: If the attack was a surprise, as indeed it was, at first there was panic among American troops, though the Germans in turn were in for a surprise because they really didn't expect the kind of resistance that followed.
BEEVOR: No, they underestimated several things. The fact, as Hitler had said to his generals, was that it depended on shock and brutality because he hoped that

through murder and terror the Americans would collapse completely and that that would leave the way open. But they didn't collapse. He also thought that Eisenhower would have to consult with London and Washington before he could react. In fact, Eisenhower was able to react very quickly. What he also underestimated was the vast mechanical cornucopia of the Americans so that they were able to shift getting on for seventy thousand troops in just over twenty-four hours, bringing in reinforcements from every direction. They also had huge fleets of trucks able to shift out of range the supply dumps of fuel which the Germans needed to capture. So, their timing basically fell to pieces very rapidly and Hitler made another mistake. He insisted on choosing all the routes they would follow without realising of course that what might look okay on the map were little more than cart tracks and after the heavy rains the Panzers chewed up the mud and the poor horses dragging the artillery behind them couldn't even get through the mud properly.

BIGSBY: You mentioned earlier the shooting of prisoners and there was a famous case in which an SS group did do that but more shocking, in some ways, because you expect that of the SS, many of whom had come from the Eastern Front, was that the American troops did the same and the British troops did the same. We have this model in our minds of impeccably behaved British and American troops.

BEEVOR: Military historians, I am afraid, have always tended to cover up the shooting of prisoners, especially by their own side, by their own countrymen. There are no statistics, but I came across enough incidents, involving quite large killings, while writing that particular book. Patton, in his diary, even acknowledged the killing at Chenogne, where the Americans rounded up sixty Germans and shot the lot of them out of anger and bitterness because they had had a really bloody fight. There are many reasons for the shooting of prisoners and I am afraid some of them are purely pragmatic. It is too much trouble to take them back. There weren't that many British involved in the Ardennes but there were a number and there were cases where they did also shoot down prisoners. It has always happened in war. It happened in the First World War, but we never hear much about it.

BIGSBY: You have mentioned American generals, particularly Eisenhower and Patton, along with Bradley, but there was also a British figure involved – Montgomery – and there was considerable tension between him and the Americans. He does not come out of this terribly well.

BEEVOR: Montgomery was given command over the top part of the bulge by Eisenhower because Bradley was below the bulge and couldn't get up there and take control of both sides. So, he had Bradley commanding the southern bit and Montgomery commanding the northern. Montgomery comes across as arrogant. There are different explanations for this. I suggested to Montgomery's step grandson, who lived with him, that Montgomery might have had high functioning Asperger's and he thought this was extremely likely. I subsequently found that there was a Professor of psychiatry at Trinity College, Dublin, who had written a whole paper on the subject back in the 1980s, so it wasn't as if it was terribly original on my part, but I do think that he had a real problem seeing how other people saw him or reacted to him or understanding their point of view. He behaved, I am afraid, in a totally humiliating way towards Bradley. Eisenhower's chief of staff, General Bedell Smith, thought it terribly funny that Montgomery was convinced that Bradley liked and admired him when Bradley absolutely loathed him and of course the trouble really came to a head on the 7th January when Montgomery told Churchill he was going to give a press conference to say what a jolly good chap Eisenhower was and how much we owed to him. So, Churchill thought 'well, that can't go wrong surely?' Oh God, it did, because Montgomery couldn't stop himself and claimed that he had won the whole of the Ardennes campaign himself. Everybody in the audience was just cringing or fuming in anger. The Germans were terribly clever because they picked up on this and did a false broadcast, pretending it was the BBC, basically exaggerating what Monty had actually said thus making it even worse. Most of the Americans who heard it were absolutely convinced it was true. As a result, the British lost almost all influence in Allied councils right up to the end of the war and probably for quite a long time afterwards because it aroused so much anger.

BIGSBY: One last question, if you were writing a job description for a military historian what would you say was required?

BEEVOR: Well there is always the debate about whether or not you need to have been in the army to be able to write about military history. It certainly helps in many ways because you have got to understand why armies work in the way that they do. Funnily enough, they have a certain emotional intelligence when dealing with a crisis, when dealing with tragedy and with death, which is quite effective, but which to an outsider may appear grotesque or ridiculous. So, it helps in that particular way, but I can also think of some women historians who have had no military experience. Catherine Merridale wrote a superb book, *Ivan's War*; Lyn MacDonald wrote excellent books. One of the dangers, of course, is when you get outsiders wanting to impose a certain ideological grid on a subject. War, of course, is a controversial subject and does attract a lot of people but if they tend to come in with their own theories from the civilian world they often get things very wrong indeed. I think one of the most important things in your job description is an open and enquiring mind. I find one of the most exciting things in archives is when you find that assumptions that you have made are totally wrong because then it means you are probably discovering something quite interesting.

LOUIS DE BERNIÈRES

Louis de Bernières was born in 1954. His name has Huguenot origins. He briefly joined the army before attending university. He taught for a while in Colombia, South American literature prompting his first three books. His best-known novel is *Captain Corelli's Mandolin*, subsequently made into a film. His books include *Birds Without Wings*, *A Partisan's Daughter* and *The Dust That Falls from Dreams*. He is the author of short stories and poems as well as being an accomplished musician.

This interview was recorded at the King's Lynn Literary Festival in March, 2017.

BIGSBY: Before talking about your writing, let me ask you abut music. When did your interest in that begin?

DE BERNIÈRES: I acquired a tiny little banjo ukulele when I was about eight and the little book that you got with it had chord diagrams. It was songs like 'All Through the Night', the Welsh hymn? The ukulele was quite hard to tune. I tuned it to my grandmother's piano, which was itself out of tune, but that is really what started me off. I didn't have any formal lessons until I was in my thirties. I had classical guitar lessons, then, later on, I had oboe lessons and got to grade two before I realised that the oboe was satanic – but now I have taken it up again, oddly enough. Then I had flute lessons for many years because I didn't have it inflicted on me as a kid, though actually I rather wish I had.

BIGSBY: What made you stumble on it when you did, then, in your thirties?

DE BERNIÈRES: The thing is people of my generation, boys of my generation, couldn't get a girlfriend unless they played the guitar or had a car. I don't know if you remember parties back in the late 1960s and early 1970s, there was always some boy in the corner getting halfway through a Bob Dylan song while nobody listened. That was me. Like everyone else I was interested in song writers like Tom Paxton, Bob Dylan, Ralph McTell and Paul Simon, but the more I played the guitar, the more I wanted to be a good instrumentalist and so I moved steadily into classical music and traditional music from all over the world.

BIGSBY: But if you had an ambition to be Bob Dylan, didn't you also want to be a cowboy at some stage?

DE BERNIÈRES: Yes, that is true. When I was a little boy my father came out into the garden when I was playing with my friend Gilbert. We were playing cowboys and Indians and I think had tied my sister to a tree and were shooting her with plastic bullets, and he said, 'There aren't cowboys any more. There is no point playing cowboys. Why don't you play soldiers?' Well, that was a bit fatal because he had been in an elite cavalry regiment and wanted me to follow him and so Gilbert and I played soldiers from then on. Ironically, when I went to Latin America at the age of eighteen I actually did work as a cowboy. My father was completely wrong. There are masses of them left.

BIGSBY: And you can throw a rope. Is it called a rope or a lariat?
DE BERNIÈRES: It's a lasso, but there are two different techniques for roping cattle. One is close range; it is the over-the-head kind because if you are close up you can't be waving a rope around you in cramped conditions. But for long-distance throwing, it is a different technique and that's the one I am best at.

BIGSBY: So, you are a horseman?
DE BERNIÈRES: I can ride Western style, yes. I think the British way of riding is a bit cissy.

BIGSBY: In terms of music it is stringed instruments largely, but not exclusively.
DE BERNIÈRES: And woodwind, yes.

BIGSBY: And you not only play them, but you repair them. In that connection I came across something where you were asking if anyone had got a dead tortoise.
DE BERNIÈRES: Yes.

BIGSBY: What do you mean yes? What has that got to do with music?
DE BERNIÈRES: I had a yen to make the ancient Greek lyre, and there is a reason why instruments from the Middle East or Greece are normally round-backed because, originally, they were made of tortoise shells, and you get some pretty big tortoises, so you can make different sized musical instruments out of whatever size your dead tortoise is. So, I was hoping that somebody would send me a dead tortoise – well… a tortoise canopy, so that I could make a lyre.

BIGSBY: Did they?
DE BERNIÈRES: I am not actually going to do this, but I had this stupid idea that because poetry was originally

always recited to a lyre maybe it is something I could try at poetry readings. I have gone off the idea now, but I still want a lyre.

BIGSBY: Worryingly you not only repair instruments but also motorbikes. Somehow, they don't go together, or do they?

DE BERNIÈRES: They do because these days instruments are precision mechanisms. There is always a reason why they are not working. The same is true of cars, and if you analyse it at enough length, with enough acuity, you can always find out what's wrong and put it right. Things like machines and musical instruments are so much easier to deal with than humans because with humans that just doesn't work, does it?

BIGSBY: Can you still play? Because you had a hand problem, didn't you?

DE BERNIÈRES: I had a terrible hand problem called focal dystonia, I also had Dupuytren's contracture, where your fingers fold over. I had the operation for the contracture because otherwise I would have had to give up playing the flute. It was after that that I realised I had focal dystonia as well, which is when a specific area of your body doesn't do what you think your brain is telling it to do so you can try and move that finger and what happens is that another one leaps in the air. So I stopped doing public performances for several years and then, just last year, I found a focal dystonia site where they gave you advice on how to cure it and it actually worked and now I can play again.

BIGSBY: It is not like writer's cramp?

DE BERNIÈRES: No, it is actually in the brain. Particularly with very rapid micro-movements, your brain gets the signals all muddled up and the difficulty of this is that you have got to use your own brain to re-educate itself which theoretically ought to be impossible.

BIGSBY: Have you cut a record?

DE BERNIÈRES: I am making two at the moment. I am recording all the songs I have written ever since I thought

I was Bob Dylan. I have recorded two CDs before which were instrumental, but one of them was crap.

BIGSBY: One of the people you used to perform with, Alison Stevens, died of cancer at the age of forty.
DE BERNIÈRES: Yes. She was probably the best mandolin player in Britain. She had a beautiful delicate and I think feminine way of playing and, yes, we used to do a lot of events together and then she died at the age of forty, a terrible waste.

BIGSBY: And so she would play and you would recite poetry. Didn't you want to be a poet from an early age?
DE BERNIÈRES: Yes, I was convinced, when I knew I was going to be a writer, that I was going to be a poet.

BIGSBY: And it was in your family?
DE BERNIÈRES: Yes, my father writes poetry. He still does. He is 93. He writes very good old-fashioned poetry which reminds you of people like Walter de la Mare or John Masefield, that kind of style, quite well structured and written in modern English. It was my father who told me to give up all this 'thee and thou' stuff. He said, 'you can't do that any more' and I was annoyed because you know 'thee and thou' rhyme with so many things.

BIGSBY: Do you still memorise poems?
DE BERNIÈRES: Yes, from time to time I do. We had to learn a poem a week at school and I still remember them now, and if I come across a poem that I really like I do memorise it.

BIGSBY: One of the things about poetry is that it tends to be written at moments of heightened emotion – birth, love, death, ways of dealing with it, controlling it in some way – and that seems to be true of your poetry too, doesn't it?
DE BERNIÈRES: Yes, definitely.

BIGSBY: And you have said you are an emotional writer. What do you mean by 'an emotional writer'?
DE BERNIÈRES: I mean I couldn't be bothered with

that cool metropolitan cynicism that I associate with places like North London. I grew up in the countryside and though I don't want to slag him off, if you have read Martin Amis's novels you'll know they are really heartless. There is just no compassion or warmth in them and I find that very alien and probably self-deceiving because I don't believe that he is a cold and emotionless person at all. It is just a façade. I couldn't be bothered with the façades that you are supposed to affect.

BIGSBY: You didn't publish your poetry when you were younger, and I read somewhere that you were glad you didn't?
DE BERNIÈRES: Very glad I didn't, yes.

BIGSBY: Why was that?
DE BERNIÈRES: Because I was confused about what poetry was and how it should be done. When TS Eliot came along with his modernist revolution it transformed the way poetry was written. It made life very difficult for other people who couldn't do it as well as he did. He knew how to write traditional poems. He wrote plenty of iambic pentameters but when it suddenly seemed that anything goes it meant that we couldn't actually tell the difference anymore between poetry and chopped-up prose and I found myself in that position. I was writing poems and then wondering if they were really just slightly pretentious prose. I was also very conscious that some of my lines were very lumpy, that they didn't have any music in them, and it wasn't until a few years ago that I finally got to grips with learning how to do metre properly in the old-fashioned way and now I can spot straightaway why one of my lines isn't working. I feel that is something that again should be taught in English classes in school.

BIGSBY: There is a record based on your novels and that is a reminder of the fact that there is music in those novels – *Captain Corelli's Mandolin* is an obvious example. Do you think the poet in you is also visible in the novels?
DE BERNIÈRES: Yes, though that is quite deliberate. For example, you can write more poetically when what you want is a heightened emotional effect in the reader.

So, at the end of *Birds without Wings* there is a passage which is a sort of a monologue where a character is writing about how he feels about his memories and really it was written as a poem.

BIGSBY: When you started writing novels you published three novels in three years, all set in South America. Were they stacked up in your mind and then rushed out?

DE BERNIÈRES: Yes. It is quite easy to write a lot when you begin because your mind is absolutely packed with all you have accumulated, and I didn't start writing flat out until I was in my early thirties. I had had a year in Colombia which was very transformative for me, the most important thing I have ever done from the point of view of forging my outlook on the world. Then, through my twenties, I read nobody but Latin Americans. When everyone else was reading Martin Amis, I was reading Latin Americans, but you tend to get out what you put in, so I am quite cautious about my influences these days.

BIGSBY: What did you find in Latin American literature?

DE BERNIÈRES: I loved the jaunty relish for language that they all seemed to have. They did sometimes write, I suppose, in a slightly mad poetic style. When Marquez came across a word he had never used before, he would stick it on the fridge to remind himself to use it sometime. There was a great love of language with those people and I liked the political realism. However absurd or fantastic the magic realism was there was always a political context, so you might have a girl ascending into heaven taking the washing with her, stark naked, but the context is the long Colombian civil war. So, it was always rooted in a political reality, however strange it was – and I admired it. Later I abandoned magic realism because I began to feel it was simply cheating. If you had books where anything can happen it is obviously cheating, and, in the end, I got really bored with it, but I loved it at the time. What I always tried to keep was the political realism and that relish for language.

BIGSBY: You moved on from Latin America to Greece with *Captain Corelli's Mandolin* and didn't that stir some political reaction?

DE BERNIÈRES: It was cooked up by the *Guardian*. 'Shameless' Milne, who became an adviser to Jeremy Corbyn, is a communist and he noticed that I was contemptuous of what the communist resistance hadn't done and had done in the Second World War and he actually went to Greece to find these old people to tell them I had insulted them and then asked them if they were offended. It was just cooked up by him.

BIGSBY: But now it is a tourist attraction?

DE BERNIÈRES: Yes, you can go to Cephalonia now and go on a Captain Corelli tour where you can find out exactly where I got all my ideas. I am longing to go on it.

BIGSBY: What is the attraction of the past to you?

DE BERNIÈRES: There are different reasons. I am of that generation whose parents went through the Second World War and whose grandparents went through the First World War and we grew up expecting to be annihilated in the next nuclear apocalypse. I remember often counting the number of years between 1918 and 1939 and then adding it on to 1945 to see when I was due to die. I think part of the reason for the incredibly brutal schooling that people like me had in English private schools was because we were being brought up as Spartan warriors in expectation of the next war. Of course, there was a plethora of black-and-white heroic war films after the war which we used to watch when I was young, like *The Bridge on the River Kwai* or *The Cruel Sea* and so on. I remember listening to my parents' stories about the Second World War and my grandfather, my mother's father, was badly maimed in the First World War. He wrecked his legs crashing a Sopwith Camel, so it was all very present to me.

The thing about wars is that they are full of drama. They bring out the greatest extremes in human behaviour and that is easier to write about than people being normal. The one reason I wrote *Captain Corelli's Mandolin* was because when I first went to Cephalonia I realised there had been an earthquake and I thought, God, I have never done an earthquake before. Greece is full of people who came from Anatolia when the Christians were expelled in the population exchange in the early 1920s and they think of Anatolia as their lost paradise, the wonderful place they lost when they were pushed out. Similarly, most of the Muslims were kicked out of Greece and sent to Turkey. They didn't speak a word of Turkish and until very recently there actually was a settlement of people in Syria who still spoke the Cretan dialect. They have probably been wiped out in the civil war, but those people always thought of Greece or Crete as their lost paradise and I have become aware that I have written an awful lot about lost paradises. That is one of my themes.

BIGSBY: You have said that this book is not only the best book you had written but the best book you would write. That rather writes off the future, doesn't it?

DE BERNIÈRES: No, it doesn't. You might grow the world's biggest marrow one year, but it doesn't stop you making nice courgettes in the future, does it?

BIGSBY: Your next courgette was *A Partisan's Daughter*. Up until then you had set your novels in Latin America, Greece, Turkey, places which seemed exotic. *A Partisan's Daughter* is something of a halfway house because there are two central characters, one from this country and another from Yugoslavia. There is a love affair, except neither of them can ever really bring themselves to articulate or even quite understand that.

DE BERNIÈRES: I once actually read the whole of *Being of Nothingness* by Jean-Paul Sartre and it has a section called 'concrete relations with others' in which he talks about how people behave in order to try and make an impression on others, for example the waiter who acts being a waiter. And he says with love what happens is that you present yourself to the other as being better than you really are because you want to attract them. They in return do the same thing and try to present themselves as better than they are and so the people who fall in love are other than the people than they really are and that is why love is doomed because, as time goes by, the pretty façade is peeled away and you are left with somebody else who isn't what you thought they were and you aren't what they thought you were either. So, I used that idea a lot in that book. Roza is trying to impress Chris with all these stories she tells him. She is like Scheherazade. You don't really know whether her stories are true or not, do you? And Chris presents himself as an almost fatherly listener when what he really wants is to have a love affair with her.

BIGSBY: They are both exploitative of one another, are they not?
DE BERNIÈRES: Yes, this is my French novel. I always wanted to write an existentialist novel about a relationship that can't work out, so there is a quote at the beginning of it from one of Camus's novels.

BIGSBY: We see from both people's points of view, and there is one chapter in which you switch multiple times within the chapter. Why did you do that?
DE BERNIÈRES: I think that was a mistake. I am interested in post-modernist technique and so I like to try out all these different tricks. I thought that might be an interesting one to try but when I look at the book now I think I should have not bothered with that one.

BIGSBY: When did that strike you?
DE BERNIÈRES: When it was too late, Chris.

BIGSBY: Sometimes when people give readings they want to revise it.
DE BERNIÈRES: Javier Marias, when he does readings, keeps noticing the mistakes in the punctuation. It is really annoying.

BIGSBY: *The Partisan's Daughter* is set in England but still has this other place. *Notwithstanding* is squarely set in this country, in a village in Surrey. It is very small and full of complete eccentrics. Is this an account of the people who actually live there?
DE BERNIÈRES: Or were there. It is hard for me to know what it is like now, but they got me to open the village fete last year.

BIGSBY: Having read this?
DE BERNIÈRES: Yes.

BIGSBY: This is surely a passing era. It is not just in a Surrey village. When I went to university I don't think I was taught by a single person I would describe as fully sane. They were eccentric.
DE BERNIÈRES: No, I wasn't either. I was remembering in the car, on the way here, a history teacher who had been in the Ghurkhas. He taught us history and geography and every single lesson began with 'when I was out in India', but I would rather have had him any day than a genuine historian.

BIGSBY: *Birds Without Wings* and *The Dust That Falls from Dreams* are substantially set during the First World War. I remember talking to Doris Lessing, who said, 'People think they know the First World War because they know of all the battles and the numbers of dead. What they don't realise is the human impact it had for decades afterwards,' and that is apparent here. There are male characters who just disappear from the story as they disappear from the story of people's lives.
DE BERNIÈRES: A good example is my grandfather who, as I say, crashed a Sopwith Camel. He smashed up both his legs and was not expected to live, but he did. Then they said he would never get out of bed, and he did. They said he would never walk and he taught himself to walk and play golf on crutches. So he was a man of immense determination and courage but he was a very heavy smoker, partly as a tranquiliser, and when he got emphysema in the 1960s he blew his head off with a shotgun. So that is a long time after the war was over, but he was a casualty of it.

BIGSBY: And was it that family history which in part lies behind the novel, that suicide?
DE BERNIÈRES: Yes, that is the reason I was so interested in writing about Gallipoli in *Birds without Wings*, because my grandfather was shot three times at Gallipoli.

BIGSBY: There is, obviously, the violence of the war in this book, but that is not the only violence. A child is killed, and you don't look away. Violence is a presence in your books.

DE BERNIÈRES: As part of the Bob Dylan generation we thought we were pacifists, and there were stupid songs by people like Donovan – 'If only there weren't any soldiers we couldn't fight.' We were really pathetic. He wrote "*The Universal Soldier*. The hippy generation was a bit like that. It had a vapid idealism with no proper political programme and I did think I was a pacifist. It is one reason I left the army, because obviously it was a bit hard to be a pacifist in the army. But when I started writing I realised that I was very, very obsessed by violence. My first three novels in particular were extremely violent. The second one is appalling. But as time has gone by I feel I have purged this. There is less and less of it in my work and if it is there I tend to write about it obliquely.

BIGSBY: You have set yourself quite something in announcing a saga. Presumably a central character will be time because time is passing, the background noise, the history is changing, and they are living within that kind of a context, also a multiplicity of characters too?

DE BERNIÈRES: That is the difficulty, actually.

BIGSBY: Do you have a wall chart, or what?

DE BERNIÈRES: What I normally do is keep an address book with their names in along with crucial facts about each character. It is already alphabetised for you, so it is very easy if you are going to look up a certain person because you can't remember when they were born or whether they have a moustache or what colour their eyes are.

BIGSBY: You are already at work on volumes two and three?

DE BERNIÈRES: Two and three at the same time.

BIGSBY: And you don't write sequentially, do you?

DE BERNIÈRES: No, there is no point. You just write

whichever bit you feel like writing and then you come back and fill in the gaps later.

BIGSBY: How do you do that? Do you keep different files on your computer?
DE BERNIÈRES: Yes. It helps if you do my kind of writing where there are multiple narrators. You can tell an entire sequence of stories from the point of view of one narrator and then do an entire sequence of stories from that of another narrator and then intersperse them, so they alternate. I think I did that with *Captain Corelli's Mandolin*.

BIGSBY: Do you know where it is going to end?
DE BERNIÈRES: Yes, I have written the ending. I have written the last two chapters.

BIGSBY: Of volume three, of which this is volume one?
DE BERNIÈRES: Yes. The difficulty is keeping track of them. There are lots of difficulties with sagas and I really regret that Elizabeth Jane Howard is dead because I could have done with her advice. She was very good at it. I almost regret taking it on because it is so difficult. One of the problems is that if a hundred years goes by obviously most of the characters will die and it just becomes a catalogue of mortality, which is depressing.

BIGSBY: And you are the one who is killing them.
DE BERNIÈRES: I am killing them. One of them gets to ninety-six, though. I was going to hold him back.

KENNETH CLARKE

Kenneth Clarke was born in West Bridgford, Nottinghamshire, in 1940. He read law at Cambridge and subsequently practised law. He was elected to parliament as a Conservative in 1970. In time, he would serve as a minister in various departments, including transport, health and education, as well as taking on the key roles of home secretary and chancellor of the exchequer. Under the 2010-15 coalition government, he became lord chancellor and secretary of state for justice. He was staunchly opposed to Brexit. As the longest-serving MP, he is 'Father of the House'. He is also a jazz aficionado.

This interview was conducted at UEA on 24 November, 2017.

BIGSBY: You have been a minister of state in various departments – health, education, employment. You have been chancellor of the exchequer and home secretary and in your spare time a bird-watcher and an enthusiast for jazz, hence the title of your memoir, *Kind of Blue* – which I take it has a double meaning.

CLARKE: About half the readers recognise it from the Miles Davis album and the others just assume it is a funny reference to my occasionally somewhat personal brand of Conservatism.

BIGSBY: When did this enthusiasm for jazz begin?

CLARKE: It goes back to my teens in Nottingham. I used to go to the local jazz clubs. It was the trad-jazz revival. People like Humphrey Lyttleton and Chris Barber were trying to recreate the music of their idols from the early days of New Orleans and it had quite a big following then. I went there really because they had a bar and you could meet girls, but I got into the music and eventually started buying LPs and extended my knowledge of jazz beyond this English Dixieland. When I get interested in things I usually get rather obsessive about them, so for a long time I immersed myself in jazz and jazz remains the only music that ever moves me. It is the only music that matters to me. I irritate all my other friends because, while I regard a night at the opera as quite entertaining, I don't regard the music as a particularly moving experience. I don't get the chance to go to the clubs much any more. I've lost touch with the friends I used to go with, so it is CDs in the car now. I have got Thelonious Monk in the car at the moment.

BIGSBY: The other side of the title, as you say, is your relationship with the Conservative Party. Is it true that Central Office once tried to stop you going on *Question Time*?

CLARKE: Quite recently, yes. These are the days of message discipline, which Tony Blair introduced. The reason the two major parties are both fading away, I think, is in part is because they have started paying huge sums of money to public-relations experts and filling the place with journalists, getting rid of all the civil service press officers, and using American-type techniques. So, you are meant to go out there and just repeat the slogans, be rehearsed. They therefore were always worried once I had left the government, with its assumption of collective responsibility. They were worried I might go off-message. So, there was one occasion when I had arranged with the producer that I would appear on the programme at Welbeck, I think, when suddenly No 10 rang me up to say that the BBC had asked them to apologise. They had made a mistake and double-booked and would have me on again soon, but not this Thursday. It never occurred to them that I knew the phone number of the producer. So, I rang her up and said, 'What is all this messing about? We fixed this up months ago,' and she said, 'No 10 have just rung me and said they are very sorry, but you have asked them to tell me that you are very ill and not able to do it. They have kindly offered us Matt Hancock instead.' So Matt Hancock was sent back, and I went on and did it. That was the most blatant attempt to get me off the air but, as I say, it was the new politics from 1997 onwards, message discipline with selected spokesmen for the government. Ministers had to get permission before making a statement. Their speeches were vetted, which I think does make the political debate more wooden and rather more artificial than it used to be.

BIGSBY: I'll come back later to your special relationship with the Conservative Party, but first I would like to know how you got into the world of politics. You were born into a working-class family, I think you called it 'an impeccably working-class family'.
CLARKE: It was really, yes.

BIGSBY: Impeccable in what sense?
CLARKE: I genuinely did have working-class ancestors and working-class parents who both came from slightly different, not particularly prosperous, parts of Nottingham, although my Communist grandfather – a shop steward at the Raleigh cycle works – had made himself quite prosperous by being an expert puzzle-solver in the magazines. He won quite big prizes. I was born in Nottingham, but my parents moved to a pit

village in Derbyshire, so for the first ten years I lived in this pit village surrounded by the tips and the collieries. My father was an electrician at the local colliery, but he was moonlighting. He was also running the local cinema in the next village, saving up to make himself a shopkeeper after the war, which he did. So we weren't impoverished. It is just that I was born into an impeccably working-class family in a pretty rough village. It was perfectly all right. Indeed, I quite like Langley Mill. It was not an alien culture to me. I am accused of being part of the elite and I have to confess that at some stage that happens to all of us: you join the establishment even though you don't notice it on the way. That is certainly true by the time you are a former chancellor of the exchequer, but it is no good claiming that I am totally out of touch with the rest of the world.

BIGSBY: You mention one grandfather. You had another who ran away to sea at the age of thirteen, fourteen, and the same grandfather's wife ran away on their wedding day?

CLARKE: That's right. 'Normal for Norfolk,' as they say, and he came from Norfolk but moved to Nottingham. He was an odd-job painter and decorator. He was a delightful but slightly feckless old soul and, yes, he never saw his wife again. He eventually had a partner who was the mother of his first three children. Then she died so I know little about her, but she was my grandmother. He then 'married' the person described as 'her sister', although all my uncles believe it was actually her daughter. No one ever knew, and the family never knew whether the marriage was bigamous because nobody knew whether either the first wife was deceased or had ever gone through any divorce proceedings. Nobody thought he had.

BIGSBY: And then your father ran away when he was fifteen after hitting his stepmother?

CLARKE: Yes. It was quite a normal family really. You are just remembering, in meticulous detail, a lot of things I have mentioned in passing. It was a perfectly reasonable family.

BIGSBY: Were you ever tempted to run away?
CLARKE: No, I never ran away. Well, I suppose I did. I went to university, but that was different.

BIGSBY: The family moved back into Nottingham, although on the border because you were in Eastwood, DH Lawrence territory.
CLARKE: That is where my father's shop was.

BIGSBY: He had more than one shop, though.
CLARKE: Yes, we moved to Nottingham when he acquired another one. We lived in the accommodation at the back of it. That is why I wound up completing my education in Nottingham.

BIGSBY: But you shared a bedroom until you were quite old?
CLARKE: Oh yes, until I left to go to university. It wasn't a very big accommodation. This was the 1950s but at no stage were we a deprived family, or anything like that. He was running quite a successful couple of shops, but it was normal. Living standards were very much lower then.

BIGSBY: You won a scholarship to Nottingham High School. That was as an independent school.
CLARKE: Yes, for some reason the then governors had declined to go to grant-maintained status after the war. So it was an independent school, an academic sweatshop. These were the early years of the 1944 Education Act. The eleven-plus normally took you to the local grammar school, and there were quite a good couple of grammar schools, but if you had done well there was a second eleven-plus and if you passed that there were some places at the local independent school. I was one of the city eleven-plus boys, who were about a third of the intake when I was there.

BIGSBY: It was the school DH Lawrence attended.
CLARKE: Yes.

BIGSBY: And Ed Balls.

CLARKE: I joined all of them. I carried on being quite actively involved with the Bow Group, which was a rising Conservative pressure group in those days which people like Geoffrey Howe were leading, but I also joined the Campaign for Democratic Socialism, which Roy Jenkins was heading at the same time, although long before I graduated I had become a Conservative. Indeed, I was on the Conservative candidates' list before I left the university.

BIGSBY: There is a photograph from your time at Cambridge and there are very identifiable people around you.

CLARKE: Oh yes, the whole lot of them.

BIGSBY: Because they would go on to be in the cabinet. Isn't there a problem about that? To this day sixty percent of Conservative MPs went to public school, nearly thirty percent went to either Oxford or Cambridge. May this not have something to do with the gap between party and people?

CLARKE: I don't think there is a gap between party and people, for a start. It is not as simple as that.

BIGSBY: Didn't the referendum show that?

CLARKE: I think it is true of an awful lot of professional occupations that Oxbridge is quite heavily present. On the other hand, I think the statistics are unreliable. I, for example, am counted as one of these public-school boys because I went to an independent school. My generation emerged during that brief episode of meritocracy which the United Kingdom had in the post-war world. When we all started turning up in government and cabinet we got called the Cambridge mafia, though an astonishing number of us had perfectly modest backgrounds. The idea we were all born to the purple is complete nonsense. Today, of course, there are public-school boys who went to fee-paying school, and that is a pity. I think there is less meritocracy at the moment than there probably was when I was young. The part of Nottingham I lived in, and the village I lived in before, doesn't produce many people who go to university now. It certainly isn't going to produce a chancellor of the exchequer, unless something quite remarkable occurs.

We were a very political generation, left and right. There were huge numbers of people in CND and on the left among my contemporaries. There was a very political phase when I was at university. Vince Cable went off and made a career in the oil industry and then came back and joined us much later. He was a Liberal but all the rest of us were Conservative and about fifteen or sixteen of my contemporaries at Cambridge wound up as Conservative MPs. That was the wave of Butler, MacLeod, Heath. Modernisation appealed to us. Britain was in a pretty bad way after the war. We had won the war and the world owed us a living and didn't understand it. We had got the Empire, but the Empire didn't do what it was told any more, and the Americans wouldn't let us resume our old role. It was a really drab country. We were being left behind. The first wave of 'let's move on from 1930s politics' was led mainly by Rab Butler, our great hero. Suddenly, the Conservative Party was the reforming party – if you were not a Socialist – and it swept us all into its net in the way that the Conservative Party has never done with the young generation on quite that scale since.

BIGSBY: Let me move you on into parliament, because you were elected an MP in 1970. This was when Edward Heath was in charge and within two years you were in government, in that you were attached to the whips' office, and this was at a time when Edward Heath took us into Europe. You have said that if your career had ended then you would have been satisfied. That was presumably because he had done the major thing that you were concerned with at the time?

CLARKE: When you say you want to be a politician it is rather like saying you want to go on the stage. Everybody wants to do it but only one in a hundred will actually make any substantial or lasting career. It requires a great deal of luck, which I have had throughout my life, I readily concede. It is a high-risk occupation. If you have any sense you would take up a political career with reasonably low expectations while if you come from outside parliament – I was a barrister and trying to get into parliament – any kind of office was the giddy heights. I was delighted to be put on the front bench and as it was quite a fascinating time when I was in the whips' office. When I had been a student if I had been told you can spend a year or two on the front bench that would be fine, that's the expectation of the average person who does get elected to parliament, but things kept going my way thereafter. I was very pro-European, as most of my generation of Conservatives were. Some people still remember Dean Acheson's comment that, 'the British have lost an Empire and have yet to find a role'. We were completely at sea in the modern world and the European project, which we should have joined from the first, really inspired my whole generation of Conservative MPs.

The post-war consensus was very cosy but gloriously unsuccessful. With economic underperformance we were becoming a second-rate nation nostalgic for its past and over-basked in its moments of glory. All that got me into parliament. The Conservative Party has been the pro-European party ever since, until eighteen months ago. When I was a whip it was the imperialist wing of my party that rebelled. We hadn't got a Conservative majority to take us in. We had about forty or fifty rebels. They talked of the Commonwealth but with a certain tinge of regret because my hero, Ian MacLeod, had given away what was left of the Empire, for which they never forgave him. So, they were against us, and on the other side was Roy Jenkins. It was the Jenkinsites who gave us the majority. That is why we had a big majority at first, but I had to negotiate with the other side because we needed a lot of them to stay away and abstain when we had a big revolt on our side to get the European Communities Bill through.

BIGSBY: But when Harold Wilson was in power he had problems of a kind which are familiar for the Conservatives. His answer to a split in his party was to call a referendum. So the Labour Party was first in the field with a referendum.

CLARKE: Wilson was a very bright man who didn't have any deep convictions about much and it was a classically Wilson gimmick. He thought, 'We will have a referendum and then the public can decide which way to go.' He wasn't intending to take that much part in it himself. His excuse was that he had renegotiated the financial terms and was putting those to a referendum for approval. As in all referendums, you could spin a coin, really. Then all his colleagues and he would agree that the policy was now to be the one that had won, and he was absolutely horrified to find that most of his colleagues in cabinet had passionate views on one side or the other so that, within a few hours of his announcing this blasted referendum, they were forming committees against each other, on both sides, with the left going off to be anti and the centre right going off to be pro. The Conservative Party was similarly split.

BIGSBY: Can I ask you a fundamental question about the idea of a referendum? Earlier you made a remark about representative democracy, and my understanding of that is that you choose someone whose judgement, at that moment, you trust, whose integrity you trust to make decisions. That is not how a referendum works. If it is a binding referendum…

CLARKE: It wasn't declared to be a binding referendum. It was an advisory referendum, and I still stick to that principle. So do the leavers. Had the leavers lost the referendum they wouldn't have taken the faintest notice of the result any more than they did in the 1970s.

BIGSBY: The phrase that really gets me is, 'the people have spoken', because the people spoke and elected Margaret Thatcher, then the people spoke again and put Tony Blair in office, and then they spoke again and we had a coalition, and then they spoke again and we had a considerable Conservative majority, then they spoke again, and the Conservative majority was cut. Why? Because they always knew that if events changed, and opinions changed, they could vote again. Today, the very suggestion is greeted with howls of complaint. What happened to representative government?

CLARKE: You and I agree on referendums. Every politician of my generation did. Michael Foot would have denounced referendums with the same vigour that Margaret Thatcher did. She said they were just a tool of dictators. You and I still espouse the model of representative democracy. I thought you were about to start quoting Burke's Address to the Electors of Bristol: 'I owe you my judgement. I am not mandated.' The public are quite rightly entitled to change their minds, and do, in reaction to events. They exercise their judgement on whether they are still prepared to accept the judgement of their MP, what the performance of the government has been like, which of the party platforms they think is most suitable in the present circumstances, and then you have an election. A working government, along with all its MPs, is answerable to its electors in the light of how it all works out, when you see how well or badly they have done. That's how a democracy works, and it does ensure a sensible system of governing a modern, complicated state. Ministers, with the instruments of power in their hands, have to deal with hugely complicated issues, most of them never remotely mentioned during the election. A referendum, particularly on a big broad question, with hundreds of sub-questions, asks for a 'yes' or 'no' answer. The things we are bogged down arguing about now weren't even mentioned during the referendum campaign. None of the public knew anything about the single market, or the customs union, because the leavers just assured everybody that our trading relationships would carry on as they are now. There was no reason to break the news. 'The Germans have got to sell us their Mercedes,' said Boris Johnson, as if nothing would change. Now we are bogged down in deadlock. Both parties are divided on details, but I am delighting in the fact that you and I are reinforcing the classic view of parliamentary democracy. I have been in many elections where I have urged my constituents to vote Conservative only for the public to elect a Labour government. When I turned up in parliament, I wasn't told that the voice of the people now ordered me to support renationalisation of steel, and that my personal opinions and judgement should now be totally suspended because the Labour Party had got forty-five percent of the national vote and the Conservatives had only got forty-one percent. That is a completely childlike, daft, way of running a country and a very dangerous way of engaging with a big, international issue.

BIGSBY: Can I take you back to those Thatcher years? She began as an enthusiast for Europe and she signed up to the single market. But things changed.
CLARKE: She fell out with Helmut Kohl.

BIGSBY: But, beyond that, why did she change her mind?
CLARKE: I think she got irritated by being patronised by the male politicians who she met at meetings. That was one of the basic problems. It was the economic Europe she was keen on and she actually furthered the liberal economic policies of Europe as a trading nation. The single market would not have happened but for Thatcher's leadership of her own party, and of Europe. It was her idea to go beyond what we used to call the common market, the customs union, and deepen it to a proper regulatory single market. The political stuff she was more wary about. She had odd hang-ups about Germans, which is why she – rather oddly – tried to resist German reunification after the end of the Cold War. I always think it was to do with the kind of hang-ups she had picked up from Alderman Roberts in her wartime childhood and she could never get on with Helmut Kohl. I think it was partly male patronising of this noisy female colleague he was trying to get on with. She was suspicious of them. Then, after she had gone, all the right-wing newspapers turned Eurosceptic.

BIGSBY: When she fell from power, people were summoned to give their advice as to whether she should continue running. You were the first one in. What was that conversation like?
CLARKE: It was perfectly all right. I was called in first. It was John Wakeham's idea, I think, trying to persuade her that it wasn't going to be straightforward to carry on, that she should summon all the members of Cabinet and see them individually. I think I was called in first because I had been rung up earlier in the day. I had voted for her in the first round and had been rung up and asked to take

over as her campaign manager for the second round of the voting. I think my reply on the phone to whichever friend it was rang me up was fairly robust: 'What second round? Tell her she has been defeated. She should pack it in. She will not win if she runs again. I regard my obligations to her as having been discharged by having voted for her the first time. I probably won't vote for her myself the second time.' So, I think she was advised to see me first because if she calmed me down she would find it was easier with most of the others, which was a mistake. Anyway, she saw me first and the atmosphere was quite calm. We had our usual robust conversation, which was perfectly friendly. I think she referred to it afterwards as my doing my usual candid friend act, so she didn't take to it well afterwards. She said I was being defeatist and I said, 'You have been defeated.' Stacks of MPs were changing their mind. 'They voted for you once, but they are all going to vote for Heseltine in the next round. You are not going to defeat Heseltine. You should retire gracefully.' I compared standing a second time to *The Charge of the Light Brigade* and she ticked me off. I think to her it must have been quite a shock to have the first cabinet colleague quite resolutely telling her that she should retire and resign; she wasn't going to win, he wasn't going to vote for her. It came as a surprise.

Then the whole evening must have become harrowing for her as one after another they all came in and said the same thing, some of them no doubt in a frightfully timid or conciliatory fashion, and others more robust. Chris Patten and I would have resigned from the cabinet if she had come back the next morning to say she was fighting. I couldn't see how I could carry on in her cabinet when in this forthcoming leadership election, I wasn't going to vote for her. Anyway, that was what became that famous conversation. It wasn't a quarrel. I had plenty of rows with Margaret. She enjoyed political rows, but this wasn't the occasion for that. We didn't raise our voices but had a vigorous exchange of views in which she got nowhere in persuading me, as she had obviously hoped she would, to change my mind. It was very sad but if only she had gone when she had finished her first ten years she would have left at the crest of a wave and retired in triumph and been spared the minor humiliation – in the context of her whole career – of having to concede she had been defeated in the leadership election.

BIGSBY: And didn't she become a rather bitter force when John Major was in power?
CLARKE: She took against John, having induced the party to have him as her successor. She became quite embittered quite rapidly, unfortunately, and I just wonder whether the dementia which tragically took hold of her quite quickly was – and it is a sort of slightly tasteless thing to say – already taking hold of her. Her judgement had gone. She had lost her former pretty impeccable political judgement and was persuaded by the worst of her friends that somehow it had all been a plot, she had been betrayed and it was Europeans who were responsible. So, she became ever more vehemently Eurosceptic, although I never heard Margaret suggest we should leave the European Union. It never crossed her mind, I don't think.

BIGSBY: But there was a real bitter internal fight?
CLARKE: There was a bit of internal strife and she spent her time trying to turn people against John.

BIGSBY: And didn't you nearly sign up to a referendum at that point?
CLARKE: John kept being tempted by referendums because referendums are always demanded by the side of an argument that knows it can never get a parliamentary majority. You have got to get round parliament. That's what they are for. The Maastricht Treaty absolutely wrecked the Major government. We achieved quite a lot, actually. The policies still went ahead but the political atmosphere, the state of the Conservative Party, was reduced to rubble really. We couldn't work a cabinet government properly because of the behaviour of the Eurosceptics in it, so people tried to persuade John that a referendum would heal things; the Harold Wilson stuff, the David Cameron stuff, the belief that a referendum would heal the party, and everybody would come together once we had held it. He got tempted occasionally but

Michael Heseltine and I, who were John's leading and most loyal supporters, were so ferociously against the idea it just got shot down.

BIGSBY: And then came William Hague and Iain Duncan Smith?

CLARKE: And then we went through ten crazy years of opposition where we just carried on a civil war as a hobby until Cameron came along. It is always the case with parties who are defeated. When you are first defeated a lot of one's colleagues, a lot of politicians think, 'Well, the public have obviously made some mistake, but they will soon realise that and we'll all be back in office, so it doesn't matter what we do.' So, instead of trying to work out quite how, we contrived to get ourselves buried by Tony Blair in a complete landslide. The party just carried on changing leaders, having internal wars. It wasn't Hague's fault. We had a bit of a rest from the usual civil war. It was the Hagueites versus Portilloistas that half the party seemed to be consumed with in the 1979/1983 parliament. Then we went back to Europe again after that.

BIGSBY: What is it like to be out of power for thirteen years?

CLARKE: I went off and had a business career. I declined to go back into the shadow cabinet. Opposition is extremely frustrating, and I had been in office for a very long time. Unlike most people when they cease to be ministers, who assume they will be back again very soon, I assumed that political history seemed to demonstrate to me that none of us would ever be ministers again, certainly not given the then state of the Conservative Party. And although I wanted to be an MP – I remained the same political addict that I am now – I was not willing to be a shadow minister. I had done that last time we had been in opposition as a junior shadow minister. You sound off but nothing you say, nothing you decide, gets done because it is the other side who are doing things. I went off and did what nowadays former office-holders get ticked off for, I combined being an MP with jobs. I had a portfolio of non-executive directorships which is the main way in which I earned my living, and my one regret was I acquired business experience *after* I was chancellor of the exchequer, which would have been of great value to me had I had it before.

BIGSBY: I will ask you in a second about business, but I want to jump to another job you had which was you were in charge of health?
CLARKE: That was earlier, yes.

BIGSBY: And you had brought in all kinds of reforms.
CLARKE: We were providers of ideas.

BIGSBY: But to jump ahead, Andrew Lansley conducted a top-down reorganisation of the NHS weeks after Cameron had promised not to have one. The King's Fund described it as 'a car crash' and when Vince Cable was here two years ago he said he thought it was the worst mistake the coalition made because it cost three billion pounds and, if you talk to anyone in the health service, they regard it as at best a distraction from what they should have been doing and a distressing loss of money. Why were you supportive? Was it because he was continuing some of your policies?
CLARKE: Everybody followed my policies. The Blair government followed my policies with enthusiasm. NHS England is modifying them quite a bit, which is fine because circumstances change. They were fiercely resisted, mainly by the BMA, who have resisted everything that has ever been done in health since Lloyd George introduced panel doctors. They always attack the secretary of state of the day. Andrew decided to go further; I am a little bit kinder to Andrew, since every time anybody drops a bedpan in a hospital in Llanelli, it is the secretary of state's fault. Every time you want to close some completely obsolete building, workhouses renamed geriatric hospitals, you have ten thousand signatures on a partition opposing it. The first time I went to health, hardly anything seemed to be decided on the basis of what was going to produce the best outcome for the patients in the light of modern medical practice. Andrew tried to address that, but I do agree he over-elaborated it like crazy. A lot of the upheaval was ever-so-slightly

pointless but very expensive whilst it was being carried out, and it was not a triumphant success. He had been working on it for years. He got very immersed in it and made a number of impenetrable speeches explaining it, but everybody now agrees it was a bit of a disaster. This is one of those areas where usually the arguments are slightly exaggerated because the complexities of the subject do actually need more sophisticated and nuanced opinions than public debate usually allows for.

BIGSBY: I want to make a connection between this field we are talking about, and the business that you mentioned. I pass over the fact that as minister of health you would conduct meetings while smoking cigars.
CLARKE: I was the last smoking secretary of state for health, yes.

BIGSBY: What I don't understand is your role at British American Tobacco, because that company manufacturers a product that kills people; it killed two of my friends at the university. In Africa, your company has actually taken cases to court to stop them putting health messages on the packets.
CLARKE: I am not sure it has. Anyway, that was my conservative-libertarian thing. Firstly, I do smoke, so I can't think of anything more hypocritical if I decided I couldn't possibly be a director of a tobacco company. That would have been bizarre. I know the health risks. It is not the most dangerous thing I do. The most dangerous thing I do is driving my car, I am sure, and I have taken other risks in my life. I have even tried motor racing. I have never tried mountaineering, but the law and society allow all kinds of people to choose to do things which are risks. Now there is undoubtedly a health risk and in government I took the view that so long as you properly inform adults of the health risks, the adult is entitled to make his or her own judgement about lifestyle and whether they are prepared to take that risk for whatever satisfaction it is they get out of smoking. So, I just don't share the view of vehement tobacco campaigners. The ethical standards of BAT were extremely high; I certainly insisted on that when I was there. I used to chair our

corporate responsibility board on the basis we had got enough trouble arguing about our blasted product so in every other way we had got to be absolutely sea-green incorruptible. Half the tobacco campaigners – on the basis that anything is justified because the cause is so noble – used to hurl things at the company which simply weren't true. We were always being accused of having child labour on our plantations, which was quite an easy one to answer since we didn't have any plantations and we tried to avoid buying tobacco from anywhere where there was a suspicion there was child labour, in any part of the world. I won't go on but if I thought there was anything morally wrong it would be if you were selling the product and denying, or trying to hide, the fact there was a health hazard.

BIGSBY: I suppose what I was saying is that smoking is down to seventeen percent in this country, so you have lost a market and are looking for another one.
CLARKE: Which has made for a good motive I am sure.

BIGSBY: Anyhow, let me ask about a different area. When you were in control of education you did away with the binary line, the division between polytechnics and universities.
CLARKE: Yes, sure.

BIGSBY: What we now call the post-1992 universities. Did it work out exactly as you expected, because what we have witnessed is the word 'polytechnic' disappearing and the invention of English departments and history departments.
CLARKE: Yes. Some of them promised me they wouldn't do that, but they did. I just decided. It was a personal decision. I just got totally fed up with having, by historical accident, two separate lines of higher education, both obsessed with status, the universities insisting on regarding the polytechnics as second-division institutions and the polytechnics all-consumed with paranoia and wanting the status of universities. We had separate methods of quality control. We distributed money separately to them. Any other country in the

world would have described the whole lot as universities while we were wasting a lot of time and money with two entirely separate organisations both delivering pretty decent standards of higher education. So I had had enough of it and got rid of the distinction. It has worked out as I expected, on the whole, in the sense that I don't think anybody would go around now saying 'You have got to go back to being a polytechnic. You are not a real university.'

BIGSBY: Well, of course, Andrew Adonis would.

CLARKE: Andrew might, but I don't agree with him. Which university did Andrew go to? Some of the ones that were most vehement were not very good universities, or the ones that had rather weak faculties in them. They were frightfully keen on their university status and didn't want places like Hatfield Technical College [now the University of Hertfordshire], which were better than they were, to be given the title of university.

BIGSBY: You have been in parliament for a long time and so are in the position to stand back and judge how things have worked out. This is surely an appalling moment. The referendum was conducted appallingly on both sides. The Conservative Party is tearing itself apart; the Labour Party has members of parliament who hate the person who is the leader, whatever the constituencies say; the Liberals have been reduced to a rump; UKIP has disappeared into the twilight. Have you ever seen a political situation as bad as this one?

CLARKE: I can give you my first short answer: No, no. I have never seen a mess like it. I think it is a turning point of some kind, unless it turns out to be just a temporary phase of chaos. The nature of democracy in the western world is changing. It is not working in the way it used to. We have a more angry, more challenging public. We don't have the set-piece party loyalties, the kind we used to have. All the western democracies are producing strange sweeping protests, clearing out their old establishment and there are very, very disordered debates in most of them. Ours is as bad as any. There is no precedent for this. It is complete chaos, accidental chaos. Trump and all these other populist movements of right and left who loom very big now, in all the democracies of the western world, are partly the result, I think, of the financial crash of 2007/2008, from which most countries have not yet fully recovered. In most countries there is a section of the population that has really been badly hit, left out and feels injured, and isn't benefiting from any recovery that has taken place.

But it also partly goes back to our earlier conversation. There is a dissatisfaction with traditional parliamentary representative democracy and a search for scapegoats who you can be angry with. People are offered simple solutions. You sweep America by saying it is all the fault of the Mexicans. You sweep Britain by saying it is all the fault of Brussels and if you are in France it is all the fault of the Arabs. Macron is the one protest man who has come forward and swept away the old parties, the Hollandes, the Sarkozys. They have all gone into the dustbin, the old prime ministers who thought they were coming back. He happens to be an economic liberal and a social liberal who rather agrees with me. Whether he is capable of delivering anything I don't know, and nobody voted for him in France because of the things he said he wanted to do. In fact, now he is trying to start doing them his popularity has collapsed. They aren't having that. They want the same old unreformed order to be left in place. But I see what is happening in British politics as an extreme example of that. We still have our tribal party politics, even though our two big parties have been hopelessly split for a quarter of a century on our relationships with Europe and, indeed, our relationships with the wider world. We don't seem able to produce any consensus on the subject to settle it and, of course, the triumphant leavers having got over their amazement at winning are insisting that the public, by a small majority, provided a simple straightforward answer to everything with the word European in, anything with EUR in, like Euratom, we must leave as that is what we have been ordered to do. What they are going to, nobody has the foggiest notion and we are all still debating.

BIGSBY: I have a different take on the EU beyond a discussion about trade.

CLARKE: Yes, so do I.

BIGSBY: It was put together in the aftermath of seventy-five years in which tens of millions of people died in Europe waving nationalist flags, fighting one another. Trade was the means, it was not the end. The end was to have peace in Europe. When David Cameron made a comment of this kind he was derided, but in fact that is what always seemed to me the point of what is now the EU. Trade was a way of knitting people together. You surrender a certain amount of sovereignty in return for a common commitment to peace. What we have seen now is the rise of nationalism everywhere. Twenty-eight countries still have not gone to war with one another in the subsequent seventy-five years while just outside we witnessed the slaughter at Srebrenica, the seizing of the Crimea, aggression in the Ukraine. So, I feel I am in this bizarre place. I believe in the European Union for reasons which have nothing to do with the reasons I hear debated.

CLARKE: We have turned to trade as the first big item but again I almost entirely agree with you. It was a political thing. The leavers always reject the 1975 referendum because, quite untruthfully, they say the public were told 'oh, it is just a common market', which is not remotely what they were told by Heath or anybody else. I campaigned in the course of the referendum. It was a political project to produce stability and peace in Europe and the common market was part of it. The arguments in the 1970s, the arguments when the Bill was turned into the Act in 1972, were all about sovereignty and our relations with the Commonwealth, that kind of thing, and it has been extremely successful as a political project. A lot of the generation before mine were pro-European. My old mother-in-law was, who was quite a right-wing Conservative. She was very pro-European because she remembered the war. She remembered two world wars. Her family were involved in the First World War so, 'never again' was the big driving force. Now – and I think it is very important – politically we are in a very dangerous world, as dangerous as at any time since the Second World War and the influence of the European states is maximised when they can operate together and defend each other's interests. If we went back to being twenty-eight separate nation states, the fact is that our influence in the world would just be that of a fading old power and Putin wouldn't bother to pick up the phone to a British prime minister if he was busy. In fact, in many parts of the world they wouldn't be interested in what British opinion was in some crisis.

    I would like to see the EU continue to be beneficial, liberalising, democratic – embracing free market economics. Trade was an instrument at first. That is why the European Coal and Steel Community was first founded. It was because they were military industries, so if you made them interdependent they couldn't arm against each other again. That is exactly how they started and that is what the first founders had in mind. Trade maximises prosperity. Our clapped-out economy of the 1950s and 1960s was eventually turned into a modern, quite competitive, dynamic economy for a long time mainly because of the single market. That is when it really took off. Others take more advantage of it than we do in the modern world, and trade obviously has a bearing on the kind of prosperity each individual government and country can aspire to, but the best political thing that Europe has achieved, and which no one foresaw, was the end of the Cold War, the collapse of the Berlin Wall – the most important moment of my lifetime. I never dreamed I would live to see the Berlin Wall having people climbing over it. That could have been followed by going back to the 1930s, to military dictatorships, revolutions, unsettled states. Instead, enlarging the European Union – in which British governments were the leading and most influential European members – gave them a model to aspire to, a model of liberal democracy, free market economics. Integrating with the western world was, I think, the great achievement. What Romania or Poland would have been had we just gone back to historic Poland, with no real democratic traditions in either of them, I hate to think – even as it is still difficult to keep it together. Unfortunately, we stopped short of the Balkans. We never could bring them in, apart from Croatia and Slovenia. Elsewhere it is extremely dangerous still. Russia is encroaching in Ukraine and so, politically, the

EU remains immensely important but, unfortunately, we are giving a lead in going back to idea of a nineteenth-century-type sovereignty. Apparently, we are going to be a great national power again. Fortunately, all the other treaties in which we have pooled sovereignty no one seems to mind at the moment, but in pulling out of the European project we are going backwards. Palmerston would be proud of us.

J P DONLEAVY

J P Donleavy was born in 1926 in New York City. During the Second World War he served in the US Navy before moving to Ireland, where he studied at Trinity College, Dublin, though without completing his degree. His career as a novelist began with *The Ginger Man* in 1955. Among his many books are *A Singular Man*, *The Beastly Beatitudes of Balthazar B*, and *The Onion Eater*. He was also a playwright. He died in 2017.

This interview was recorded at the King's Lynn Literary Festival in March, 2006.

BIGSBY: I confess that when I heard you talk I was surprised by your accent. I expected to hear bits of American and much more Irish and although I can hear faint evidence of that how would you describe your accent?

DONLEAVY: I have been puzzled by this. I can't figure it out. I can recall it once being said to me, when I first arrived in Ireland off the plane, and it was universally said, 'you don't sound like an American' and I am not sure how that has come about. Various people said it when I was at school. Incidentally, though I didn't exactly hate going there, I have had a letter from that school, Fordham Preparatory school, dated 26 April, 2004. It said, 'Dear JP, Greetings from Rose Hill and Fordham Prep. Sorry your first experience in Fordham Prep came to such a sudden end. We will welcome you back next time you are over here.'

BIGSBY: That is because you were thrown out?

DONLEAVY: Yes, I was thrown out by some stupid body, but I do remember that at the school there was a special course in public speaking, and how you presented your voice and it did occur to me that maybe I was slightly more conscious of the fact that we use some poor language. The same thing was true of my friend from Trinity College, Gainor Crist, and, of course, of Sebastian Dangerfield in *The Ginger Man*. The same things were said of our mutual friend George Roy Hill, director of *Butch Cassidy*. He came from the mid-west, Minneapolis somewhere, and, like Gainor and myself, and was trying to accommodate this evil, short, refined or whatever accent. We were all conscious of having accents which you don't associate directly with America. But if you go to Boston and Charles Street you will see elderly ladies from Beacon Hill, with their canes, going in to buy something in the apothecary using their English accents. Americans are very conscious about it. Southerners quite rightly change them when they get to New York because people tend to mock them.

BIGSBY: Both of your parents were immigrants from Ireland, although they came in under rather different circumstances?

DONLEAVY: My mother may have emigrated to America but she in fact went to America with an Australian uncle who had made a lot of money in Australia and had five sons. He gave each son a farm and then decided himself to travel the world, so he stopped off in Ireland with his family and my mother was fifteen or sixteen years of age and he looked at the children and said, 'which one of you wants to go to America?' When no one said they did he just pointed to my mother and said, 'why don't you come?' She described her trip to America in a very brief sentence, 'a barefoot girl from an Irish field one day and living on Park Avenue the next' working as a companion. So, her life in America was nothing but private railway cars and she didn't know any other style of American life than this.

BIGSBY: How did she come to meet your father then?
DONLEAVY: He was a spoiled priest. I suppose he spoke a bit of Latin and Greek. So, he wasn't one of the destitute, but he did come from a large farm in the middle of Ireland and I believe he went up to study for the priesthood and then there was some crisis on the farm and when the crisis was solved decided that America was better. He was a great horticulturalist and ended up growing orchids on top of the Ritz Carleton Hotel where he had these glass houses, though they didn't belong to him. He became a slightly eccentric gentleman. He kept alligators and monkeys and my mother ran into him because she may have been staying at the Ritz Carleton. So, they met on that level and were a little bit strange in their backgrounds in America. I remember friends of mine, who grew up with me, said 'they had never met people like my mother and father.' This was news to me but evidently they had old world manners. Any young child who came along, or they were introduced to, was always received like an adult and made a fuss of as if they were important, which is unusual for Americans who would say, 'get the hell out of here and stop annoying me.' That's the natural American reaction, which is rather bad.

BIGSBY: You were born in Brooklyn.
DONLEAVY: Yes. The address was no. 8 Willow Place.

BIGSBY: But you were raised in the Bronx.
DONLEAVY: That is true, but it is the worst thing you can say about your background, born in Brooklyn, raised in the Bronx, because it is presumed you lived in poverty, in the slums. I had never gone to Boston, an Irish slum, and didn't know what they were like. I had no idea.

BIGSBY: In fact, as a family you were reasonably well off.
DONLEAVY: Probably, yes, indeed.

BIGSBY: And then you got thrown out of the school. Was this a matter of shame or pride to your parents?
DONLEAVY: Oh, horror. It was disastrous but growing up in America I don't think I really did get along with America.

BIGSBY: When the war broke out, at least when war broke out in Europe in 1939, you were thirteen years old but towards the end of the war were you drafted into the navy?
DONLEAVY: You had to enlist in the navy. You couldn't be drafted. You were drafted into the army and to avoid being drafted in the army what you could do is enlist in the navy.

BIGSBY: You didn't go out to the Pacific while you were in the navy.
DONLEAVY: I went a little bit of a distance. I was assigned to the Amphibious Corps.

BIGSBY: Not a good Corps to be in I wouldn't think?
DONLEAVY: Not a good Corps to be in. The ships I was on were called tank ships, landing tank ships. They converted them to be rocket ships. They closed the deck over, filled the tank deck with rockets and then had the fire power of a battle ship for three hours. As a result, they were the targets for the kamikaze and if they did hit one, that was the end. One hundred tons of rockets went up. But while I was training in the Amphibious Corps, and we were just about ready to go off to the Pacific, we were alerted to the fact that you could sit examinations for the

Naval Academy and so I did sit for them and managed to get through. I was told that there was no chance of my gaining entrance to the Naval Academy, but I did.

BIGSBY: And it was at the Academy that you developed an interest in writing.

DONLEAVY: Yes. What they did first was to send you to a strange school, the strangest school probably ever put together in the history of humanity. It was called the Naval Academy Preparatory School. They would call the most brilliant professors from all over to come and teach at this school and it was a plum thing. They set it up to spite one of the English public schools. It was a beautiful school that used to be a prep school on a beautiful hillside overlooking a cesspit and a river and it was run just like a prep school with all these privileged people. I was one of them, but the other people were either appointed by the President or a Senator and you had this power class of folk the like of which the world has never known because if one of them went to have a meal and their tooth sheared as they bit on something that was a very hard they would phone their Senator right away and complain and their Senator would come up, one Senator after another. There was no control over the school. It was quite an incredible business because of the political power that they had. They all had influence because they had political appointments.

BIGSBY: But there was a culture there that enabled you to be interested in writing.

DONLEAVY: That is exactly it. One of the professors who turned up from the fleet had been a professor at Yale, or some place, and he actually took an interest in writing. His classes were fascinating, and he would encourage people to write their themes because a lot of people in the navy hated to write anything at all on paper. I would write for them. I would have to write for five or six different people and so this professor announced one day, 'there is a ghost writer in this class.' That is really how it happened, and he said, 'I note with this ghost writer there are overtones of James Joyce' and suddenly I had to go down to the school library and look up James Joyce.

BIGSBY: There was an enormous advantage in being in the military because that qualified you under the GI Bill which meant that you would get money for education. How come you ended up not going to an American university but going to Trinity College in Ireland?

DONLEAVY: Initially, it could have happened because my grades were so poor. I might have demonstrated intelligence by getting into this naval academy but otherwise I wasn't having it easy in America. One day I casually asked my mother, 'are there any universities in Ireland?' Men on some of those ships had said things about Dublin which fascinated me, so I wrote off to Trinity.

BIGSBY: Your low grades were good enough for Trinity?

DONLEAVY: They didn't care. They simply said, 'come over.'

BIGSBY: How did your parents feel when you moved to Ireland more permanently, because you were moving against history?

DONLEAVY: It amused my father. I am not so sure it did my mother, though, amazingly, she bought a house there not far from where I lived in Kilcoole which is in County Wicklow. When they came over to visit she was staying in a local hotel and would go out for a constitutional in the morning. She saw this marvellous house standing on the coast of grey stones with a 'for sale' sign. She went in and talked to the lady, had a cup of tea and said, 'Take the for sale sign out of the window.' So that became her summer house and it is still there to this day.

BIGSBY: You don't strike me as having been a very assiduous student?

DONLEAVY: Not tremendously, no.

BIGSBY: It was more a base from which you sallied forth?

DONLEAVY: That's right, but I kept my room somehow and bought myself a piece of land and became a farmer while I was still at Trinity.

BIGSBY: This was in the time you could spare from drinking and having fights.

DONLEAVY: I wasn't as much involved in that as most people would imagine. Certainly, the fighting would happen because I was the only man in Ireland with a beard chasing after the ladies so that they got sick of the chase as it were. I was outnumbered from the very beginning and that did lead to lots of fighting and getting stuck in. I had no choice.

BIGSBY: In one sense Ireland was obviously liberating, but it must also have struck you as a rather curious society, subservient in certain ways?

DONLEAVY: Oh, yes. We had a word that was coined. I haven't seen it used since but people like George Hills and Gainor Crist used the word 'crut.' Someone was 'covered in crut.' They dismissed everyone by just saying they were 'utter crut,' which meant that it was religion, and all the overpowering things that frustrated us. If a woman went to hospital and there was a difficulty in the birth it was the mother's life that would be sacrificed. So, they chose the protestant church.

BIGSBY: Did that oppressive atmosphere inspire an element of rebellion in you?

DONLEAVY: I think so. It was a pretty terrible business but there were enough people around so that places like The Catacombs came into being, places where people made a lot of noise and got in trouble.

BIGSBY: You were ambitious in many ways. You didn't spend all your time in bars, but your ambition might just as easily have led you in the direction of painting rather than writing. In fact, you are a painter. So, was it possible that you might have gone in that direction?

DONLEAVY: It is possible, yes, but I was fascinated by writing. I remember a man who came in and would read things over my shoulders. I might be trying to write on a typewriter, but he was already a graduate of Harvard, a fascist, and so on. I said, 'well, what do you think of that?' He said, 'it stinks,' so finally I got a couple of pieces out of Horace and Virgil and got those printed out and typed out on a typewriter and said, 'how about that? I am trying to really improve now.' He looked at it and I said, 'read it carefully now' – 'That stinks too.' I said: 'well, that is Virgil.'

BIGSBY: If some of the prose which you were now writing was sexually provocative, so were some of the paintings, were they not?

DONLEAVY: Oh probably, yes. I think pubic hair had something to do with this. Some lady came in with her umbrella and was swinging it around the place and she came up to the table where people were selling the tickets. There were three people there and she smashed these people on their heads with her umbrella and said, 'you filthy, filthy people.' I happened to have asked them to mind the desk while I went out and had a drink for five minutes. It didn't seem right.

BIGSBY: By now you were beginning to write *The Ginger Man* and Brendan Behan played a small role in that, did he not?

DONLEAVY: Yes, he did. He must have broken into the cottage when I had gone away for two or three days and, when I came back, I found the hearth blackened and so on. I went out to the studio where I had a desk and a typewriter and next to it was lying a manuscript which I began to read and as soon as I saw the word 'Borstal' I knew who had been, who had broken into the house and vanished with my shoes. Brendan had departed with twenty-six pairs. Americans always have a lot of shoes some would say, and when he came back he was singing down this very isolated farm track. I said, 'Brendan, where are my shoes?' He said 'ah well, I hate getting my feet wet, so I took all your shoes. I wore a pair until they got soaking wet, threw them into a field, put on a dry pair and went down to the pub with dry feet.'

BIGSBY: He was a very strange man with a very ambiguous relationship to the IRA.

DONLEAVY: Yes, he was 'out there,' he said, 'staying at the pub because he had been sentenced to death by the IRA in his absence.'

BIGSBY: I suppose ambiguous doesn't quite cover that does it?

DONLEAVY: But he would say, 'I am glad they didn't sentence me to death in my presence'.

BIGSBY: After a while in Ireland you went back to America and were trying to sell *The Ginger Man* which you could say was something of an uphill task.

DONLEAVY: Yes, it was. In those days in America McCarthy was in full power. I submitted it to the best publishing house, Scribner's, who had me come in and talk about it. Then I moved up to Boston and was working further on it, but they had had a lot of trouble over obscenity with James Jones's *From Here to Eternity* and Scribner's didn't want any more trouble. And, although I tried to see if the book could be in any way changed, and the head editor was very sympathetic given that I was just starting out, I realised that, if they turned this book down, there was no one in America that was ever going to publish it.

BIGSBY: Is it right that it went to forty-five publishers?

DONLEAVY: Probably, something like that over a period of years.

BIGSBY: Then you were back in Ireland again and this is when your contact began with the Olympia Press in Paris, which had a double reputation, that is to say it would publish avant-garde work but also pornography.

DONLEAVY: Yes.

BIGSBY: Were you an innocent abroad? Did you actually realise what was going on?

DONLEAVY: They had a group of young Americans who were quite serious and genuine, and Maurice Girodias looked out for these books under the imprint of the Olympia Press, so it never occurred to me that anything other than this was going to happen to *The Ginger Man*. It was going to go out in this list of pornographic works. Each season there was a new collection of works put out by Girodias and there was talk that the French Government would sue them.

When it came to *The Ginger Man* a small section of eight thousand words had been taken out and published in the *Manchester Guardian*. To Girodias, this meant that, when the government brought in the new act, on the new set of books, he could present this book as having been published in a respectable place. I found a letter just a couple of weeks ago that I must have written at that time. I finally went over to Paris to see what he was saying about the book. He took me out to dinner and apologised for some of the things that he thought he had done with the book though he had been surprised that Nabokov's *Lolita* was being read by people.

BIGSBY: You subsequently had an epic battle with Olympia Press and ended up owning it.
DONLEAVY: I have the greatest stable of writers in the world. Just ask anybody. I buy any writer open for business.

BIGSBY: *The Ginger Man* didn't appear in America until about thirteen years after it had originally been published.
DONLEAVY: It probably would have been, yes.

BIGSBY: And even then there would be more battles to get that edition out?
DONLEAVY: Yes. I only met lawyers in those days.

BIGSBY: Is that where the letters come from in *The Singular Man*?
DONLEAVY: Yes, indeed. I was writing *A Fairy Tale of New York* at the time and couldn't do it because of the amount of litigation. But *A Singular Man* I found I could write.

BIGSBY: You mentioned *A Fairy Tale of New York* and that was staged as a play before the publication of *The Ginger Man* in Britain?
DONLEAVY: Yes, that's right.

BIGSBY: When *The Ginger Man* was put on as a play in Dublin it had to be withdrawn?

DONLEAVY: Yes, after three performances.

BIGSBY: Because?

DONLEAVY: The nature of the play and I believe an insult to religion and insults to all Catholics and disgusting and –

BIGSBY: This is the son of a person who trained to be a priest? Were you tempted to become a playwright because that was very successful. You won an award for it.

DONLEAVY: I am not sure, though I remember that somebody said to me, 'one thing is for sure, you will never make a play out of *The Ginger Man*,' and I just thought to myself, 'I wonder.' So, I had to sit down to see if I could revise it and do something with it as a play and that is how I started off as a playwright.

BIGSBY: When I read your prose I feel that you ought to be writing like Kerouac on a great roll of paper because it flows so easily, and yet when you are writing do you still work in these small notebooks?

DONLEAVY: Yes, indeed I do and in a strange way some of my manuscripts are written like that. When I have a whole draft, it gets to thirty or forty feet long, but that only applies to about three or four, maybe four or five of my books. Maybe *The Destinies of Darcy Dancer, Gentleman.*

BIGSBY: *Darcy Dancer* books are a bit surprising for me because they are about a different kind of Ireland.

DONLEAVY: Yes.

BIGSBY: An Ireland that is still there or has gone?

DONLEAVY: It has gone but suddenly you will get reminded of it still. Something will crop up and it is very disturbing if it does. The old Ireland is there, the odd glance.

BIGSBY: You have a double profession now. You are a writer but also a serious farmer.

DONLEAVY: Not serious perhaps but I must confess I have a very strange herd. It is one of the few herds in the world which never has had anything to eat but grass, nothing but straw, and they graze around and grow to old age. Some of the cows are fifteen or sixteen and they cheat all the young animals out of the hay. It is quite a remarkable thing when you see this herd. It is one of the few herds you can walk through and they might look at you, but they continue on grazing. I have discovered that some farmers in Ireland, serious farmers, would buy animals and bring them back to their farms just to look at them and stand near them. No cow in Ireland will normally stand near to a farmer, especially when he is quick.

BIGSBY: You live in a huge house.
DONLEAVY: Yes, Levington Park.

BIGSBY: And you live in it on your own, which surely creates certain problems. If you are in one part of it and you want something from another part of it what do you do?
DONLEAVY: Well, then you have to go for a hundred yards' walk.

BIGSBY: This is surely not the life style you would have anticipated when you were living in the Bronx, though not in poverty as we have established. You have moved into a wholly different world?
DONLEAVY: Yes, it is true, but I did frequently live in the country when I was in the United States, but I didn't grow up in America. In Ireland I was never allowed a drink of coca cola or drinks of that nature. No food was ever brought into the house because we had food cellars. Everything was bottled, everything was preserved, nothing was ever bought. I had to take cod liver oil always and a draught of iodine and a glass of water every day, all kinds of things that Americans never engaged in. I used to feel embarrassed if I visited some friend's house and saw his refrigerator full of all these fizzy drinks and things though my parents knew all about what we know about today, organic things, while I am an organic simpleton.

BIGSBY: *The Ginger Man* has, as far as I know, never been out of print. So that is more than half a century from the original publication, though not the version that you particularly like. There is something odd about having such a dominant book in your life. I confess I have always liked *The Singular Man*. Do you just take pride in *The Ginger Man* or is there something oppressive in the fact that that is your first of your books that comes into people's minds?

DONLEAVY: I think I am lucky to have any notice at all. The reason I ever got anywhere is because somebody might say to another person, 'have you ever heard of *The Ginger Man* or J P Donleavy?' and they will say, 'No, I have never heard of him.' Then the other person gets very angry. People get angry who had read, say, *The Onion Eaters* which is one of the sleeping books in all my work and is out of print, though actually almost all my books have stayed in print the years. They are not in print in Britain, but they are in America. *The Onion Eaters* has always fascinated people because that is a book that does circulate around. Few people had heard of it before there was *The Ginger Man*, but the wider reading public came with *Balthazar B*. That opened it up to the general reading public. Nevertheless, some people think of *The Ginger Man* as a tag which identifies me, and other authors have had that happen. Think of Joseph Heller's *Catch-22*.

RICHARD FLANAGAN

Richard Flanagan was born in Tasmania in 1961. He is a graduate of the University of Tasmania. His first novel, *Death of a River Guide*, was published in 1994. Subsequent books include *Gould's Book of Fish: A Novel in Twelve Fish*, *The Unknown Terrorist*, *Wanting* and *The Narrow Road to the Deep North*, which reflects his father's experience on the Burma Death Railway. *First Person* appeared in 2017. He is also an essayist, a columnist and a screenwriter. His many awards include The Commonwealth Writers' Prize and the Man Booker Prize for fiction.

This interview was recorded at UEA on 1 November, 2017.

BIGSBY: Nearly two years ago, you wrote an extended essay about Syrian refugees. You went to the Lebanon, to the Beqaa Valley, and ended up in Central Europe. What was the impetus behind that?

FLANAGAN: I was contacted by World Vision and they made this offer that they would facilitate the trip and give me guides if I wished to go. I thought about it and agreed. I asked a friend to come, a very well-known painter in Australia, but I had been thinking about doing something like it for some time. The real impetus was really a photograph I have in my writing room. It shows my three daughters looking across the Julian Alps from Slovenia to the Austrian border. It was over that mountain pass, in 1958, that their maternal grandparents fled as refugees and my wife, Maida, was conceived in an Austrian refugee camp in southern Austria. That same route was the one that the Syrian refugees were seeking to use to get to Germany and I felt I didn't feel that they were distant, or different. I felt that they were you and me. They were my family and I wanted to go and discover what their stories were and write what I saw.

BIGSBY: There is a striking phrase you use in the essay, and in a very short video in which you are doing a piece to camera. You say, 'They are not like us, they are us' and I think that applies to a lot of your work, especially, perhaps, to *The Narrow Road to the Deep North*. It was chilling looking at that video because it had been raining and was now snowing and these people were living under plastic covers with the water cascading through. The water was almost up to their ankles as they walked around. One man was dying and, rather than have food for themselves, they put money into buying medication to help him while, of course, ahead lay the Beqaa Valley and the journey they had to make.

FLANAGAN: That family had a five-year-old son who was stunted because they couldn't afford food for him. I met another family who were marrying their thirteen-year-old daughter off because they couldn't afford to feed her. I met a nine-year-old who was working illegally in a welding shop seven days a week to help support his refugee family in the Beqaa Valley. I met a Kurdish family from Darat Azzah, in Lesbos, and the day before crossing that fatal sea between Turkey and Greece and Europe their boat had sunk and they had lost a three-year-old-child. And the extraordinary thing about all these people who had not just seen but lived under the savagery of ISIS, who had had their own government barrel-bomb them, was that they all had hope and refused to renounce hope. That moved me more than anything and made me also think that for any of us to give into despair is a terrible crime.

BIGSBY: The segue from that into *The Narrow Road to the Deep North* might not be immediately obvious, but this is a novel with another kind of terrible violence at its heart. You have said it is the novel that you had to write but the novel you didn't want to write. How does that work?

FLANAGAN: Well, badly. It took me twelve years to write. I didn't want to write it because I didn't know how to write it, but I knew one thing. It was a much easier novel to write badly and an almost impossible novel to write well. It bore no attraction for me, but it was like a boulder inside me and the boulder grew and grew until it was choking me and I couldn't write anything else. I was possessed by two utterly illogical ideas that nevertheless I felt to be compelling and true. The first was that if I didn't write this book I would be unable to ever write another book, and the second strange conceit that took hold of me was that if I didn't finish this book before my father died I would never finish it. So, over several years, I wrote it as a number of different novels, not just a number of different drafts but each novel was many drafts and, in the end, each one failed. I would burn them, and I would wipe the hard drive. I would destroy any remnants of them but, I guess in the same way that Cortes, when he arrived at the New World, burned his boats so that there was only one way and that was forward with no prospect of retreating to what you knew, I had to strike out afresh each time.

BIGSBY: *The Narrow Road to the Deep North* is mostly set in Thailand and Burma and is to do with the building, for the Japanese, of the railway there. Huge numbers of people were involved, including the British, but the Australians are the focus of your book because your father was involved in building that railway. People starved to death, were worked to death, died of diseases. About a quarter of them died, though your father survived to return home. Did nothing of those five novels, which you burned, survive into the finished version?

FLANAGAN: I guess some things did, but they were different in that they share some characters and some elements. What essentially they share is the idea that it would be about prisoners of war. What finally alerted me to what I must do was the thing that sparked the novel in the first place and that was in 2001, when I had finished a novel called *Gould's Book of Fish*. I found myself in Sydney walking across Sydney Harbour Bridge – which on a late afternoon is a very beautiful thing to do – and while I was walking across I was reminded of this story that my parents were fond of. It was about a Latvian immigrant who had come to live in the little town where I was born, in Tasmania. This Latvian man had been caught up in those great cataclysmic movements of people that beset Eastern Europe in the final years of the war and he got swept away from his village. When he finally made it back to the village at war's end it was to discover that it had been razed to the ground. He was told that his wife was dead, but he refused to believe this and spent the next two years journeying through that apocalyptic landscape that was post-war Europe, going to displaced persons' centres, refugee camps, searching for his wife. In the end, after two years, he had to accept that what he had been told was true, she was in fact dead.

He emigrated to Australia and ended up in the little town where I was born. He married another woman and had a family. Then, in the late 1950s, he went to Sydney, which is very distant from the island I am from, and was walking down a crowded street when he saw, walking towards him, his wife with a child on either hand. He realised he had only a few moments to decide whether he would acknowledge her or not. Growing up, I always thought that was the most beautiful story about love that I knew because it was about what someone would do for love, about the wound of love, and about the cost of love, and about how love can exist beyond morality, how it can be a hell as much as it can be a paradise. So, walking across the bridge that day, this image came to me of a prisoner of war who many years after the war is walking across the Sydney Harbour Bridge and sees the woman who is the love of his life walking towards him and is confronted with the same dilemma that confronted the Latvian man when he saw the wife he thought was dead. I felt this was the thing that would drive my novel and I rushed back to The Rocks, which is the nearest suburb, found a pub and went in. I had nothing to write with, so I got a pen from the barman and I wrote a draft of that chapter on beer coasters, and I took the beer coasters home and then forgot about them for a long time. I started trying to write the novel other ways, and each one failed. Then I rediscovered the beer coasters and realised it wasn't really a story about war at all. I wanted to write a novel about the many forms of love, so I started again with that as the catalyst and finally that unlocked something within me and I was able to finally finish the novel.

BIGSBY: And love is, in a way, a balancing factor set against the violence which has to be in the book because of the treatment that was metered out, but there is another kind of love which is the comradeship of those people who were suffering these privations together. But I wanted to ask you about the violence. You have to describe it, and do so in a very detailed way. A man is beaten to death in front of the assembled prisoners of war. They can do nothing and there is a moment when you say that one of the men was thinking that this was delaying the moment when they would be fed because they were subject to terrible starvation so that the desire for food dominated them. At the same time the man who was beaten to death was a real person, a friend of your father's.

FLANAGAN: He was my father's best friend. We never really heard the full story. We just knew that his best friend, Micky Hallam, had been dragged out of what passed for a hospital, very ill, and beaten to death in front of the assembled prisoners of war.

BIGSBY: When you are writing a passage like that can you detach yourself? Zola said that a writer should be as cold as a vivisectionist at a lecture.

FLANAGAN: I hadn't heard that Zola line. It is very good, and I would agree with it. I think the greatest sin a writer can commit is the sin of empathy. What you should do is simply describe what you see. If you were telling the story of being in a car crash, say, you wouldn't pretend you knew what it felt like. You would describe what happened. Because we live in a material world, we see things, we touch things, we hear things, we smell them, and we assemble all these impressions. Then, over time, we decide that they are tragic or erotic or comic or whatever. That is your job as a writer, to describe what happens and then allow the reader to form his or her judgement because if you tell the reader what to think you are destroying the other half of the creative act that is a book, because books only come alive in that communion of reading.

BIGSBY: That reminds me of something Hemingway said which was that you should never describe emotion but write the thing that will provoke the emotion. The emotion is felt by the reader because you have described the thing so precisely.

FLANAGAN: And also because you don't know what the emotion is. You pretend you know what the emotion is. It is better to allow the mystery of other people to enter into it. I think a good novel is one that you go to again and again and find fresh meanings. There are some novels I re-read every couple of years and discover an entirely different book. I find fresh meanings because the novelist doesn't tell me what the meaning of it is. Chekhov said that a writer should describe what their characters do and say and think but it is for the reader and God to judge.

BIGSBY: There is a challenge in writing this kind of book, which is not dissimilar from trying to write a novel about the Holocaust, and you refer to this in the book. A novel can give shape and form and apparent meaning to things which in truth lack shape and form and meaning. Terrible things happen but once they are brought into language that normalise those things while at the same time language arguably lacks the capacity to capture extremes of experience. The Yugoslav poet, Miroslav Holub, in a poem, talks about the fact that the word pain can never communicate the experience of pain, substituting language for experience, and you do refer to this problem of giving shape and order and purpose to something through writing.

FLANAGAN: I think it is the fundamental paradox of writing because there is this myth that if you work hard enough, revise long enough, you can find the exact phrase, the precise word, exactly describe what it is you wish to describe. But even Flaubert, who was the one who promoted this idea above all others, recognised that it was in fact a lie. In the middle of *Madame Bovary,* he suddenly steps out of character, steps out of the novel entirely, and says, why is it that none of us can ever express the exact measure of all our thoughts and needs and sorrows and loves, that all human speech is like a cracked kettle upon which we tap crude rhythms for bears to dance to when all the time we long to move the stars to pity. That is the dilemma writers face. They want to move the stars to pity but they know that, at their best, they are only tapping crude rhythms on a kettle for bears to dance to. I think Whitman was right when he said, 'The words of my book nothing, the drift of it everything.' There is something beyond style. Flaubert writes, enraged I think, to George Sand, saying, 'Why is it that all the great writers achieve their affects without style?' I think that happens because the really great works have a soul and what that is is mysterious, but it is what allows a book to survive the fires of translation, the passing of the years, go into other languages, other cultures, and other times and still have meaning. It has some soul that keeps on communicating the mystery the writer was seeking to communicate in the first place, but it exists beyond words.

BIGSBY: Is that what you meant in addressing the survivors of the railway when you said, 'this is only a fragment that I can offer you', because anything you were going to write was going to fall short of the experience that had lived on the pulse for them?

FLANAGAN: Yes, of course. I thought very deeply about the vastness of just that one experience of being a prisoner of war, which for many of them spanned not only the death railway but being put on what were called 'the hell ships' that took the survivors to Japan. There was a man living in Tasmania until recently who ended up five hundred metres from ground zero at Nagasaki and survived. He was just an ordinary man who happened to have lived this extraordinary few years as a young man. You can't capture any of that in a novel. I spent six months trying to write his story, about someone who survives Nagasaki, but, in a novel, it looks histrionic because really God is allowed the good stories while a novelist has to make do with the merely plausible and the merely plausible, for me, was to reduce it right down. So really all that the reader gets of that vast experience is one day in a prison camp and what happens is actually very little – a man gets rifle-butted in the morning, gets progressively sicker and debilitated, and then finally is beaten to death. In the annals of violence, and violence on the death railway, and the greater violence of the last century, these are very small things, but I thought if I could concentrate on the material details of what that day might look like then perhaps that fragment might allow readers to find within their soul something of the universe of suffering those people lived through.

BIGSBY: Is that one of the reasons that you went out there? You have said elsewhere that you are not a great researcher. You mentioned an American writer who explained, at an event in California, the spreadsheets detailing the research she had done receiving huge applause while you said, 'I just make it up.'

FLANAGAN: To which I should add that you found it funny but the two thousand Californians who had come to see the famous American didn't. Nobody laughed because she had gone on for geological periods of time and I thought people would like a joke, but nobody laughed. It is a terrible thing in North America to be guilty of indolence and I longed for the San Andreas Fault to open up and swallow me.

BIGSBY: You did, though, go out to see where the railway had been built. Was that because you wanted to nail down details or was there the sense that some of that experience adhered in the place itself and could communicate something to you?

FLANAGAN: Such research as I did over the twelve years consisted of occasionally asking my father a few questions about very mundane details. I went to the death railway in the manner, I felt, of a poet. I just wanted to be open to what the material world there was, what the heat felt like, what the insects were, to have a strong sensual impression of that world. There was nothing mystical about it. I didn't want to have any sense of feeling. I just wanted to record as best I could. I didn't take notes. I just wanted to have an impression of what it was like to exist in that world.

The final bit of research I did was I learned that there were some prison guards who had been guards on the death railway who were still alive, so I went to Japan to find them. I found a group of extraordinary Japanese women who had worked for some years to try and document the war crimes of the Imperial Japanese Army and they led me to these prison guards. I met three and each of them, as it turned out, had been a guard at one of my father's camps. I hadn't expected that because the death railway was a pharaonic project of a quarter of a million slaves, along a four-hundred-and-twenty-kilometre length of railway. But I met a man who had been a medical orderly who had been to my father's camp in the jungle in Thailand and he recalled entering the camp. He said it was like a Buddhist hell, and I said, 'What do you mean?' He said there were pyres on which corpses were burning, and in front of the pyres there were skeletons crawling around in the mud. They were the prisoners of war and I asked him, as a medical orderly, didn't he feel that he should help these people and he said, 'We didn't see them as people.' He also told me that the Japanese had good hygiene and used to have a hot bath every day and the Australians didn't. I paid for his tea and for a taxi home. Then the next day I went to meet a guard. I didn't recognise his name. It was a Korean name and about five minutes before I got there I realised that this man was actually the Ivan the Terrible of my father's camp, a man known to the Australian prisoners of war as 'The Lizard'. The Lizard was sentenced to death for war crimes at the end of the war but later this was commuted to life imprisonment. He had then been released in a general amnesty in 1956. My father was a very gentle man, a man without hate, but the only person I ever heard him speak of with violent intent was The Lizard, but when I got to meet him I was greeted by a gentle and dignified ninety-three-year-old man who did his best to answer my questions respectfully.

He told me many things but had no memory of violence. It may be that he was lying or it maybe he had no memory of it because I think we too often think that memory is testament while memory is also an act of creation. So, we had been talking for about an hour and a half when I had this very odd thing I asked him to do. I don't know why it came to me, but I asked him to slap me because, in the Japanese army, the immediate form of corporal punishment was 'binta'. Binta was this violent slapping with both hands until you dropped to the ground in a fairly bad state. Sometimes the Japanese guards would do this to the prisoners but sometimes they would actually line the prisoners of war up in two rows and they would have to beat each other until one dropped. If they thought you were just playing around a bit and going soft they would come and give you a hiding. So, he stood up, and I stood up. He flexed his arm and cupped his hand in a particular way. Then he curled his body and you knew that even if he had forgotten the violence his nerves, and what remained of his muscles, hadn't at all. He slapped me three times and I remember how soft the skin of his hand was but on the third time the whole room started moving like a boat in a wild sea. It was rolling around and there were these taxi keys on the wall and they all started shimmering, making a strange ethereal sound, and I thought I had gone completely mad because it had been a very strange time for me. I thought something had gone within my mind but, by coincidence, a force seven point nine Richter scale earthquake had hit Tokyo, though I didn't know it. I had never been in an earthquake and it is an unusual thing, I have to tell you, but The Lizard did know what an earthquake was and as I looked across at him, with chairs falling over and cupboards falling, he was frightened and I suddenly understood that wherever evil was, it wasn't in that room with me and this old man.

BIGSBY: But when you told your father this, it was not something he wanted to hear, was it, that he had turned into this gentle person?

FLANAGAN: My father had seen enough of this life to understand the strangeness of the world. I didn't say The Lizard was a good man, I didn't say he was a truthful man. I had just encountered a gentle, gracious and dignified man, but you can reconcile that with a reformed man or a wicked man. It is impossible to say what he was.

BIGSBY: Just now you talked about asking your father questions. Many people that came back from these experiences, or, indeed, from the Holocaust, remained silent, sometimes for decades, and for reasons you can understand, but your father didn't remain silent. When he was talking to you did he talk about the violence or about other things?

FLANAGAN: Yes, many remained silent, many remained silent until death. They were encouraged in that, certainly in Australia. The army psychologists advised families and loved ones not to talk to them about it, and also the culture of the day which, in my country as in yours, was one of reticence and not the confessional culture we have now.

BIGSBY: It didn't fit the Australian narrative either in the same way that in Israel victims didn't fit their narrative. That was not what the culture was now about. it was leaning into the future.

FLANAGAN: No, it didn't. They didn't speak for all sorts of reasons. One is that it just didn't fit the conventional stories of war. This was such a profound and complex human experience it didn't fit the normal stories of heroism and courage and so on. I don't think they had a language for it. Also, I think you have to accept that man survives by his ability to forget. They had lived through an extraordinarily horrific experience and when they came back they had no language for it and they needed to get on with life. It was necessary to forget, but equally freedom exists in the space of memory and at a certain point you have to go back into the shadows and confront these things if you are ever to live in the light. The problem is that for some of those who bear these deep wounds that moment never arises in their life and those wounds pass through them into their families, communities, sometimes whole societies, and then the job of communicating the incommunicable, of going back into those shadows, falls to others, others in the family, historians, public figures and sometimes artists and writers. Then they are the ones that must go back into the shadow.

BIGSBY: There was something almost Sisyphean about this project of the railway because by that stage in the war the Japanese were not going to win. They had lost in the Pacific so that defeat was only a matter of time, not that that stopped them. I have just been watching Ken Burns's series on Vietnam and for nine-and-a-half episodes it is terrible violence. Two million Vietnamese died, fifty-eight thousand Americans died, but in the final section an American who had served in Vietnam went back and met somebody who had served in the North Vietnamese army and they were buddies. After the death of so many you get this moment of reconciliation. And few traces of the war remain. Your book is now finished, now out of your system, and in your new one it is as though something in you was released because this is a different style. It is partly comic. It is as though a duty had been fulfilled and you could move in another direction, though oddly the direction you move is backwards. I was going to say it takes you back to the beginning of your career except that you didn't have a career. Nonetheless, you were commissioned to write a particular kind of book.

FLANAGAN: Yes, I was. I think, is it Homer who says, 'the gods weave misfortune in order that later generations have something to sing about' and in my case it wasn't the gods but Australia's most notorious conman and corporate criminal, a man called John Friedrich who, in 1991, rang me and asked if I would ghost-write his memoir in six weeks and if I did he would pay me ten thousand dollars. Now this odd request arose because John Friedrich had taken over a very small charity, of four or five people that, in the days before Occupational Health and Safety, became a national blight. They used to go around putting up posters in workshops about the wisdom of wearing hairnets if you were operating a lathe or ran workshops on the necessity of bending your knees if you were lifting heavy weights. Friedrich came into this organisation and, within a few short years, it had been transformed into this paramilitary business of some five or six hundred employees, of whom four hundred were like a small army. He had helicopters, an air wing, submarines. He even had Idi Amin's helicopter. They had a certain notoriety. There were dark rumours of CIA connections but then the whole thing went belly up and there was the biggest manhunt in Australian history. It turned out that Friedrich had embezzled about a billion dollars, in today's terms, and all the money had vanished. They finally found him in West Australia, extradited him back to Melbourne and within about an hour Australia's leading celebrity agent, a man called Harry M Miller, rang him and said, 'Don't sign anything. I'll cut the deal,' and he cut a very handsome deal, a lucrative publishing contract for a memoir, and he got released on bail.

A year and a half passed and, being criminally indisposed to recording anything on paper, he produced absolutely nothing, so the publisher set ghost-writers and editors to work with him and they all gave up very quickly because he could be a very abhorrent individual. So, they said, if you won't work with our writers you find a writer who you will work with. Well Friedrich, being of a criminal disposition, had surprisingly not met any writers, but his bodyguard, a Tasmanian, said, I have got this mate in Tasmania who wants to be a writer. At this point I was working as a builder's labourer so I could write my first novel. Then the phone rings and it is Australia's most wanted offering me ten thousand dollars to ghost-write his memoir. My first thought was, what damage would this do to my literary reputation? until, fairly rapidly, it occurred to me that not having written a novel I didn't have a literary reputation to damage and so the next day I flew to Melbourne and began work with this very unusual man. He was a man of many secrets. He immediately turned up in disguise. We were to work in the publisher's offices in Melbourne and he turned up in this disguise like Yasser Arafat dressed up as Austin Powers. He told me I was not to tell anybody what we were working on, so I said, 'Well, what do I say?' and he looked around as though people were listening in, or watching, and he thought about this and then he said, 'Tell them we are co-editing an anthology of medieval German folk verse.' So, we began work, which is a generous description that encompasses me asking questions which were never answered. Then, after three weeks, he shot himself dead, and this forms the beginning of this novel, *First Person*, but there has been one early review in England, in the *Daily Mail*, which says, 'It is a good book apart from the very implausible set-up.' I don't want to point out to a purveyor of truth like the *Daily Mail* but that is actually the only true thing in the entire book.

So, he is dead, and it was front-page news. The publisher did what any good publisher does in that situation, which was go everywhere saying they had a tell-all memoir that would answer all the many questions being asked about where the billion dollars had gone, the CIA connection, and so on, but that they weren't going to divulge any details. Well, that was as well because by this stage I was back in Hobart sitting in a pub desperately trying to make them up. It is often said of a writer's first novel that it is autobiographical, but I was discovering that my first autobiography was rapidly developing novelistic tendencies. So, then the book came out to immediate failure, which was less than surprising given it was about a man who had spent three weeks never telling me who he was, and then had shot himself dead. I had been left to ghost write a ghost and there was a campaign by an organisation called 'Don't buy Books from Crooks' which I would have found offensive in other circumstances but since by then I had the ten thousand dollars it seemed not much of a concern, as Woody Allen once said, 'for financial reasons'. And with that I was able to stop working and, or, builder's labouring, and I spent six months finishing what became my first novel, *Death of a River Guide*.

BIGSBY: The real question is why you are coming back to that moment in your life now?

FLANAGAN: What happened was that years and decades passed and this strange new world came into being where lies became alternative facts, truth became worthless and the more implausible the lie the more likely people were to believe it. There was an attack not just on particular truths but about everything from climate change to how much money the EU was stealing weekly from your budget, or the size of the presidential inauguration crowd. Public figures have always lied, there is nothing new in that, but what we have now is a fundamental attack on the very concept of the truth, on the idea of the truth, and if we decide that there really is no objective truth then all we have is opinion and, in that world, the loudest opinion, which is the opinion of the most powerful and the richest in our society, is the one that prevails. Then I think we have gone to a very dark place because ever since the wall went down and communism ended in the late 1980s, early 1990s, there has been a foolish presumption, on the part of us in the west, that freedom and progress go together but if you look to the example of China you can see that this is a nonsense, that you can have progress without freedom. I think that the hinge, the rusty hinge that holds freedom and progress together, is truth and if we abandon truth then we are lost, so I wanted to write a book about truth and lies, about our need to believe stories, about how we can have poisoned stories which can pervert whole societies, or we can have stories, which I think fiction at its best does, which can be liberating and transcendent. It is not that literature has the power to change anything but, at their best, novels may have no answers, but they do ask the necessary questions and with this new book I have asked some of the questions that I think matter.

BIGSBY: I was watching an interview with someone talking about Facebook. It is now possible to go back to previous postings and change them. In other words, you can change history, but of course you have always been able to change history. The Poles, who were used to books suddenly appearing with people airbrushed out of them, or sections removed, had a saying, 'The hardest thing to predict is the past.' We are in a world in which those lies can actually seep back and the narrator, like Scott Fitzgerald's characters, is slowly corrupted, contaminated by association with this person and then ends up drifting off into reality television, a contradiction in terms if ever there was one.

FLANAGAN: Mark Zuckerberg said a few years ago that 'privacy is no longer an acceptable social norm', and then he said that, 'Henceforth we won't have one identity at work and another identity with our friends and another at home, we will only have what he called 'the integrity of a single identity which will be your online identity.' Gabriel Garcia Marquez said, 'Each of us has a public life, a private life and a secret life' and I think if you deny people their private and secret lives you deny them the multitudes that each of us contain. You deny the essential humanity of people. In this world where privacy is so under attack I think that books and reading in particular, which remain deeply private acts, become much more important. They become subversive acts and books have come to occupy a very strange position in our culture now because they are largely ignored in the mainstream media and yet they seem to be of growing importance to people who read. I think that is because other forums for defining our world collapse around us, be it politics or the media, be it the early promise of the internet souring into something much darker. In that world, novels assume a new power and if you think this is hyperbolic, this idea of reading being subversive, the idea that books are actually the new counter-culture, I would ask you to ponder the story, a couple of weeks ago, about an American actress called Shailene Woodley. She was walking the red carpet at the Emmys and was thrown the question, 'What TV shows are you watching now?' to which she made the entirely innocent reply, 'I don't watch television. I don't even own a television. I prefer reading.' For that innocent comment she was condemned everywhere, social media, old media.

I think this antagonism to reading, and to books, is a very new thing. I think it is because books are a private act and we go to novels because we understand that each of us contains multitudes. We go to them because we understand that each of us contains possibilities, to be far worse people and far better people. We understand that we are both Anna Karenina and Hannibal Lecter. All these possibilities exist within each of us. When we are granted the integrity of one single online identity we become reduced to something that can be monetised, as that ugly new word has it, or surveilled, as the other ugly new word has it. A dogma that has taken hold that literature now has worth in so far as it is grounded in lived experience, something you can quantify and qualify. People are now fearful of story, of invention, but I think the novel is not just an entertainment, it is an entertainment that comes out of a profound spiritual, intellectual and aesthetic tradition, and when writers have done their work properly it expresses a truth of their soul, and in this world of lies we need that truth more than ever.

DAVID GROSSMAN

David Grossman was born in Jerusalem in 1954. As part of his national service, he served in military intelligence. He studied philosophy and theatre at the Hebrew University of Jerusalem and worked for Israel Broadcasting for some twenty-five years. His many novels include *The Smile of the Lamb*, *To the End of the Lamb*, *Falling Out of Time* and *A Horse Walks into a Bar*. His non-fiction works include *The Yellow Wind*, *Sleeping on a Wire: Conversation with Palestinians in Israel* and *Writing in the Dark: Essays on Literature and Politics*. His books have been widely translated and he is the winner of multiple prizes.

This interview was conducted at UEA on 8 November, 2016.

BIGSBY: Your mother was born in pre-Israel, that is to say Mandate Palestine, and your father came from Poland when he was quite young, nine.
GROSSMAN: Nine-ish.

BIGSBY: Why did his family leave Poland?
GROSSMAN: My grandmother, the mother of my father, was a widow. She lived, they all lived, in a very small town, between a town and a village I think. It is called Dynów. Usually when I say this word in front of an audience I pause for a second hoping that someone will know this place. Nobody? She walked in the street and was harassed, not arrested but harassed, by Polish policemen. She was then, I think, thirty-five, and was already a widow. She was a very tiny lady and she took her two children, my father and his sister, and they travelled all the way to Palestine. From the moment she arrived in Palestine, before the State of Israel was created, she almost never left her home, but she did this amazing journey for a woman. I think it was the first time she had left her home town and she took a bus, probably for the first time in her life, and a train and a boat, and I don't know what else, and landed in Israel where she started her life. It was lucky for all of us because those of her relatives who stayed in Poland were murdered and this small lady was the centre of our family for sixty years, and I feel indebted to her.

BIGSBY: Yours wasn't really a wealthy family when you were growing up, was it?
GROSSMAN: No. My father was a bus driver and later, when he had to quit driving because of problems in his eyes, he became the librarian of this transportation organisation in Jerusalem, so I had a private library. I would ask him to order this and that book and he did it. I was the first reader always. He himself did not get a proper education because at the age of fourteen he had to quit his studies to be a garage worker in this transportation organisation, but he gave me books. I think it was a way for him to complete what he has missed in his own life. He gave me, for example, the books of Sholem Aleichem. Sholem Aleichem, I am sure you know, was a Jewish Yiddish writer at the beginning of

the twentieth century. He wrote about the life of the Jews in the *shtetl*, little towns or villages like my father grew up in Dinov. He was a humourist, a great humourist. He had a wonderful sense of humour, a very Jewish sense of humour. So, one day, when I was eight years old, he gave me a book of Sholem Aleichem who I had never heard of until then, of course, and he told me 'read it, Davit' – at home I am Davit – 'read it. It is about our life over there.' I remember a very short and thick book with a red cover and I climbed on the window, which was where I liked to sit and read, and I read and was swept immediately into a reality that was totally foreign for me. I was a very Israeli child of the state of Israel at the beginning of the 1960s. Israel had started to build itself and was a country totally tuned to the future deliberately being very reluctant to look back at the traumatic past of the Shoa, of the humiliation of masses of people, and I didn't know anything about this reality that I read in the stories of Sholem Aleichem. Suddenly there was a whole world with the codes of this world, the rules, the language, the melody, the characters, the institutions, all these things about the Jews who had to live among the non-Jews and be afraid of them, the Gentiles. Who are the Gentiles? I never knew that there were people who were not Jewish. I thought there were only Jews.

BIGSBY: But he wrote in Yiddish. Did you read him in Yiddish?

GROSSMAN: I read him in translation to Hebrew of course. His son in law translated his books in a wonderful way. I think it was like a child today reading *Harry Potter*. This world had the wholeness and solidity of the real world and I was sure that this world continued to exist in parallel to my life in Israel. I had no idea that it had perished and been totally obliterated. I inhaled all the stories of Sholem Aleichem that were for children and grown-ups and just felt that this was my world. One thing I knew was that I was not supposed to talk about it with my classmates or with my friends because it was not cool to say that I was being immersed in this enclave of the diaspora, so contradictory to the 'Israel is strong' and the militant existence of the 1960s. Then, one day

I heard on the radio that there was a competition about knowledge of the stories of Sholem Aleichem, a national competition, and I came to my parents and I told them, 'I want to go there' and they said 'What do you mean? You are a child?' I said, 'but I know Sholem Aleichem,' and they said 'No, no, no, don't do anything.' But against their order I went and bought my first postcard. I didn't know how to fill a postcard in, but I just said, 'I want to come to the auditions that they announced on the radio.' A week later an official letter came from the radio station – the radio was governmental then – asking me to come to the audition. My parents literally almost fainted. It was like David Ben-Gurion himself was pointing at me saying, 'Give me your son, the one you love.'

My father took me, very reluctantly, and when we came to the room they said, 'Okay, keep the boy out.' 'No, no the boy is the thing here,' so then they auditioned me, they tested me, and I had a very fresh memory which I do not have now but had back then. Then they started to be embarrassed, which I only learned about later because they rigged the radio. There was only one radio station in Israel, and they thought it was not educational for such a young boy to win such a big money prize. It was something like one hundred dollars but in Israel, in the 1960s, a hundred dollars was regarded as a lot of money. So, they made a deal with me that I would sit in the studio when they aired the programme and if one of the competitors did not know the answer to one of the questions they would turn to me. So, they did, and the people from the radio spotted me and suggested that I should become a kind of a child correspondent. So, at the age of nine, I used to travel around Israel interviewing the people who interested me the most, which were mainly football players. But, as a lip service, I had to interview the President and all kinds of writers, poets and theatre actors. That was the beginning of my professional life as a radio person which I continued until I was in my thirties, when I was fired from the radio because of political reasons, but that is another story.

BIGSBY: You mentioned theatre and you became an actor, a child actor, so your time seems to have been packed. You had school and then were off to the studio to be in a play.

GROSSMAN: Yes, and at this time the radio was very popular in Israel. We didn't have television so every day there would be three, four radio plays. Until I came along it was usually women who played children's parts. I was very short, not like now when I am a giant, and when we recorded all the grownups were much taller than me so there was an empty orange box with my name on it and I would stand on this box in order to reach the microphone. But through acting in all these radio plays I started to open myself to all the treasures of culture. All the best literary and theatrical creations were adapted as radio plays and I was able to read them. Suddenly I felt the power and I think this was undoubtedly one of the things that directed me towards writing.

BIGSBY: You said something just now about not knowing about Gentiles and in fact you didn't meet a non-Jew until you were what… nine, ten?
GROSSMAN: I guess even more than that.

BIGSBY: What did you think of those other people?
GROSSMAN: I think like most Israelis of my generation we knew that there was Israel and there were the Arab countries which were against us so probably I likened everyone who was not Jewish to the enemies of Israel. In Hebrew it even sounds the same. The word for Egyptians and Christians mizraim, notzrim, sounds the same and I remember that, probably until I was ten, I confused the two. I think only after the Six Day War, which happened in 1967, did I start to be much more aware of the complexity of the world.

BIGSBY: At university you did philosophy and theatre?
GROSSMAN: Yes.

BIGSBY: Does that mean that acting was a career you might have followed?
GROSSMAN: No. I really loved radio. I think radio is a wonderful thing. I loved the sweetness of the intimacy that one can have in the radio, unlike in television which

I really didn't like. Having a programme of your own at midnight, for example, when you know that very few people will listen to you, that actually, after a while, you start to think maybe there is only one person listening to you, creates this intimacy, this bubble that I really loved to be in. Later I became the anchor man of the main news magazine in Israel for four long years and that was really tough because everything in Israel is political and, of course, to be the anchor man of this morning news magazine was very political and, since I never made a secret of my political opinions, which are very much to the left in Israel, I had to face a lot of criticism, a lot of pressure from my superiors in the radio. More than once, more than thrice, maybe more than a hundred times, the moment I finished the broadcast at 8 o'clock I got a call from the General Director of the radio inviting me to his office, demanding to know, for example, 'why did I smile when I asked those sarcastic questions to Mr Ariel Sharon?' Don't laugh, it was exactly like that. Then, one day, in 1988, 15 November, 1988, Mr Arafat declared that he was willing to accept the two-state solution. I came to the radio to see what would be the least of the topics for the next day and I saw this listed as number twelve, something like that, and I said, 'No, it should be number one' and they said 'No, no, no, we have got a special instruction from the Minister of Defence, who was then Yitzhak Rabin, to play down this announcement because we don't want to provoke the Territories, 'Territories' being the occupied territories. I said, 'but the Territories don't need us. They listen to the radio from Jordan, or from Damascus,' and they said, 'No, you are not supposed to give it high profile' so I said, in that case I will not deliver the news tomorrow morning. Please find someone else to replace me.' The next morning, when my wife opened the *Haaretz* paper, it was on the front page that I had been fired. That was how I learned.

BIGSBY: You are jumping ahead a bit in time because this is Israel and people had to serve in the military. You were in military intelligence, I presume because you had done Arabic at school. What did that consist of? Was that sitting in a back-office thumbing through papers or what?

GROSSMAN: Very boring things, yes.

BIGSBY: But while you were serving you were writing some stories but didn't show them to anyone.

GROSSMAN: I didn't show them to anyone. I didn't know anyone who was close to the world of literature that could give me any advice or look at them, but you are right, I wrote because in the Intelligence, in my unit, one of the advantages was that we always served in the most beautiful places, in high mountains, and we were sometimes three weeks in a camp unable to go out. It was all very cramped. You didn't have a place of your own and whenever I got to a new camp while normal soldiers looked first for the canteen or the dining room or where their bed would be, I was looking for a place that would be hidden from the base itself and I would be able to walk to. When I write I always walk. I almost cannot sit. When I have to sit and write something I sit but then if I want to think I must walk. I walk for hours every day, even in a corridor. My wife says I am like a prisoner leaving marks on the carpet, but I cannot sit so I needed to find a place where I would be able to walk back and forth and not to be seen from the outside. I think this was what really saved my sanity, the fact that every day I had an hour or two when I could be totally alone by myself and think of my imaginary world that was totally remote from the actual reality in which I lived, the reality of the army. Only later did I start to write something about life as a soldier or my experience in the army. This is something that was important to me because the feeling is always that when you are in the army the army confiscates you. You belong to the army, and I did not want to belong to the army.

Later, I was a reserve soldier in the war in Lebanon in 1982. I served deep in Lebanon, in the border between Lebanon and Syria. It was not a pleasant place for us to be and I was very glad when we withdrew after many years. I was there for, I think, thirty-five days and I remember that every evening, after I finished my daily job, I used to climb on the roof of the tallest building, without my protective vest, without my helmet, sitting with my back to the village which was, naturally, hostile to us, and from which snipers shot at our people, and every evening I sat there for five, six, seven, ten minutes with a book by Romain Gary –*Promise at Dawn*. Romain Gary is a French Jewish writer, also known as Emile Ajar, and *Promise at Dawn* was a book that I loved deeply when I was young and used to read every year as a kind of a periodical medication, and I sat there reading it. Then, when I finished a chapter, I ran like a mouse back into the building to be safe again, but I felt needed to do it because I needed to have a reminder of who I was before this war and who I wished to be after this nightmare was over.

BIGSBY: But you were going to be changed in another way because another important thing happened while you were serving. You met the person who you would marry. Earlier you referred to yourself as on the left, but you weren't on the left until you met her?
GROSSMAN: No, no.

BIGSBY: So, what happened?
GROSSMAN: I am really a late bloomer in so many ways. My parents were very much to the centre with some tendency towards the right wing, then I met this wonderful young woman and immediately fell in love with her and the first evening she suggested we should go to the Khan Theatre, in Jerusalem, to see a political cabaret of Hanoch Levin. He was an Israeli playwright, a genius really, who died some ten years ago. He was very, very political, very leftist. I knew nothing about him. So, we went to this little cabaret and I sat there and started to freak out because he was saying terrible things about Israel and about the army and about the occupation. I didn't say a word but when we came out I asked her, 'so, what did you think?' and she said, 'It was amazing, marvellous. He says exactly what I think,' and I thought 'what will happen now?' It was her and her parents who really taught me another way of looking at our reality.

BIGSBY: Her grandmother was in the Communist Party.
GROSSMAN: Yes, and thanks to her I think I really opened my eyes to see the reality that until then I had preferred not to see and not to know.

BIGSBY: Your first book was for children, but the first adult book was *The Smile of the Lamb* which was set on the West Bank. It has a central figure who is a survivor of the Holocaust and who believes he has nonetheless retained human and humane values which are, though, slowly corroded by the situation in which he finds himself. Later, the Holocaust is significant in your second novel, *See Under: Love*. The Holocaust is a difficult subject in itself in that simply to talk about it is almost to normalise it, to bring it into an ordinary urbane language when it defies that. Elie Wiesel said that you can't have a Holocaust novel because it is either not about the Holocaust or it is not a novel. On the other hand, it exists and permeates the whole world in which you exist, especially in Israel. But Israel responded in a very strange way. It was vaguely hostile towards survivors and they were silent for almost traumatic reasons because presumably their narrative didn't fit that of the new Israel. Is that right?

GROSSMAN: It is right, and also I think many of them felt guilty to have been spared while all their loved ones perished. As you said, they felt that their being in an Israeli reality that is tuned towards the future, they reminded Israelis of things that most Israelis preferred not to know. I myself was haunted by the Shoah from a very young age. I mentioned Sholem Aleichem, and he would be important. I remember in a very vivid way the moment I understood what the Shoah really was. It was on one of the memorial days for the Shoah that we commemorate every year in April or May. When I was a child the teachers did not really know how to convey knowledge of the Shoah because it is something too big and too terrible to burden a young child with. Yet they had to commemorate it and to explain things, so they found shelter in clichés, in generalisations, in words that meant nothing. How does a child understand the meaning of the murder of six million Jews in the Shoah? This number is just a number. It says nothing.

But I had my characters from Sholem Aleichem and I remember the moment when I was standing on the blazing asphalt in my school in Beit HaKerem, a neighbourhood in Jerusalem. I was ten and all of me was immersed in Sholem Aleichem and suddenly it occurred to me that those who had been murdered were my people, the people of Sholem Aleichem who he described in his books and who were now gone. I remember how I was shocked by this memory and that is why I also wrote *See Under: Love* because I felt that I must understand how I would have behaved had I been there in the time of the Shoah as one of the victims and as one of the killers. What do I have as a human being that I could place in front of this total obliteration of my uniqueness as a human being, of all my abilities, my intimacy, my connections with my family, with my friends, everything? What do you do? What is the thing that allows you to maintain your humanity, the thing that cannot be taken from you in any circumstances, cannot be obliterated? I also wanted to understand how a normal human being becomes a mass murderer. What do you have to erase inside yourself, so you will be able to erase others? What are the processes needed in order to stop seeing human beings as such and look at them as easily destroyable, without any remorse, without any second thought? What is the psychological process that one has to undergo in order to become a murderer?

    The book is mainly or partly about that, but it is also about the question of how are we able to believe in mankind after everything we know about the atrocities of mankind. How is it possible that we bring new babies into this world knowing what people can do to each other? I remember when my eldest son came from the kindergarten, when he was three or four, and it was the day of the commemoration of the Shoah. He was shocked when he came back and asked, 'What was it?' I thought it is terrible that they had to be exposed to such knowledge at the age of four. In normal places children are exposed to the facts of life at this age but our children had to be exposed to the facts of death at the age of four and I felt that I did not want to tell him anything, that I really wanted to protect him from this knowledge because I had the feeling that if he was exposed to the horizons of human evil he would be polluted in a big way, he would never be the same child again, never be a child again once these atrocities are formulated within him.

In my book there is a boy called Momik. He is eight, later nine, years old, and he is the only son of two survivors from the Shoah, and he, like myself, is haunted by the question of the Shoah because it is really so hard to understand. Sometimes I think it is like looking into the sun. You cannot really look into the sun; you cannot really look into the essence of the Shoah, the fact that something like that was possible. My Momik is surrounded by grownups most of whom are survivors. They have numbers tattooed on their arms and he hears cries during the night of people who are shouting from their nightmares and the memories that they have and everybody is talking about the Nazi beast. He goes to Bella, who is the owner of the grocery store and who also has a number tattooed on her arm, and asks, 'Bella what is the Nazi beast?' and she wouldn't answer because she also wants to protect him from that. But Momik is such a child that once he is pushed back he will push forward. He is so terrified that he must know, he must investigate, and, in the end, he pressures this owner of the grocery store so much that she takes a puff on her cigarette and with a very deep and profound sigh tells him that the Nazi beast can come out of any animal if it gets the right food and the right nourishment. She, of course, says it ironically but he is only eight years old and takes her very, very seriously so he decides that he will collect animals, all kinds of animals – a hedgehog, a wooden cat, a bird that he found, a turtle, a little dog – and cages them in boxes in the cellar. They are underneath his parents' apartment, parents who are survivors from the Shoah. Momik is raising the Nazi beast and he wants it to come out because he wants to domesticate it and to tame it so that it will stop torturing his parents and all the other grownups, but the animal doesn't come out. So, he comes to believe that just as his sleepy turtle comes alive when he smells the peel of the cucumber, so he must give the beast the food it likes the best, which is a Jew. The problem is that he is very Israeli. He belongs to the new Israel and doesn't know what it means to be a Jew, so he has to learn what it is to be Jewish.

BIGSBY: Before talking about another novel, I want to mention a non-fiction book, *The Yellow Wind*. As a journalist you went to the West Bank and observed for a couple of months and then wrote a book which seems to have shocked a lot of people in Israel because it saw the relationship between Palestinians and Israelis differently. Behind it is the notion that those in Israel did not know how Palestinians felt, how they lived. They couldn't imaginatively put themselves in their situation. It was a report from the other side. Did it shock you when you went there? Were you similarly naive before you went, or did you already know what you were going to find?

GROSSMAN: Probably I was naive but not so much because this came four years after I published my first novel about the occupation, *The Smile of the Lamb*. I was aware of this reality and I was even more aware of what it means to be 'occupied,' and what a whole society has to erase from its knowledge in order to be 'the occupier,' to establish a very efficient 'occupation.' What are the manifestation of the occupation in the most intimate fabric of the life of the occupied and the occupier? This is what brought me to write first *The Smile of the Lamb* and later *The Yellow Wind* because I started to feel that there is a whole reality that we are responsible for because we have the upper hand, we are the occupiers, we are the Israelis, and it fascinated me to see how we learned to live together, to co-exist with this knowledge without suffering at all from it because I thought that a normal moral society, as we are, is a strange and tricky thing. How we can believe that we are moral when we are totally immoral? To have an occupation for fifty years takes quite a piece of denial. I went to the Occupied Territories just to expose myself to this reality and I started one morning, a very hot day I remember. I left my home in the south of Jerusalem, in Talpiot neighbourhood, and I drove twenty-five minutes, something that I never did, towards the south of this neighbourhood, to the refugee camp of Dheisheh. This was one of the most terrible places to live where Palestinians, hundreds of thousands who either ran away in the war of 1948, which we call the War of Independence, when Israel got its independence, or were expelled from it, from the land of Israel, and found themselves in huge refugee camps created by the United Nations. Today it is almost seventy years that they have been there, while their problem could have been solved easily by Arab countries and the whole world. But they refuse. They want to remain there as a reminder, as a mark of shame against Israel, and, of course, they are trapped between larger powers than themselves. I went there because I wanted to see what it means to be a refugee? I come from a family of refugees. My grandmother was a refugee when she came to then Palestine.

I went there and planted myself in the middle of this camp. Immediately I was surrounded by some of the youngsters of the camp, who were in a way their military leaders, and they started to ask me questions and they did not understand how it was that I could speak Arabic. They were very suspicious and kept me there for almost three hours under the very blazing sun. They kept asking questions and more and more people accumulated. There were children for whom I was the first Israeli they had seen without a gun and without a uniform. There was also an old woman who deeply reminded me of my grandmother and she burst through the lines that surrounded me and took me by the hand. She said, 'Doll, come with me' and she took me to her hut and started to tell me about her life and about the night she had had to run from her home somewhere in a place that is now Israel and found herself a refugee. She lost all her property and all her dignity and some members of her family. Then her daughter-in-law came and started to talk with me and tell me her story and I had my notebook and was writing for some hours because they would not let me go. More and more people came and started to tell me their stories and I really don't want to be presumptuous, but I think it was the first time, in the relationship between Israelis and Palestinians (it was twenty years after the occupation that this dialogue took place), that they were able to tell their story to an Israeli, to tell her story without interruption. I did not argue with them, I did not oppose them, even when the facts that they told me were unlike the facts that I knew. I was just listening and absorbing their story. I was very attentive. When I came back to Jerusalem that evening it was quite late and I remember walking in Ben Yehuda Street, one of the major streets of Jerusalem, and around me were my fellow men, Jerusalemite Jews, and I looked at them and thought, 'how is it possible that you do not feel that there is a huge fire that will eat us very soon' because the anger and the suppressed rage that I felt among the Palestinians, and the deep national and personal insult that they felt, were so vivid to me it was so clear to me that very soon there would be a huge explosion.

BIGSBY: And there was, the Intifada.
GROSSMAN: There was the Intifada. A very few weeks after I published this book the Intifada burst out.

BIGSBY: I want to talk about three more books, very quickly. *To the End of the Land*…
GROSSMAN: You have seen now why I write such thick books and not Haiku poems…

BIGSBY: We are going to come on to a short one in a second, but first, *To the End of the Land*. You had two sons who served in the military and this bears on *To the End of the Land*. You have described this as 'a walkie talkie novel,' that is to say it is about a woman whose son is in the military, coming to the end of a period of service, but then goes back again. She fears the moment that someone will come and knock on the door with bad news. So, she gets it into her mind that, if she is not there, if she goes on a walk through Israel, it can't happen. It is a kind of spell she casts. You actually did such a walk yourself, but the terrible thing is that, before you had finished the book, one of your sons died. He was a tank commander. He knew about the book, but you hadn't finished it when he died. Eventually, you went back to it. Can you feel the bruise in the book that resulted from going back to it in the knowledge of what had happened, because surely, in a sense, you wrote the book for the same reason that the woman went on her walk, nor is that kind of fear restricted to you? It is felt by everybody in Israel who has people serving in the military.
GROSSMAN: Yes. I told a friend yesterday that when you have a baby born in Israel immediately the parents

calculate what will be the date when he will be eighteen and go to the army. I started to write this book very soon before Uri my son went to the army because I felt I wanted to accompany him as much as I could. I knew he was going to have a tough service in the Occupied Territories. I wanted to be there as much as I could, and I had this idea about the mother who, as you described, decides she will not be there when they come, the notifiers. She will not be a sitting duck. As she says, 'I will not allow them to drill their notification into me.' What she does is to refuse to collaborate with the machinery of the military, of the state. She will not be there, and she goes to the end of the land, which has double meaning. She goes to the place which is the border between Israel and Lebanon and she starts to walk there, a very long trail which is called the Israel Trail, but on her way she kidnaps a man, Avram, who was the love of her youth and probably is the love of her life even though she is not married to him, something that happens only in Israel. She met Avram when he was sixteen. When she met him, he was like a volcano of ideas, imagination, fantasies, sexuality and creativity. Then when he was twenty-one it was the time of the Yom Kippur war – we count our decades according to the wars – and he fell captive to the Egyptians who tortured him brutally and he came back to Israel later broken in his mind and in his body. He doesn't want to have any contact with her, or with life, but she makes him come with her and gradually we understand that she has a purpose in that he is, in a way, very close to this son Ofer who went to the war. She walks with Avram, who is a total zombie at the beginning of the book, and starts telling him the story of the life of Ofer, about all the small details from which we accumulate one human being in this life, all the minutiae of life, all those moments of effort and devotion and mistakes and frustration in love that we infuse into the veins of our children. I think she tells about all these most intimate moments because this is her way to protect her son, to infuse solidity and vitality into him when he is out there in the hard war when the air is full of military slogans and passwords and clichés and generalisation, as it is always when there is war, believe me. She is using the most intimate fragile tender multi-layered language. Her way of resisting is to say, 'I' in a reality that confiscates the 'I'ness and sanctifies the weakness. The book is about their journey – for me it was five hundred kilometres along Israel – the people they meet, but more about everything that happens between them and their joint effort to save the life of Ofer.

BIGSBY: After your son died you were almost stunned into silence. You said that it took words away from you in some way. When you did return it was to write a book which is not long, and which is effectively in verse. In it you write, 'I cannot understand this thing that happened nor can I fathom the person I am now after it happened and what is worse is if I do not write it I cannot understand who he is now either, my son. No getting around it I can't understand anything until I write it.' Later you write, 'he is dead, I know now, I now can say though always in a whisper "the boy is dead." I understand almost the meaning of the sounds 'the boy is dead' I recognise these words as holding truth, he is dead, I know, yes I admit it he is dead but his death it swells, abates, formulates, unquiet, unquiet is his death, so unquiet… it still breaks my heart my son to think that I have, that one could, that I have found the words.' It is very difficult to read that without getting moved by it because it seems to have been an impossible book to write but a necessary book to write. Having written it, though, it seems to leave you with a sense of guilt that you could write it?

GROSSMAN: I would not say guilt. While I was writing I was quite torn between these two urges. One is not to write. How can one dare write about something like that? How can one pigeonhole it into words because it is really an experience that, no matter how much writers write about it, remains such a 'mystery,' though that is a small word and I will not try to find a better one. At first the reaction is to be silent, or to shout, to cry out, or to do something physical like running to the end of the land. Then, later, I realised that if I do not find words for what has happened the channels between me and this loss will be gradually closed, and I did not want them to close.

It is not that I am a masochist or something, but I just felt that it is so tempting to avoid feeling and to avoid having words that will make this loss more tangible, more nuanced, but like everything that happens to me in my life I understand it through writing. This is my way to understand my life. I realise there are so many things that I only started to understand – the situation that I describe and what my feelings and opinions regarding it are – after I have written about them. My family and I got many letters of condolence from Israel and beyond. Many were written by writers from Israel or elsewhere, writers who I knew by their books or personally, and it was so interesting to see that most of the letters, let alone three or four, said the same thing: 'We are speechless. We have no words,' and they were really masters of language and yet at such a moment people either remain mute or start to talk in clichés, but cliché is the last thing you need or want in such a moment.

You want a reaction that will be totally tuned to your need and since I did not find something that could express what I felt, I said, 'I will try to write something.' I said, 'if I was sent to this island of exile – and grief is an island of exile, an island because it is the most isolating human predicament – then it is exile because you are exiled from everything that you knew before. Nothing can be taken for granted anymore, nothing.' And I said, 'at least I will have met this island of exile with my own words. This is the way I know how to make things mine and to 'Be' in my life with a capital B, not to avoid my life, not to run away, to be there.' Then I was able to start writing it and to find words and yes, the centaur in this book – and the centaur is the story teller, the writer who is unable to write about the death of his son and will not write – after a while assimilates with his writing desk and becomes half writer, half writing desk. Only when he is able to conclude the book is he able to make this separation because I think that there are probably people here who have experienced something like a loss of a very dear person in their life. There is always the delicate question of how to forget parts without killing the one that we loved and how to remember without dying of it and in this book I tried to find this very thin line to tread and to find a language to talk about what has no words, finding words for it that will still be fresh.

I just want to say one more thing about the writing of this book. People who are religious can benefit from the belief that there is an afterlife. I am a non-believer, very Jewish but absolutely atheist, and I hope it is not a spoiler, but I don't believe in an afterlife. There is no afterlife, okay. Even more than that it is so important for me to know that there is no afterlife, that what we have here is what we have, that there is no second chance, that's it. This burdens us with a lot of responsibility towards our time, towards the preciousness of our time. There is no chance for another quantity of time, but I learned that there is one thing in which we can really be and at the same time 'Be,' with capital B again, be with the wholeness of life and vitality and creativity and with the total nothingness of death. And this, for me, can only exist in art, in writing prose or poetry or making movies or music or theatre. I think that every serious piece of art that I have read or watched or listened to took place in this place, in this very throbbing and undefinable place that consists of the two things.

BIGSBY: I want to ask you a question about language, which you have mentioned several times. In a sense the writer's language, your language in this context, is a resistance to other kinds of language because you are surrounded by it. Mario Vargas Llosa ran for the Presidency of Peru and was dismayed by the language he had to use. Suddenly all the ambiguity, the finesse, the beauty of the language shattered in shards because that wasn't a language he could use. You live in a country which is almost permanently at risk of war where the military language, perhaps of necessity, suffuses everything, so that the art of writing is an act of resistance, holding on to another language, a language which transcends that of daily life. In your case it is Hebrew, a strange language because it went to sleep for a long time and was only revived at the turn of the nineteenth into the twentieth century. Actually, the British made it an official language before Israel did. Writing in Hebrew, though, means that it may take nine years for a book to appear in English. I don't suppose you are ever tempted to write in English but what are the qualities of Hebrew that appeal and does it have its limitation because of that history?

GROSSMAN: First I just refer to the beginning for your question. The first thing that is manipulated and distorted and forged in a situation of war is the language. There is a special language that is created in order to justify what we are doing and to demonise what the others are doing. They are words that are meant deliberately to buffer between the individual and the things that are being done in his name and on his or her behalf. When I write articles – which I prefer much less to writing fiction, of course – articles which react to the situation in my country, I stick to a very personal, private and intimate language, and it is important because of the thing that you said, because the air, the whole verbal air is confiscated by the situation, we call it 'the situation,' '*HaMatsav*,' a euphemism for an ongoing bleeding of a hundred years. We say '*Hamatsav*,' this situation, as if it is a kind of objective situation that fell on us from heaven and we can do nothing to change but I think that especially in such a poisoned reality – poisoned by fears, by animosity, by the narrow mindedness that a long state of war imposes on the individual and on the society – it is so essential to go back to a vital language, to a language that is nuanced that insists on no answers and therefore also when I write I don't think that I am doing a kind of political act. I just want to tell a good story. But the fact that Hebrew literature, movies and music and art are so blossoming now I regard as a kind of a compensation for the general paralysis in the political field, as if the vitality of the society must burst out somewhere and it goes through the language.

You spoke about Hebrew. When people see how I write from right to left they say, 'ah look you write in the opposite way' and I say 'no, you write in the opposite way. We were first' and we write from right to left. Hebrew was dormant throughout the almost two millennia of our diaspora. Hebrew did not exist as an active, live, living language. It was only a sacred language used in religious rites or holy books and then, at the beginning of the twentieth century, a crazy genius guy named Eliezer Ben-Yehuda came from Russia to Jerusalem and decided to kiss the sleeping beauty, the dormant language, and he started to create a newspaper in Hebrew. He forced his wife to speak Hebrew with him and she had to agree that if she bore a child they would only speak Hebrew to him. And they had a child and spoke Hebrew to him. Sometimes I think he was the only Hebrew-speaking child on earth. Can you imagine what kind of solitude he suffered? And now we have two granddaughters and they have just started to acquire the language, and for them it is taken for granted. They speak Hebrew, but he had to overcome so many problems because for two thousand years merchants did not do business in Hebrew and soldiers did not have a military slang in Hebrew and lovers did not make love in Hebrew and children did not play in Hebrew. So, he had to reinvent the language based on the Bible and the Talmud, but, of course, in the time of the Bible we didn't have a tomato or giraffe or crane or ice cream, so he had to re-invent on the basis of something that had never existed.

He was really a genius because I think one of the greatest achievements of Israel, among many, many achievements – and don't get me wrong, with all the criticism that I have of Israel I do not forget for a second that the fact that we have a state of our own is a miracle and I know that it's not very fashionable to say good things about Israel or about the Zionist idea – the story of the return of the Jewish people to this land and the things that we have created there against all odds, living our life in the most hostile environment that really hates us and doesn't want us to be there and wages war upon us time and again, all the economic, terrible situation, and the fact that Israel had to absorb millions of people that were sometimes much more than the population that absorbed them, all this is one of the most exciting, meaningful and profound human stories that we have. I see what happens to Israel now and it really kills me to see how it has been distorted, the idea of the state, but I do not for a second forget that the fact that we have a state is a miracle.

BIGSBY: Your new book is called *A Horse Walks into a Bar* and if that sounds like a joke, this is full of jokes.

GROSSMAN: It is.

BIGSBY: It is about a stand-up comedian in a rather run-down club who is telling jokes, but it gets darker and darker as he goes on. People begin to leave because he is circling around an event in his own life which was a traumatic moment when he was fifteen. He was at a camp, a vaguely military youth camp, and they call him out and say he has to get to Jerusalem for a funeral, but they don't tell him whose funeral it is. He thinks it may be his father, but it might be his mother. They don't tell him. There is, therefore, this curious sense of indifference, the inability of people to put themselves in the place of somebody who is having that kind of experience. Surely this has a resonance going beyond that particular story.

GROSSMAN: First of all, I am glad that you are my reader because this is really for me one of the hearts of the book. There are plenty of people who are indifferent to the suffering of others, the ability that we develop in order not really to become committed to pain when we see it. We all like to peep into the hell of others. It gives us a nice stimulation as we see the wound of the other exposed, but we do not really allow ourselves to become committed to it, to carry the burden of it on our shoulders.

The whole story takes place in one session of stand-up comedy in a rundown nightclub in the city of Netanya in Israel. When he was fourteen he was sent to this funeral for a journey of four endless hours with a half-crazy military driver who kept telling him jokes, but in the end we understand that this driver was the most humane character because he really wanted to make his journey more bearable and to make the boy laugh, to forget for a second the tragedy that awaits him. After some time, though, the boy starts to believe that, if nobody told him whether it is his papa or mama who has died, it is up to him to decide. And when he thinks of that, his mother and father start to quarrel in his mind begging him to keep him or her alive and since they were a very symbiotic family, like the Bermuda Triangle, as he describes it, and the papa and the mama are totally different from each other, he has to choose which life he wants to have and maybe all his life he will continue to pay for this experience, for what happened when he made up his mind eventually. The question is how was it possible? And cases like this happened: it is based on a story that somebody told me when I was writing another book, back in 1991, and for twenty-four years I was haunted by this idea of a boy going to the funeral not knowing whose funeral it is. And each time I finished a novel I said, 'okay, now I am writing the story of this boy' and I was unable to because I didn't find how to find a situation that would allow this story to burst out. Then one day, suddenly, some three or four years ago, I had the idea that it should be told in a stand-up comedy session, in the most unlogical, unreasonable situation to tell such an intimate story. But, on the other hand, here he is again, Dovaleh, my stand-up comedian, talking to a totally indifferent audience, an audience which does not really want to listen to his troubles but want to be entertained and to hear good jokes, finding a way to tell them his tragic story, but all the time having to bribe them with jokes, to keep them there. So, it is this tender line between tragedy, horror, and laughter, as they find themselves laughing, even as the reality becomes more and more dark.

RICHARD HOLMES

Richard Holmes was born in London in 1945. His first biography, *Shelley: The Pursuit*, appeared in 1974. Among his many others are *Coleridge: Early Visions*, *Dr Johnson and Mr Savage*, *The Age of Wonder* and *Falling Upwards: How We Took to the Air*. He has also published reflections on the nature and role of biography from a personal perspective: *Footsteps, Sidetracks*, and *This Long Pursuit*. His awards include the Whitbread Book of the Year, the Duff Cooper Prize, the James Tait Black Memorial Prize, and the Royal Society Book Prize.

This interview was recorded at UEA on 16 November, 2016.

BIGSBY: Your book, *The Long Pursuit*, has a sub-title, *Reflections of a Romantic Biographer*, as *Footsteps* has a sub-title *Adventures of a Romantic Biographer*. Does that mean you are a biographer of the romantics or by nature romantic?

HOLMES: Biographers deal in ambiguity. The romantic period, in the wider sense, from the mid-eighteenth century to the early nineteenth century, is one that has fascinated me all my life. The very first bit of work I did was on the poet Thomas Chatterton, who died in 1770. I had written an essay on Chatterton's brief tragic life in Bristol and London and the great publisher John Murray liked it and put it in the *Cornhill* magazine. This was an amazing break for me to get in 1970, aged twenty-four. This period of romanticism is so rich in literature and, as I later found out, in science. The people are so fascinating. They travel, they go abroad, write wonderful letters and diaries and write not only astonishing poetry but the mist vivid prose. So it is a tremendously rich period to work with.

BIGSBY: You are not the first writer in your family, are you?

HOLMES: No, that is right. My mother was a short-story writer and a children's poet and used to publish in DC Thomson's Scottish magazines for young people, as well as an anthology of war poetry published by Virago. Actually, at the end of his life, my father, who was a solicitor, also published a series of autobiographical short stories. He had a wonderful, crisp, lawyer's style. So those were powerful influences but of a completely different kind. My mother was what I would describe as an Anglican agnostic and her world view was tender and also very romantic. My father was, by contrast, a Roman Catholic and great rationalist. That tension had quite strong effects on me I think.

BIGSBY: When you say severe?

HOLMES: His own father had been an Anglican vicar, but he was a Catholic convert. He was converted while an undergraduate at Cambridge, a time of great struggle for him I suspect, and they always say converts are the most dangerous believers. Anyway, that was a kind of tension.

BIGSBY: As a result, you were sent to a Catholic boarding school, a fairly well-known one which is so Catholic that only now has it got its first lay headmaster; so, profoundly Catholic. What did that do to you? Were you deeply religious or did you rebel against it?

HOLMES: The best thing Downside did for me was teach me the value of long-distance cross-country running, which is not entirely a joke. That is the one sport I was any good at, and I loved it. I loved the notion that every time you went on a run potentially you were escaping. You might never come back. Also, it is lonely, and you are competing against yourself, which is something that, for writers, is quite important to learn. But the school also had two quite brilliant lay teachers, John Coulsin, who taught English, and Desmond Gregory, who taught history. Together, they taught me to read, write, research, and think for myself. Otherwise, I found it a rather difficult place and I was very pleased when I left.

BIGSBY: You left it for Cambridge to read history, but you went to a college which was more to do with science than the arts.

HOLMES: Yes. I had a great break there. It was the freezing winter of 1963 and the whole of Cambridge was as cold as only Cambridge can be. It was under ice, and the place seemed grim. I was interviewed at Trinity College by a distinguished historian. I can remember him poking the fire and asking me searching questions about fourteenth-century England, which I knew nothing about, so all my answers were hopeless. All he said was, 'Very pleased to meet you, Mr Holmes. Don't you think you should do some more medieval history?' And he continued poking the fire. That was the glorious end of my Cambridge interview. But quite shortly afterwards, I heard that there were people at Churchill College, the brand new science college founded in 1960, who would see me. Perhaps there was something I said; I had a completely different kind of interview at Churchill. I remember trudging through the snow to the new college, only half of which was built, but it was warm and modern and thrilling, and I thought, 'This is more like it.' I was interviewed by a sympathetic don called John Morrison, who later became president of Wolfson College, who simply said to me, 'You don't have to read history. Why don't you read English, because we have got this extraordinary chap called Professor George Steiner.' George eventually became a sort-of mentor. So, again, a wonderful lucky break. In the first interview I ever had with George he said, in his slight German accent, 'How many languages do you speak, Mr Holmes?' Then he said, 'Okay, go away for a year and learn another one,' which I did. I went to France.

George was an inspired, passionate teacher and lecturer. The fact that he was also rather difficult, and intellectually demanding, was tremendously good, as I was so ignorant and my spelling was so bad. I remember the first trembling essay I turned in on George Eliot and all he said was, 'There is a general agreement in British civilisation that George Eliot is spelt with only one "t" at the end,' so it was a very sobering experience. He had a real passion for the whole breadth of European literature and that's what you want aged eighteen or nineteen, and I marvelled at it. We would be given passages of poetry, with absolutely no context, and we would have not only to explain them but place and date them. I remember at his first seminar he said to me, 'By the end of your degree you will be able to date any passage whatever within ten years.' Then he added, 'And then it will be your turn to test me.' The whole thing was a joy to me, a mind-expanding experience, and in addition many of my friends were physicists and engineers who spent their time testing things.

BIGSBY: The world you entered was that of the 1960s. Were you a part of that or an observer?

HOLMES: I think the idea was that I should stay on and do post graduate work at Cambridge. But I did not do well in my part two, and only got a first on was what was called 'a free paper' where you could just write your own stuff. I submitted a collection of my own poems for that, and some translations. So that set me free to go to London and then I knew writing was the one thing I wanted to do, even though I didn't know how on earth I would live off it. I went to the Labour Exchange and the first job I got was compiling the Electoral Register. That sounds very humdrum but actually it was a wonderful bit of further education. I was sent round the Pimlico area, which was all very poor in those days, and knocked on doors and started talking to people. I was simply getting their names so they had the right to vote. But they would frequently take me in and tell me what their troubles were, and I learned to listen. So, it was a year-long social education. And all the time I was trying to write.

I went up to Liverpool, met the young Liverpool poets, and wrote a piece about them and their poetry. I sent it in to *The Times* and to my amazement I got a letter saying, 'Come in and speak to us.' William Rees-Mogg was the editor and he looked me up and down and said, 'Are you eating enough?' Then he added, 'You had better see the literary editor.' They were just launching *The Times Saturday Review* and looking for young writers. The first piece I wrote was about JG Ballard, the new science-fiction novelist who was creating a great stir. I remember the literary editor saying to me, 'Read everything he has written, and then everything written about him.' It is that discipline I thank *The Times* for. I worked freelance with them for probably twenty years, under three marvellous literary editors: Michael Ratcliffe, Ion Trewin, and Philip Howard. There is nothing like that basic journalistic discipline: do your research, get the pieces in on time, and make sure that you do not write bad first paragraphs.

BIGSBY: You mentioned writing poems and your first published book was a slim volume of poetry.
HOLMES: It was. It was called *One for Sorrow*. How very well-titled that was.

BIGSBY: I have it here. One of five hundred copies.
HOLMES: It is very thin, isn't it?

BIGSBY: Yes, but dense. That was your first publication outside of newspapers and magazines. Were you tempted to see poetry as your future?
HOLMES: Yes. The person who helped me was the poet Christopher Logue, whose wonderful Homer translations and modernisations, later collected as *War*

Music, hugely impressed me. He wrote to me because I had been reviewing his poetry saying, 'Maybe you ought to think about a collection yourself.' But the letter got misfiled in *The Times* and they only found it after six months. The final result was that book, published in 1970. I still go on writing poetry, but not for publication. It is the writer's equivalent of going to the gym. You are testing your use of language. I even use rhymes and stanza forms and it is a terrific discipline.

BIGSBY: You have said that after you had left Cambridge you went through a period of being suicidally depressed. Is that just an expression or is that Winston Churchill's black dog?

HOLMES: My father used to refer to Churchill's black dog. I think many writers do have a kind of black dog who circles round and it is most noticeable that the black dog arrives when you are not writing. Writing seems to immediately open the door and let the dog out and the light in. I don't think it is that unusual.

BIGSBY: You mentioned France. How long were you there?

HOLMES: I stayed there for about six months and walked round the Midi, from the hills of the Cévennes to the marshes of the Carmargue, and learned French. I think many writers, maybe everybody, has this other country of the heart. To me it is France and the French language and French literature. That's my other country. The very first time I was taken by my parents when I was about nine. We drove down in the ancient Wolsey as far as the Pyrenees. That journey has always stayed with me. I went again as a teenager and then again, later, after I had written the Shelley book, for two years to Paris and then again, later, many glorious times.

BIGSBY: Was it in France that you wrote a novel?

HOLMES: I had written a novel, yes, which we shall not mention again, but I did once publish a short story called *Doctor Johnson's First Cat,* and it was broadcast by the BBC. You learn a lot from the way fiction is written when you are writing biography.

BIGSBY: You have written literary criticism, poetry, a novel. Surely all that feeds into biography because it is a hybrid form.

HOLMES: Absolutely, it does feed in and you do need to practise those skills and keep them alive. I suppose one of the definitions of biography is that it is a hybrid form. Part of writing biography is being able to orchestrate different types of evidence. That's quite a scholarly task but it also requires the ability to tell a clear story that holds the reader. That is parallel to a novelist's task and it is something I absolutely love doing. Even in the shorter pieces in *This Long Pursuit,* each one is meant to be like a short story and have a particular voice and shape to it, and a particular ending. One of the early things to decide is whether the voice is to be tragical, comical, pastoral, historical, whatever. Very often the biography you finally write turns out to be a mixture of those forms.

BIGSBY: I mentioned a novel which never broke surface, but you also wrote a book about French writers which suffered a similar fate.

HOLMES: Yes, that is right. I wrote a complete book about the nineteenth-century writer Théophile Gautier and his great friend the poet Gérard de Nerval. They interested me because Gautier was a journalist who worked all his life for newspapers and had a solid career, while Nerval was a footloose poet, one of those friends that you have very early on in your life whose career gradually gets wilder and wilder and ends in disaster. He travelled abroad, wrote a lot of poetry and in the end was incarcerated in an asylum and committed suicide. So, you had this deep friendship but these two contrasted stories, and that fascinated me. I did write that biography but I could never get the balance right. So instead I separately wrote several short pieces about Gautier, particularly one of his very, very funny visits to London, in the great tradition of French mockery of things British. The height of English cuisine, he declared, was 'the steamed potato'. So that was the best I could do with Gautier. But in *Footsteps*, the fourth section becomes a complete study of Nerval and his poetry and also what went wrong when he committed suicide. I try and trace it right back to his childhood, and that is something biography can do very well.

BIGSBY: Enough of books that you didn't publish; let me move to one that you did. How did you find your way to *Shelley*?

HOLMES: I don't think I read a word of Shelley at Cambridge. But when I was working for the Council in London, I happened to read a rather elusive poem of, his set in Italy. I remember I was waiting for my washing in a laundromat off Baker Street. So, there I was, reading the high drama of Shelley's *Epipsychidion* in the laundromat, and I suddenly thought, 'this is the place I want to be, not the laundromat'. At that point, in 1971, I was writing regularly for *The Times*. I was their official poetry reviewer for two years, which was very good in one sense but in another it was quite limiting and I took the decision to write a biography of Shelley. So, I gave up that job.

BIGSBY: You were stepping off a cliff because that was the source of your income.

HOLMES: Yes, it was, absolutely. I remember having a talk with my nice editor at *The Times*, Michael Ratcliffe, and he said, 'Well, it's a risk but we will still be here when you come back, Richard.' So I did that for two years. I travelled around, lived on a camp bed and went to all the places that Shelley had been.

BIGSBY: And that raises the question which you explore in *Footsteps*, namely your conviction that to write a biography you have to go the places that that person went to, not just where they lived but the places they visited. What do you derive from that? Is it simply a sense of the geography or is it more metaphysical than that?

HOLMES: It is a mixture. *Footsteps* is a book trying to look into that question. The first time this happened to me was when I was eighteen in the south of France, in the Cévennes region, not down by the beaches but up in the wild Cévennes, when I had followed in the footsteps of Robert Louis Stevenson. I had a copy of his book and a little map in the front and for something like two weeks I just followed that track and an extraordinary thing happened. I was eighteen, walking alone, just learning the language, quite isolated, and the effect was that Stevenson, who had been there a hundred years or so before, became vividly real to me, extraordinarily real, and that is a basic function of the biographer, walking back through history. While I was down there every night I slept out under the stars exactly like Stevenson. I was visited by various snakes and insects and some nights there were fantastic electrical storms. Occasionally, I went to the little auberge and produced my passport and signed in and always the same thing happened. In those days, in your passport, you had to write 'occupation'. I had written 'writer'. But of course I had published nothing. What happened was that Madame would open the little book and say, 'Oh Monsieur, I see you are a *waiter*.' Then I imagined it being 'travel writer' and then she would say, 'Oh Monsieur, I see you are a table waiter.'

The point of this parable is that it taught me a kind of humility about what the biographer's job was. In a sense you are at someone's service, you are waiting upon them, paying attention to them. So, from the Stevenson time on I realised that you didn't just go to the archives, you went to the places that your subjects had travelled. And they being the Romantics that took me all over England, France, Scotland and Italy and, in Coleridge's case, to Sicily, Malta, Italy and Germany. You travel with them and that is a way of reimagining their lives. With Shelley, I remember his white beach house near Lerici, in fact at a little tiny village called San Terenzo. I went down there in November. My travelling was still pretty rough; just finding somewhere to stay was hard. By chance, I went to a little café and started talking and somebody said, 'Oh, I know someone who lets rooms.' This was a sweet elderly woman who let rooms to the car workers from Turin in the summer. So in the winter they were very, very cheap. She said, 'I used to be a cook in England; I quite like the English. You can have a room,' and the room turned out to be right next to the Casa Magni, which is where Shelley's last months were spent. So, I was sitting there for days, just imagine, on the balcony reading his letters and poems, looking directly across to Shelley's balcony and I could see all the things that he saw, and what the storms were like in the bay of Spezia. I learned very simple things too: for instance, swimming there I realised, climbing up, that the volcanic rock is lethally sharp. Anyone drowning there would be torn to pieces by this. These very simple, physical things came to me and that sort of research has gone on with everything I have written.

BIGSBY: We will come back to Shelley, but first let me ask a seemingly simple question. When does a biography start and when does it finish? The natural instinct is to say, 'It begins when the person is born and it ends when he or she dies,' or does it begin with their parents or with their grandparents or the social movement that was the context? Where does it start?

HOLMES: There is a wonderful essay by Virginia Woolf in which she says that one of the grand problems is to decide how long anyone's life lasted, 'whatever the *Dictionary of National Biography* may say'. So, yes, the idea of where a life begins and ends is problematic. Then there is the question of the afterlife of the subject, which is also significant I think. In every case you have to choose very deliberately. I remember Michael Holroyd ringing me up and saying, 'I can't get Bernard Shaw to die,' and in fact his solution was to put the death on the very first page of the first volume of the biography. Similarly, I thought Coleridge would begin dramatically at the worst time of his life, in 1814, when his opium addiction was at its worst. Everybody had lost faith in him, even the Wordsworths, and he had disappeared to a secret cottage at Calne in Wiltshire, which I subsequently found. I thought I would start there at the darkest mid-point and then move backwards and forwards in time. Actually, Coleridge's life is so rich and complicated, his notebooks are so good, that what I finally started with was him just reminiscing in old age about his own childhood, saying how exceptional he was and how he talked endlessly right from his earliest years. So I was able to present this and simply add, 'And then, like the Ancient Mariner, there was no stopping him.' That became the beginning of the book. So, you do have to decide where the story begins.

Also, in a biography there are what I call 'time panels'. There are 'back stories'. Let me give an example. When Shelley meets Byron, in 1816, near Lake Geneva where they were going to live at the Villa Diodati, there is a problem for the biographer. How much does Shelley know about Byron? How much does Byron know about Shelley? Are you going to go into the full back story or are you going to try and introduce it gently over sections? And in fact, at Diodati, Byron – and his physician, Doctor Polidori – themselves gradually question Shelley about his life and Shelley tells them about his childhood and his sense of persecution by his father and so on. So all that can then come out in the story, gently. So you may have panels of narrative which slide backwards and forwards through time, though you need to plan that carefully, always holding the attention of the reader. Then there is the question of the afterlife, the subject's changing reputation after death. A lot of *The Long Pursuit* is about afterlives because biography doesn't end with a death and it doesn't end with one biography either. It is my belief that there is no such thing as a definitive biography. One of the characteristics of the form is that it is a cumulative process.

BIGSBY: Publishers always want to call them 'definitive'.
HOLMES: Yes, well they are always wrong and one of the reasons why biography is such a wonderful subject to teach and to study is because such a thing as comparative biography exists. Take the case of Mary Wollstonecraft, who died in 1797 as a result of childbirth fever, the child being Mary Shelley. Her distraught philosopher husband William Godwin, to cure his grief, writes this extraordinary biography in the space of about three months. It is shockingly honest. Robert Southey said, 'He stripped his dead wife naked,' and yet it reads now with wonderful honesty. So, there is this first biography in 1798, but then there is a whole tradition of nineteenth-century biographies of Mary Wollstonecraft. Then there are modern feminist biographies of her going right up to the present time: Claire Tomalin's or Janet Todd's,

for example. So, you study how biography has altered the reputation of a particular subject, maybe over several generations. It is comparative and cumulative. It is quite unlike the novel, which is unique. In that respect biography is always a cumulative process.

Let me tell you a story from when I was footstepping Coleridge. He was born in the west country, at Ottery St Mary, and as a small child wandered all along the river at Ottery and found this weird cave, called Pixie's Parlour. He crawled into it as a seven-year-old and went right to the back where he carved his initials, STC, in the stone. Then, when he was an undergraduate, he went back to see his initials 'carved by the hands of childhood'. He later described this cave, comparing it to his researches into metaphysics, going into darker and darker places and the stone would give a magic 'mineral' glitter when he raised his visiknary candle. So, this cave, with these initials on it, was very important to me and, on the footsteps principle, one dark November I went down to Ottery. The river had meandered and I thought the cave wasn't there any more, but the river had simply moved away and there it was, very sinister, very dark, and I thought, 'Okay, I will crawl in.' I had my lighter and I crawled further and further in and then at the back, to my amazement, I found the initials STC. I straightened up suddenly with delight, banged my head on the top of the cave, a sliver of stone came down and I realised it was soft sandstone. So those initials could not possibly have lasted for two hundred years. I came out holding my head in pain and biographical grief. Then I realised why the initials were still there. Of course, it was because previous people had crawled in like me – maybe biographers, maybe just souvenir hunters – and they had re-carved the initials, so it was carved and re-carved. And I thought that in many ways, this is the image of how biography as a form works. It is a carving and re-carving of a subject's reputation. So, when you are teaching you can look at the way a subject's reputation has altered through time, maybe over two hundred years.

BIGSBY: But isn't it also a reminder that, just as science fiction may be set in the future it tends to be about now, so a biography tells you something about the moment it was written rather than simply revealing its subject?

HOLMES: Yes, absolutely right, which is another reason why it is such an interesting subject to study. It reflects the time the biographer was writing it, just as you can tell that science-fiction films made in the 1920s are definitely 1920s films, in the same way early Victorian biography is very different from late Victorian biography, or eighteenth-century biography. In fact, I invented something called 'Holmes's Law' which is that as a biography gets older it becomes more and more autobiographical because it becomes clearer and clearer that it is also about the narrator who tells the story. Boswell's *Life of Johnson* has never been out of print. It is still a wonderful book, but has it really become *James Boswell: My Life*? To some degree, it is now about its author and this shows up more and more clearly with time and that process inevitably continues. So, my Shelley book, which was 1974, has after only forty years become very much a post-1960s biography.

BIGSBY: I raised the question of endings. On the face of it, Shelley's life ends with his drowning but something happened after that. There is the question of what happened to the body, what happened to the missing heart.

HOLMES: This was provoked by a wonderful essay by Hermione Lee called *Shelley's Heart and Pepys's Lobsters*. It was about the drowning of Shelley. She said, absolutely correctly, that in my biography, the moment he is drowned was the end as far as I was concerned, while it turns out that there is a long history about why the boat sank and grotesque things like the burning of Shelley's body. Supposedly Trelawny raked out the heart, though there is a modern view that it was actually Shelley's liver. Well I thought, 'No, I can't get into all that.' But much later I thought how interesting that that had happened. So, I wrote an essay called *Shelley Undrowned* and it looks at what happened, at the way that drowning was turned into legend. For example, a very simple thing: Mary Shelley, when she published the collected poems of her husband Shelley, wrote these very moving notes, prose notes about the circumstances of each poem. But, more and more, she said Shelley had predicted his own drowning, that in the early poems, like *Alastor, or the Spirit of Solitude*, you can see shipwrecks and boats. Then she says because he was an aerial unearthly figure, like the name of his boat, which was actually called the *Don Juan*, not the Ariel, he was a spirit doomed to leave us. Gradually this Victorian image built up and Edward John Trelawny, who was actually responsible for a lot of the design of the boat, wrote twelve versions of the cremation of Shelley's body, between about 1850 and 1875. In each one Trelawny has a more and more important role, and he introduces Mary Shelley into it. But Mary Shelley was never at the cremation. There are Victorian paintings of the burning of Shelley's body in which Mary is depicted kneeling there. She was never there. So, this develops a particular Victorian view, a Matthew Arnold view, of the ineffectual angel 'beating in the void his luminous wings in vain'. It is an instrument for getting rid of a lot of Shelley's political radicalism. Victorian biographers made him into this beautiful unearthly suicidal figure who was doomed to drown.

BIGSBY: So, writing a modern biography is a bit like getting the varnish off a painting. You have to remove the varnish outside in order to start again with a fresh picture.

HOLMES: A good image.

BIGSBY: Let me turn to your study of Coleridge. When you set out, you said you were thinking one volume but ended up with two big volumes spaced out over about a nine-year period. So, you had no idea when you started how big it was going to be, and it is worth reminding people that writing biography can be a long-term venture and that any income has to be divided by the number of years it takes to write. it is actually not a richly rewarding job.

HOLMES: I can't say that as a young biographer that particularly concerned me, as long as I could do the travelling. So, yes, I wrote volume one and the publishers were very good. They said, 'All right, we will publish it as the first volume one' and then I went off and did a completely different book, *Dr Johnson and Mr Savage*. Then I took another deep breath and went back to Coleridge and as I said, 'both of us had aged considerably in that time'. So, yes, you have to pace yourself and it is long. I often compare it to the length of time a feature film takes to make. And you keep your faithful notebooks. I think I have got two hundred of these now and they take you through. Perhaps I should explain about the notebooks, because I use them in a very particular way. I treat them as two-sided, a sort of double accounting. There are entries on both sides of the notebook. On the right-hand side is where you put the archival, the factual, the objective material, everything you can find about your subject and pin down as accurately and scholarly as you can. You are assembling a life as you go along. The left-hand page is for your completely subjective feelings about your subject, which might include excitement, irritation, impatience. It might include dreams about your subject, frustrations that you cannot find particular kinds of evidence, doubts about their political or other beliefs. You are also trying out the way you are going to tell the story on the left-hand page. So I always say to my students, 'don't put everything down you are thinking about your subject. Later you can decide what stays in.' goes into it.' Coming back to this critical question of empathy, how far you identify with your subject. Empathy is very important and has some parallels with portrait painting, some parallels with acting. You try to put yourself in your subject, but you must also take yourself away from it. Self-identification, in the end, is the most dangerous trap. It produces terrible books, but by using the left-hand side you can be are aware of what you are feeling. I remember once giving a talk to the Society of Psychoanalysts and I was referring to this and said, 'so I include my embarrassments', at which they all immediately sat up, wanting to hear more. The notebook allows you your whole range as a writer and is one of the things that help you pace yourself over this long period of writing.

BIGSBY: Tell me, why did you say that you can't love both Wordsworth and Coleridge?

HOLMES: Ah yes, well there is a natural biographer's

instinct to set one person off against another and you have got to be very careful of that. I think in the end I felt the temperamental difference between them. Either the chaotic temperament of Coleridge really appeals to you or the egotistical sublime appeals to you, which is what Keats had. Or called Wordsworth. I felt that the power relationship moved between them. The west country Coleridge really was the dominating figure but gradually that changes. Gradually, Wordsworth becomes the controlling figure and Coleridge's life becomes more and more chaotic. I think biographers identify with that rich chaos. He goes on his perilous travels to the Mediterranean while Wordsworth is almost literally dug into the Lake District and Coleridge is off in Italy and Sicily and Malta keeping his wonderful notebooks. There is nothing equivalent in Wordsworth to the Coleridge notebooks, of which there are over seventy. They take you right into his heart, I think. So, gradually, I warmed to him and maybe I was unfair about that, quite possibly, but, yes, I am a Coleridge man more than a Wordsworth man, it's true.

BIGSBY: You have talked about the irrecoverability of the past. What are the problems that confront a biographer in going back over the centuries?

HOLMES: There is an argument that the sources now for a modern biography are so complicated, so rich, because of all the electronic media, recordings, internet, email, let alone blogs. But letter-writing, on which nineteenth-century biography is so dependent, has declined. Each period presents different problems. For instance, writing about Richard Savage there were very few letters, but there was Samuel Johnson's wonderful essay, along with a lot of contemporary pamphlets. One of the most interesting documents is the court register and record of Savage's trial for murder at the Old Bailey. It is extraordinary with various witnesses describing him. Savage himself gives evidence, and you hear his voice. That kind of document is unique to then, 1724, whereas with the Victorians you get a great collections of letters that you can work through. The type of resource alters with each century. For a contemporary biography

I imagine it is very different but that is not something
I want to take on, unlike, say, James Atlas on Saul Bellow.

BIGSBY: But there are going to be gaps in someone's life, periods when there were no diary entries, when you don't know what was happening in that period. You mention the importance of the word 'perhaps'. How do you fill those caesuras, those breakages in knowledge about somebody? Do you just say, 'we know nothing of this period', or what?

HOLMES: You need to take the reader into your confidence when there are problems with sources. Very often you are given two or three accounts of the same event and the fascination of the biography is to show those and to show the contrasts between them. I think particularly, for example, of a wonderful book by Claire Tomalin called *The Invisible Woman*. This is about Dickens's mistress, Nelly Ternan – who, incidentally, in John Forster's huge, two-volume *The Life of Dickens*, published in 1872, shortly after his death, makes no appearance at all, except one in the index. Her figure just doesn't appear in that great Victorian biography. Claire Tomalin researched this very emotionally revealing story about Nelly Ternan, but she could find no evidence on the crucial question of whether Dickens had set Nelly Ternan up in a house outside London where he could visit her in secret. In the New York Public Library, however, she found a neglected Dickens notebook which had a series of mysterious timings, and she couldn't make any sense of it until she realised they were railway timetables. By going back to Bradshaw, she found they were the timings of the train leaving Paddington to go to the little market town of Slough, where Nelly Ternan had her secret cottage. From those records she could establish exactly the beginnings of that passionate relationship. There are, though, many other gaps, so there is always the possibility of something else turning up. But you do have to play fair with your reader, absolutely.

BIGSBY: I'd like to ask you about the relationship between biography and fiction because, as you have pointed out, a biography is not an accumulation of data, it is a story, which is why you can have so many different biographies about the same subject, each one with a different narrative, telling a different story. You talked about inhabiting sensibilities, but that is also what the novelist does and you happen to be in a house with your partner, who is a novelist. Is that a permeable membrane or impermeable membrane between biography and fiction?

HOLMES: There was a time when we both had the old-fashioned typewriters and I could hear her typewriter going down there and mine wasn't going at all and I thought 'Oh, fiction has it easy.' Rose Tremain's novels have actually taught me a great deal about fiction techniques. As a narrator of a biography one has to be very aware of the story, in terms of suspense, the sequence of events and the order in which people are introduced, and things are explained. The central sections of *This Long Pursuit* consist of five studies of women writers, intellectuals and scientists who, I have felt for a long time, have been neglected. When I began as a biographer forty-five years ago I felt women subjects were not being given proper attention. It has altered now, but even so it seems to me biography still owes them a debt. So, there are these five studies and the section is named after Rose's superb novel called *Restoration*. The studies include Margaret Cavendish, Lady Newcastle, the brilliant eccentric seventeenth-century scientist and poet, the first woman to attend a Royal Society meeting. Then there is Zelide, the Dutch intellectual and novelist, who was a great friend of young James Boswell. Boswell proposed marriage and Zelide wrote a crisp letter back saying, 'Dear James, I don't approve of your translations from the French so I cannot marry you.' I then go on to Madame de Stael, who became a great friend of Byron's, and launched that great tradition of the French feminist intellectual… which moves on to Simone de Beauvoir. Then there is Mary Somerville, the Scottish mathematician, who wrote the first real popular science book in 1834, and who was the woman who mentored the computer genius Ada Lovelace. But let me add a feminist fiction. When Margaret Cavendish goes to the first meeting of the Royal Society, in 1667, Samuel

Pepys is there and he writes in his diary a totally mocking account of her among the Fellows of the Royal Society, which is almost entirely concerned with what he calls her 'unordinary dress'. All the other Fellows are incredibly rude about her. Even the kindly Dorothy Osborne says, 'There were many soberer people in Bedlam.' So, I describe this scene and then I find one person, one person only, who speaks up for Margaret Cavendish. That is Sir Robert Merivel, Physician to the Royal Dogs. He says: 'My Lady Newcastle was greeted by much *yapping and barking* by the learned Fellows of the Society, but seems to keep them all *at heel* in a very easy manner.' However, this speech is a complete fiction, which I wrote myself. Merivel is Rose Tremain's invented character, Sir Robert Merivel from *Restoration*. I put him in there, and also in my index, and I hope generations of biographical scholars will be in total confusion for years to come.

KAZUO ISHIGURO

Kazuo Ishiguro was born in Nagasaki in 1954 and came to England at the age of five. A graduate of the University of Kent, he studied for a master's degree in creative writing at UEA, working with Malcolm Bradbury and Angela Carter. His first novel, *A Pale View of Hills*, was published in 1982. It was followed four years later by *An Artist of the Floating World*. Subsequent novels include *The Remains of the Day*, *When We Were Orphans*, *Never Let Me Go* and *The Buried Giant*. He is also the author of short stories, screenplays and lyrics. His many awards include the Whitbread Prize and the Booker Prize. In 2017 he was awarded the Nobel Prize in Literature.

This interview was recorded at UEA on 11 October, 2017.

BIGSBY: When you won the Nobel Prize you didn't have much notice.

ISHIGURO: No, the Nobel Prize people think it is a good idea to announce it to the world's press and then try to get through to you on the phone several hours afterwards, and, when they finally get through, they are rather miffed that your phone line is engaged all this time. They say, 'we have been trying to get through all this time though for some reason you are always engaged but we wanted to give you the Nobel Prize. Do you want it?' That is basically what happened. It was totally unexpected, but it was kind of nice.

BIGSBY: You have won the major British prizes, but the Nobel means something more, and not just in terms of prestige.

ISHIGURO: I think that is right. I have been coming to terms with that in the last few days. I am used to winning literary prizes, but it is important to remember that the Nobel Prize is not only bigger than me, it is bigger than books and literature, particularly as things are at the moment. I think people need emblems or symbols that stand for certain kinds of values. I think it is one of the ways in which, as a society, we have a conversation with ourselves as to which kinds of values we want to exalt. To some extent a Nobel Prize winner is a symbol and has got to stand for something bigger than himself or herself. So, I think it is much bigger than a literature prize. I don't just mean there is a political dimension to it, it is a question of cultural value and what kind of direction we want to go as a world, as a civilisation. So, I think I have got to be aware of that. I can't go around just being an author all the time. I am not sure what on earth I am going to do but I have got to understand that it is not just about me and my writing. I have been given a symbolic role which I may or may not fulfil. But I am a writer and the important thing is what
I do in my study day in, day out, just me and these papers and these ideas. I have got to try and hold those two things in my mind. The literary world is ultimately about some person on their own writing his or her stuff, some person on his or her own reading this stuff, very simple

things. That is where the real literary scene is, not in the showbiz bit, the Awards bit.

BIGSBY: I never thought I would use this phrase but let's put the Nobel Prize on one side. Since you were last here, you have published a novel, *The Buried Giant*. It is a novel that you began a long time ago.

ISHIGURO: It is very difficult for me to precisely track back any project like that because I work in a very odd way. I have ideas and I put them down in a little notebook. I literally have a little notebook full of ideas and actually the notebook I have been using since 2000, I bought in the Sainsbury Centre here at UEA, and I stuck a postcard from the Centre on it and that is where I have been recording ideas since. I often go back to an idea, or find an idea that I have had brewing for five or six years. But this one I can remember talking about back in 2001 when someone in the audience asked me, 'what are you thinking of doing next?' I remember saying that a lot of my work until then had concerned individuals, looking back over their lives and trying to come to terms with memories that made them uncomfortable about themselves. There were some memories that made them proud but there were a lot of things that make them feel that perhaps they had fallen short. And I remember saying to this audience, in 2001, that I would like to write a book about how a nation, or a whole community, goes through the same process. How does a nation struggle with this idea of what to remember and what to forget, and what are the equivalents of the memory banks of an individual, of you and me? If we are talking about a nation, where are the memories kept? Who controls them? Who suppresses them? How are the nation's memories, or a community's memories, manipulated for the needs of the present and the future? Is talking about a country's memories like an individual's memories just a metaphorical thing or are there real parallels? These things really interested me and so for a long time I wanted to write that book and I spent a long time trying to figure out a setting and a concept and a conceit that would allow me to talk about both individual and national memory.

BIGSBY: And you did start writing it, but a year-and-a-half in you stopped because your wife said it wasn't any good.

ISHIGURO: More or less, yes. She didn't say 'just stop,' she said, 'the way it is at the moment just will not do. It is not that you need to change this passage, or tweak it, it is fundamentally flawed.' I found this a bit disconcerting, so I put it to one side and wrote *Nocturnes*, a short story cycle, for light relief, then I went back to the project.

BIGSBY: Let me come back to *The Buried Giant* a little later because the other thing you did, besides the short stories, was to go back to music. Until your early twenties, indeed, it wasn't a writer you wanted to be but a lyricist, a singer/songwriter. If we fast forward, when you appeared on *Desert Island Discs*, one of the discs you chose was by the singer Stacey Kent and that led to a meeting with her and a collaboration, you writing the words to her music. It was a very successful collaboration, one of those records going gold in France and platinum in Germany. One of your songs won a prize. I am interested in the connection between that and your writing. In one way of course songs sound like poems. Do you ever write poetry?

ISHIGURO: No, to be honest I don't understand poetry. I really don't. If it wasn't for the title I wouldn't have a clue what it was about. I rely heavily on the title to figure out, 'oh, this is about a funeral' or something like that. I have got a complete block about poetry. However, all my life I have been passionate about how words are part of a song. There was a lot said about last year's Nobel Prize winner, Bob Dylan, and whether he should have won it or not. I have always believed that that is a very important art form, which came of age I would say in the 1960s and 1970s, what you called loosely the singer/songwriter thing. Whatever it was that Dylan does, or Leonard Cohen did, or Joni Mitchell does, I think some sort of an art form grew up then which is part performance, part poetry, if you like, part music. It was a new art form. I understood the giving of a Nobel to Dylan last year as a recognition that this art form, the singer/songwriter, or the songwriting art form in performance, deserved to be put up there as a literary art form alongside fiction, poetry and drama. I still absolutely believe in that art form. I don't particularly excel in it, but it is a great thing for me that I can collaborate with my songwriting partner, Jim Tomlinson, to write for Stacey who is a great singer. Though I wouldn't pretend that I do it well, my career as a novelist has always had, somewhere, a very important little corner that has been about being a singer/songwriter. I have always tended towards first-person. I veered away from it for the first time a little bit in *The Buried Giant,* but I am usually a first-person writer. There is a voice I go for where I try to create an intimate relationship between the narrator and the reader. Somewhere I still think, when I am writing, that I am this one guy with an acoustic guitar in a folk club with about six people listening and I am presenting this quite intimate thing.

BIGSBY: The thing about Stacey Kent is that she is almost whispering in your ear when she sings. It is that kind of direct relationship which I suppose is what the first person enables you to do. By the way, is it right that you have got eight guitars?

ISHIGURO: Probably more, actually. Some of them belong to my daughter. I am confused as to which are hers and which aren't because I thought some of the guitars were mine, but she tends to come in and play them.

BIGSBY: If I listen to your songs, read the lyrics, there is a kind of melancholy to them. They are about things that were good but aren't anymore, a kind of bruised nostalgia.

ISHIGURO: Yes, I think there is a bit of an overlap there. To some extent I am a servant in this. I do what Stacey wants me to do and I remember when I started to write song lyrics she said, 'I want love stories.' They had to be love stories and she said, 'some of your novels are very bleak and I would like a little bit more hope in my songs than you are accustomed to.' She said, 'as a singer, I need a tiny bit of hope to work with. It can be pretty miserable but just give me a tiny bit of hope. As an artist that is what I work with.' I came away thinking that although she says my novels are a bit bleak I think I have always had a very similar thing, a tiny bit of hope, a hopeless bit of optimism. I find something pathetic, but ultimately quite admirable, about the way human beings, even after they face the fact that perhaps their lives have been a waste, or that the world around them is very bleak, can muster some sort of a consolatory hope. I always like to end on that kind of note in my books.

I think up until *Never Let Me Go* when I looked at characters I was looking at their weaknesses, I was looking at how human beings fail despite their best efforts. In *Never Let Me Go* I set myself the opposite task. I wanted to celebrate human beings and say for all the bleakness of the world they face there is a decency in the way they care about each other to the bitter end that you can't touch. So, for me it was a celebration. To put it another way, I think it is the one book of mine that has nice people in it. I tried to make a real case that there was something about human beings, and their relationships with each other, and the love that they are capable of finding for each other, that makes them remarkable. I set myself the opposite task to usual, so I came out feeling quite cheerful about it.

BIGSBY: But surely melancholy is a part of the Great American Song Book: "Every Time We Say Goodbye," "One for the Road."

ISHIGURO: Yes, the jazz song. I love that kind of jazz song, the great American Song Book. I love that era musically and lyrically but if we are talking about the relationship between music and writing fiction, one of the things I find really valuable about keeping music close to me, both as someone who is a fan, and as someone trying to help create it, is that, if you are working in song forms, even if you are writing lyrics, you work much more instinctively. Just to take a clear example, if someone plays a saxophone solo, and then they do another take of that saxophone solo, it is quite hard for anybody listening to choose one or the other in a logical way. Everyone says, 'no, no, the first one was more beautiful,' or, 'the first one came from the heart.' They have different ways to say it but, in the end, they are just saying, 'take A is more beautiful than take B' or, for some reason, it is closer to what you intended to say, but it is very difficult to build a logical argument for it. The trouble in fiction, because you are dealing in words, dealing in a medium that is also used for polemical argument, for scholarly debate, there is a temptation to think you have to justify an artistic decision, perhaps because we increasingly live in a creative writingly world where people are very self-conscious about the decisions they make. Why does the main character have four siblings rather than two? Why does this happen? People like you, forensically interrogate writers and say, 'I have noticed this particular strain going through your work. Why is that?' And so, writers can become very conscious of the artistic decisions they are making and sometimes feel they have to come up with a logical justification for why they made the particular decision. Sometimes it is reasonably convincing, and I have got quite a few of these explanations for these moments. But in the end, I think it is very important, if you are a writer of fiction, to still understand that you have got to make your artistic decisions in the same way that a musician says, 'that's more beautiful than that. I don't know why, but that's the case.'

BIGSBY: Is that to do with your sense of a sentence being right?

ISHIGURO: I am not really talking about the beauty of a sentence. I am talking about bigger decisions – why does that happen in that scene, should you go for a different kind of ending? I mean the big architecture. The big important artistic decisions can be subject to this just as much as why you write your actual words in a certain way. I think it is dangerous to always make your decisions having worked out some intellectual reason why you should do this or do that because in the end it is very important that you retain that ability, as a writer, to fall back on some instinct. Part of you has to be guided by what you want to convey, what you really feel is the most beautiful thing you could do or what is the closest to the emotion you are trying to convey, without having to justify it too much. I think staying close to music, and staying close to artists who do that day in and day out, and who can build a consensus about why one solo is better than another without anyone having to come out with an articulate reason for it, is very important. That is one of the things I really value about working with musicians.

BIGSBY: And the connection is there in your book of short stories, *Nocturnes*, which has a subtitle, *Five Stories of Music and Nightfall*. They are about musicians. It is not quite the book of short stories that we are used to, though, in that they often consist of stories which have been published in various places, at various times, and are then brought together. You wrote these all in one go.

ISHIGURO: Yes, I wrote it all in one go. I loved the idea of a short story cycle. I think it is sad that short stories are this Cinderella form in fiction. There are superb short story writers and some of them are celebrated – Alice Munro, Raymond Carver, Anton Chekhov – but there are many, many fantastic short story writers who nobody reads because of the nature of the form and that is a paradox because we are told that people have less and less time to read fiction and yet the short story, for some reason, doesn't seem to thrive, and I don't know why that is.

BIGSBY: Publishers don't like them.

ISHIGURO: That's because they don't find a big readership. I don't know what it says about us. It could be about the fact that we don't like to invest a lot in building a relationship with characters if we know that it is only going to last for a few pages. The interesting thing is that storytelling seems to be going for longer and longer forms. Even film seems to be moving away from the cinema film to the long TV serial and I am interested to see if fiction follows, if we are going to go back to the kind of Victorian model of the long, serialised novel.

BIGSBY: There is a little bit of that in your short stories because characters recur. Was there ever an impetus to expand any of the stories to become a novel, or were they always going to be contained?

ISHIGURO: I was fascinated by the short story cycle. Instead of having a continuous narrative you have a series of stories that reflect on each other, refract each other. It was another way of writing a fiction book, I wouldn't call it a novel. You ask readers to think about how these stories might relate to each other. I enjoyed doing it. I don't think I am a particularly good short story writer. It is not my specialism. I think the forms are quite different. You have to have a certain kind of temperament for the short story. The great teacher I had when I was a Creative Writing MA student at this University was Angela Carter. She was a fantastic teacher, along with our friend Malcolm Bradbury. Those were my two teachers here, but Angela was a really inspiring teacher and an extremely eccentric one. She never asked to see my work until I wanted to show her, which meant that, for most of the time, she was my teacher she never saw anything of my work. We just had long rambling conversations about anything I wanted to talk about. She is an example of someone who is an extraordinary short story writer. I am probably less fond of her novels than of her short stories, but I think it is quite difficult to do both well. I don't want to sell myself as a short story writer, so if you are thinking of writing short stories, or you do write short stories, don't use me as a model. I am a novelist.

BIGSBY: One of the things about the stories is that they are about a series of failed relationships, about people whose future is their past, when they seemed to really have lived; often those who have been quite good at something, but never quite excelled. That could have been you as a singer/songwriter when you were nineteen, twenty, twenty-one What would have happened if you had not switched to literature? Might that have been your fate?

ISHIGURO: It could have easily been my fate as a writer. The distance between being somebody who doesn't quite get published, or who does but doesn't find a readership, and being a bestselling writer who wins huge awards is tiny, absolutely tiny. Sometimes it comes down to luck, sometimes to what the society of that time wants. Sometimes within a writer, himself or herself, though they have everything else, there is just some little trajectory they lack, the angle is slightly wrong, and it is that which makes the difference. It is not an incremental thing. We don't all learn and get better and better. I don't think it is like that. It is crazily arbitrary. I find in reading some other people's work they are almost a great writer but at the moment they are quite crappy.

On the other hand, if people ask me, 'how do you write novels?' I don't know. Every time it is like a fluke. I always think, 'God, I just got away with it this time,' and the next time I have to do it in a completely different way. I don't have a system. I am not even very good at writing prose. There are lots of people who write much better, but where I am good is between drafts, because whether I am going all the way through and then drafting again, or whether I am doing forty pages and then doing that over and over again, I have developed a weird ability to revise in quite a serious way. My drafts are not cosmetically improved versions of the previous draft. I take them completely apart. Things are very different from one draft to the next and that's the part I really enjoy, when I have written a ton of rubbish and sit back and break it down and ask myself, what have I got here? What do I keep? Should it be the other way around? That is my strength, my secret weapon. I try not to be inhibited when I am writing for the very first time onto blank paper. It doesn't matter how bad the prose is. It doesn't matter how corny it is. I just get all the ideas down on the paper and because I am confident that I can be quite strict and cold blooded when I am between the drafts I try to be utterly uninhibited and not think about anybody reading over my shoulder.

BIGSBY: I want to ask you, briefly, about movies, because that was something else you did, having laid aside *The Buried Giant*. You wrote the screenplay for *The White Countess* which featured most of the Redgrave family. It begins in 1936, in China, and then moves on to the Japanese invasion. You have been there before in *When We Were Orphans*, a novel set in that location, or nearly that location, and at that time. What drew you to that time and place?

ISHIGURO: I have a family background in that period. My Japanese grandfather was sent to Shanghai in the 1930s to set up Toyota in China. Toyota wasn't a car company in those days. It was a textile company. This was also a very interesting time in history. Chinese

Communism and Chinese Nationalism were having a civil war. The place was quasi-colonial. Various foreign powers had carved up the middle of the city. People called it the Paris of the East. There was a lot of decadence and huge amounts of money were going through it. I have seen photographs of my grandfather looking like a Conrad figure in a white suit. He carried a pistol everywhere. My father was born there and so I was always quite interested in that period. It should be a fantastic setting for some sort of gangster film with ceiling fans and people sweating everywhere. *When We Were Orphans* is the only time I started with a setting and then tried to figure out what I could do with it. I have always regretted that because normally I start off with a theme or story that could be set in all kinds of places. I have a story that is not peculiar to any time or place and then I go location-hunting for the setting, when and where would it work best, in what kind of world it would work best. Should it be a historical, realistic, place, or should it be some sort of weird futuristic place, or a disturbing place. if you are a novelist, you don't have to go and ask a producer for money, you can choose anywhere. So, I tend to start with a very abstract storyline and then try and figure out where I can put it down. So, *When We Were Orphans* was the only time I was so seduced by the actual historical period, and my own link to it through the family, that I chose Shanghai in the 1930s.

I did a lot of research on that period. Some people might think it is one of my least convincing novels. Some people like it but my wife says it is not very good. But I did all this research and some of it I hadn't used. I was working with James Ivory on a completely different project and was really fed up with it and I said to him one day, 'you know, this film we are trying to do in New England, set in the 1970s or something, why don't we try changing the setting to Shanghai in the 1930s? Then you can shoot in China.' This was about fifteen years ago, so it was a great idea. It seemed really exotic and he said, 'yes, it will be fantastic.' So, I wrote this screenplay.

BIGSBY: One reason I was asking is because it ends with the Japanese invasion, and that is also in the novel.

It was a particularly brutal occasion, for some people the beginning of the Second World War. It has a central character who at one stage is in tune with history, in fact partly shaping it, and then thinks he can step out of it and merely observe, but he can't because it contaminates him. We have been there before in your work, surely.

ISHIGURO: Yes. We have been there. What you say about the Second World War is interesting. I have been thinking about this recently. For my generation, and I am sixty-two going on sixty-three, when we came along, I think many of us tended to refer back to the Second World War. We wrote about a world that was in the shadow of the Second World War and there was a part of me that thought that the reason we did that, beyond the fact that we were living in a post-Second World War era, was that if you came from one of the rich, wealthy, stable countries – Britain, France, Japan, America or Italy – the problem as a novelist was that if you wrote about what you knew directly on your doorstep it was a bit boring. You had a kind of envy for Iron Curtain writers, writers who were in dictatorships, who had secret police chasing them all the time. They had something really important to write about, as did those in the developing world, or the Third World as we called it then. I remember thinking that V. S. Naipaul knows about all this stuff that is important and I only know about going to rock gigs in Camden Town or campus life at UEA.

I think our generation wanted to write stuff that was as big as the people who were writing about the big wars that were going on, the big fractures between the Communist world and the Capitalist world, the Third World and the rich world. But I felt I wasn't qualified, so I think our solution was to go back a little bit to a time when everything was up for grabs in Europe and in Britain. It was a natural place to go, back to the Second World War, and I think one of the challenges that must face the generation that is emerging now in fiction is that the Second World War is too far back. For us, it was only one generation back. Our parents had lived through it. I have often wondered what my responsibility is as a writer of my generation. Do I have a duty to keep alive the memories of the war generation, to make sure that things aren't forgotten, or do I not have that responsibility? What of the generation that is emerging now? Are they in the shadow of the Second World War? Are they in the shadow of post-colonialism, or are they addressing something else altogether?

BIGSBY: Perhaps that leads us back to *The Buried Giant*, which is set in the fourth century. There are Britains and Anglo-Saxons. There is a peace reigning and an elderly couple set out to see their son, except that there is a mist of forgetfulness. Nobody can quite remember their own past or the past of the nation and the question is, when mist thins, which is the right way to go? Is it better, as individuals or nations, to forget, to move on, to lay things to rest, or is it necessary to go back? You and I have both separately been to Auschwitz-Birkenau. It is a place of memory, yet David Grossman explained that in Israel the people from the camps were treated very badly because Israel didn't want the memory of the camps, the Jew as victim. Israel was not about Jew as victim. It is hard to think of a society that doesn't choose forgetfulness, erase aspects of its history, or evoke memory as a weapon, as in Serbia, as in Ireland. So, though *The Buried Giant* is set in the fourth century, it is surely about now.

ISHIGURO: Yes. I was tempted to set it in a real place but then the trouble is it becomes particularised. People think, 'oh, this is a story about Bosnia.' One of the ideas of setting it in a mythical place was that it could be applied to many places. I didn't want to write a historical book but essentially, yes, I am suggesting that every community, every society, has its buried giants, I think Britain does. I think the French still have a buried giant about their role in the Second World War. They had this idea that they were all heroic resistance fighters. I think America has buried the story about what it did to African Americans and this is leading to terrible problems now. There is a real debate about whether it is it better to bury the past in the hope that the terrible friction that is occurring now would heal itself, or can you only do that by resuscitating it all from the depths and having a look at it.
Or would that make it worse? Every country has these things as every family, every friendship and relationship

does. Is it better to just keep it hidden because that is the only way you can go on, the only way you can stop civil war, but sometimes if you just keep it hidden there is a poison that never goes away. When is it better to remember, when is it better to forget?

BIGSBY: I want to ask you about genre, science fiction in *Never Let Me Go,* the detective novel in *When We Were Orphans.*

ISHIGURO: I think this whole question about genre is very interesting because personally I just write my stories in the only way I can. I genuinely panic, usually about two thirds of the way through, that it is not going to work, this machine will not fly, and at that point I am prepared to do anything. I am prepared to steal from the neighbours, anything just to make this machine fly, and when it finally starts to fly and flap about and takes off then people look at it and say, 'oh, that looks weird? What is that? Then they say, 'that looks like sci-fi' or they start to categorise it. I swear to you I am not playing clever genre games. I am just a desperate guy trying to get my machine to work. Then people say, 'is that this, is that that?' and it always seems to me interesting. After the publication of *Never Let Me Go* people came at me with questions about genre and I think we should all have a think, all of us who care about books and literature, about who decided these genres in the first place? Who decided on the boundaries? Who set the hierarchy of them so that some aren't supposed to be important or serious, and some are supposed to be childish? Who decided these things? The more I look at it the more I think we have become too obsessed with genres and it is actually impeding the way we create things and the way we read. Readers become prejudiced against certain kinds of books because they pick out a few things that are signifiers of something belonging to one genre or another. They say, 'I never go there,' which seems to me a perfect definition of prejudice. It is an exact parallel with racial or religious prejudice. 'There is a saree. I am not going to go there;' 'There's a flying saucer.' I can't go there.' It seems to me exactly the same mentality. You are not looking at the real content of the thing, the meaning of the thing, the real identity of the thing. You are looking at the surface trappings.

I was having this conversation with Neil Gaiman and he said some very interesting things. He said that somebody told him this thing about Borders, which used to be quite an important book chain and has now disappeared. They decided one day that 'horror' is no longer a genre, and somebody was given the task of going to the horror shelf and deciding which of these would go into science fiction and which would go into fantasy, which underlines how arbitrary genre is. The other thing I would say about genre is that I think there has been an enormous change in the status of things like science fiction and fantasy in the last fifteen years and that is because society has changed its mind about what kind of things it wants to encourage. My theory would be that, for a long time, when we were children, we liked fairy tales and played imaginary games in the garden, and this is alright. But as soon as you get to a certain age parents, teachers, neighbours, everyone starts to say, 'you have to stop playing those kinds of games. You have to grow up.' So, once you are twelve, thirteen, you can't go around pretending to be Superman or whatever. You have to play a different kind of game. I think for a long time we had the kind of society where we brought our children up from a certain age so that they could fit into a particular kind of economic model. We had to prepare them to be factory workers, white collar workers, soldiers. There was no room for what you might call fantasy. It had to be discouraged, so if people clung on to their love of reading some kinds of fiction they were derided.

But something changed recently. We have moved out of being that kind of manufacturing type of world in the West. What we admire are the weird, geeky, blue-sky-thinking superstars of Silicon Valley. We are now suddenly trying to encourage our children to think in this kind of strange way, this speculative way, keep that kind of fantasy alive. Neil Gaiman told me that he had been invited to a conference in China about sci-fi despite the fact that in China, for generations, it was almost illegal because sci-fi was a way of smuggling in political messages that were not allowed by the regime. But the Chinese government decided that the reason they weren't having as many inspiring entrepreneurs and genius inventors as they could have had was because there wasn't enough sci-fi in their society and they started to push sci-fi like mad. They invited people like Neil to come to big state sponsored conferences. As people who care about books, I think we should try and free ourselves of these boundaries.

BIGSBY: How do you go about revising a novel?
ISHIGURO: I haven't actually settled on that question. Is it better to go all the way to the end of the story in rough and then start again and do a neater version? Sometimes, with books like *The Remains of the Day*, I tended to take chunks. I would go thirty or forty pages, a whole identifiable sequence of events, and then go over and over it before going on to the next bit. *Never Let Me Go*, though, was one where I did a wild messy draft that took me all the way to the end of the story. I think there are pros and cons to both. I think one of the reasons I am sometimes drawn towards doing each little bit over and over again before going on to the next is so that I don't commit myself to something that I later regret. Every time I do something I do it in a different way. I never feel that I have got a certain way

BIGSBY: You are working on a new novel.
ISHIGURO: I am writing a novel, the usual kind of stuff. However, I am very interested in comics. I know people often tend to call these things 'graphic novels' but I think that is very pretentious. They are comics. I grew up as a kid on the Manga tradition in Japan and long beyond the five years I was living in Japan, I carried on reading things from there. At the moment I think there is something very interesting going on in what Waterstones call graphic novels.

BIGSBY: Are you just interested or are you actually tempted?
ISHIGURO: No, I want to work in that form because you collaborate with artists. There is a whole spectrum from superheroes with weird underpants and capes, to things that are more like the European art movies scene.

I am very interested in how you tell a story and I see some of the most interesting radical ideas and experiments on how to tell a story at the moment going on in the graphic novel section. There is something quite radical going on in some of these forms and I think it is something to do with the very nature of it. It goes back to what we were saying earlier about genre. Particularly in the West, you associate comic books with children's comics. I think we have gone way beyond that and already the commercial film and TV industry has cottoned on to it. So much of television at the moment consists of adaptations from a comic book series, particularly in America. I think there is a lot of energy there which comes from the fact that it is the one form of storytelling where you can't really follow a character just physically. You see a static image and another static image, and the reader has to imagine what happens in between. A huge amount of what happens when you are reading in that form is not actually shown and I think this in itself makes for some quite radical interesting storytelling. I think some very weird things are happening in that form and so I am quite excited by the idea of having a go, as a kind of side-line, like my songwriting and my screenwriting. But yes, I am writing a novel. That is my day job.

PENELOPE LIVELY

Penelope Lively was born in Cairo in 1933. She later read modern history at Oxford and published her first work, *Astercote*, a book for children, in 1970, her first novel for adults, *The Road to Lichfield*, following seven years later. Among her many novels are *Moon Tiger* (which won the 1987 Booker Prize), *City of the Mind*, *Cleopatra's Sister*, *The Photograph* and *Family Album*. She is also the author of memoirs: *A House Unlocked*, *Oleander, Jacaranda* and *Ammonites and Leaping Fish: A Life in Time*. In 2012, she was made a Dame Commander of the Order of the British Empire for services to literature.

This interview was recorded at UEA on 2 November, 2016.

BIGSBY: You have written a book called *Ammonites and Leaping Fish*. What were you setting out to do in this particular book?

LIVELY: It's my view from eighty. It would be coming out the year I was eighty so I was writing it in my late seventies and I realised that I was now one of a new demographic. Never before in human history has there been a whole tranche of old people as there is now in the western world and I thought it was quite interesting to be a part of this, and to report what it felt like, but also to look back over my own eighty years and compare what the traumatic, big events of the last century have been that I had lived through. I wanted to compare what I could remember them feeling like at the time, and what they looked like now with the wisdoms of historical hindsight, what the historians were now saying about Suez or the Cold War. I also wanted to discuss the nature of memory itself, which is a subject that has much enthralled me and that has driven various novels, looking at things in my own house and realising that anybody is identified by their possessions. So, I took six possessions to see the way in which they have identified me.

BIGSBY: You mentioned the demographics. Twenty percent of the population are now beyond the old retirement date and one in fifty beyond eighty-five, but our notion of what old age is has changed fairly dramatically. Long ago there was a programme on what used to be called the BBC Home Service, now Radio Four. It was called *Have a Go*. People were invited to come up and answer questions and if they got it right they got a sum of money. When they came up they were asked their age and if they were over sixty there was spontaneous applause. I was very young when I heard this but it baffled me that you would be applauded for your genetic makeup until I checked what the average age was when this programme started. It ran for twenty years starting in 1946, when the average life expectancy for a man was sixty-four, while for women it was sixty-eight. So, our sense of what old is has changed.

LIVELY: I agree. It has completely changed, though whether that means that attitudes towards old age have changed, I am not sure. I am not tremendously conscious of ageism, I must say. There is a sense also in which you achieve a certain sort of anonymity in being old. When you are walking around the streets, people don't look at old people on the whole. We are not very interesting. Young people look at each other to size each other up, but the old are invisible and anonymous and I rather like that. But with respect to your story about congratulating anyone who was over sixty, I can remember that on my first flight to Australia, which was probably about thirty years ago, an announcement was made that, 'We have two passengers on board today who are over seventy', and the plane burst into applause.

BIGSBY: This book lies three years in the past now but age is surely an almost complete irrelevance. What matters is health, and you have had a fair range of problems. You have had breast surgery for cancer. You have had arthritis of the spine. You have had a collapsed part of your back and went on to have an operation that left you in acute pain for months on end. You have macular degeneration, a clouding of the eye. You have had torn tendons. The thing about illness surely is that it narrows the world suddenly.

LIVELY: Yes, but the curious thing is – and nobody young would believe this – you get used to it. Yes, I have had slightly more than my fair share. When I was getting background material for *Ammonites*, I read a lot about old age, both technically and in other ways, and there is an extremely good book by a gerontologist, Tom Kirkwood, called *Time of Our Lives*. He is very good on the technicality of old age and what he says is that in his clinic he took a sample of patients between eighty and eighty-five and not one of them was without one of the age-related diseases and most had two or three. So that is par for the course. He was using this in the book as an argument to say that if you have a demographic that is going to be afflicted by various ailments of one kind or another, much more has to be done to address age-related diseases. They are not glamorous, like cancer and heart surgery, but not enough is done about this so one has to hope that in the future perhaps something will be.

BIGSBY: You are glossing over it a bit, because when you had the operation on your vertebrae you had real pain for a long time.

LIVELY: You don't get used to that, no.

BIGSBY: You don't, and it really must close things down. Other things close down, too, because you used to travel a lot. You would get a phone call from the British Council and be off. You don't do that any more?

LIVELY: One of the pleasures for me of old age, actually, is the thought that I shall never see Heathrow again. I only travel within this country. I have just turned down an invitation to go to a literary festival in the Channel Islands. Even that is a bridge too far now, and this is wonderful. I probably wouldn't feel like this if I hadn't done a lot. I have been fortunate in the sense that a lot of travel was offered back then and I did a lot, although I have some regrets about places I have never been to, but there is no way I will be getting there now.

BIGSBY: And the other way is that you used to be a very keen gardener. Now it is pots in a small courtyard.

LIVELY: I still am a keen gardener. Yes, I can't do what I would have done. I used to have a large Oxfordshire garden and a vegetable garden on an almost industrial scale. There is no way I could do that now, but I certainly have a garden and I keep at it and indeed the next book, the book I am writing now, is about gardening. I realised that, aside from writing, the two things that I have spent most of my life doing are reading and gardening and there was a curious way in which they meshed in. I wrote a talk for a literary festival called *The Writer in the Garden* in which I looked at the ways in which various writers, literally from Beatrix Potter to Virginia Woolf, have used gardens in fiction and I had fun doing that. My agent asked to see it and said, 'There's a book here,' and I said, 'No there isn't, because I would get completely bored with trying to find more instances of this,' but then I saw that actually there was a different kind of book, a book in which the use of gardens in fiction would be prompts but it would be a book about what gardens have done to us, what we do to gardens, from the Garden of Eden onwards. So, it is about all sorts of things. It branches out in all directions but basically it is a book about gardening.

BIGSBY: So that's the response to a closing world but literature, reading, writing, surely open it up and there are no limits to that because you just ride the imagination. David Lodge has said that as he has got older his reading has tended towards non-fiction rather than fiction. Is that true of you?

LIVELY: I always have, actually. I read history at university and I read it very badly. I didn't get a good degree. I wasn't an assiduous student but it has absolutely conditioned the way I think. It didn't turn me into a novelist but it determined the kind of novels that I eventually started writing and I have been reading history ever since: history, archaeology and related areas. So, I probably read more non-fiction than fiction but perhaps it would be evenly divided. If I look at the pile on the table it will probably be about half and half.

BIGSBY: And it is reading non-fiction that has often fired your novels.

LIVELY: Absolutely. If I hadn't read a certain book I wouldn't have written a certain novel and that has always been a non-fiction book. Stephen Jay Gould's *Wonderful Life*, which is a book about palaeontology, prompted my novel *Cleopatra's Sister*. There are other examples where reading about something, getting passionately interested in something, then prompted a novel.

BIGSBY: David Lodge has recently published a memoir and I asked him if his had been a continuous self, in other words whether the David Lodgeness of him had always been there, consistently, throughout his life or whether he had changed. What do you think of yourself?

LIVELY: What an interesting thought and an interesting question.

BIGSBY: Well it came from reading your book, because you do say something about identity. At one stage you quote from Sir Thomas Browne on the different selves he contained?

LIVELY: Yes, I see exactly what you mean. My reading probably stemmed from initially not having any formal education. I didn't go to school until I was twelve. I grew up in Egypt during the war and was educated at home in a sort of ad hoc way by somebody who turned herself into my governess and who herself had left school at sixteen. She had discovered something called the Parents' National Educational Union, which sent out books and a curriculum and timetable to expatriate parents. The books duly arrived, and the timetable, and it was entirely based on reading. Before the child could read well, she had to tell back the story in her own language and, when you could write, you wrote back, so of course it was a marvellous act of discipline in language. It was distinctly short on the science side, I remember. The book that we had was called *Eyes and No Eyes* by Arabella Buckley and it was published in 1890. It was about the fauna of the English pond and streams. So, armed with this, I used to go out and delve with a net into our Nile-fed ditches and then confront the monstrous catch and try to identify it against the pages of Arabella Buckley. So that was science. And it wasn't too hot on maths either, I remember.

BIGSBY: I notice you have adroitly avoided the question I asked, which was whether you had a continuous self?

LIVELY: Yes, well exactly. I got carried away thinking about that, but you see I think I was that sort of child, a reading child, and then I went to an absolutely appalling boarding school where one of the punishments was to be sent to read for an hour in the library. The library had hardly any books in it so that this was neither here nor there. Well, I somehow survived that but was a complete fish out of water there. I was quite academic and it was a completely un-academic school, but I could feel an identity there early on. Yes, I can almost feel a self waving back, as it were. It is rather strange, too, if you are a writer. You go back to read a book written a long time ago and it seems as though it was written by somebody else. I have a children's book called *The Ghost of Thomas Kempe*, which is now forty years old, and I had to go back and read it recently and I read it, quite literally, as though somebody else had written it. I knew I couldn't possibly have written it now and yet I seemed to recognise something vaguely familiar. There was a sense of the same person having written it while knowing that I couldn't do it now.

BIGSBY: In writing *Ammonites and Leaping Fish* you had to go back to that child that was you but you say you found it very difficult to get into her mind.

LIVELY: That is virtually impossible. I tried to do that in a childhood memoir called *Oleander, Jacaranda* and that was exactly what I was trying to do and I did it by just jotting down everything I could remember of childhood, those shards of memory that we have all got which are in no sense linear, just all sorts of different slides. I was just putting them down as they were, Wordsworthian splendour in the grass moments without any kind of commentary or anything, then trying to look at them with the wisdoms of adult hindsight to see what it was that that child saw. That was an interesting thing to do, particularly because I had been growing up in Egypt during the Second World War, with the Libyan campaign raging not very far away from Egypt, then at one point going to Palestine as it then was when it looked as though Egypt was going to fall. We were living in interesting times, but of course I wasn't aware of that, because they were the only times I had ever lived in so they seemed perfectly normal to me. So it was interesting to try and put down what this child had seen but was unable to perceive and what one could now see, knowing as an adult what had been going on.

BIGSBY: And of course, you are a writer of children's books, which means you have a sense of the kind of book that children like. What is your conception of what a child looks for in a book?

LIVELY: When I started writing for children it was with great temerity. I just thought this was an extraordinary thing to try to do. I don't know, I still don't know, but I remember thinking that what you don't do is patronise. You don't write down to children. You write straight out of your own adult interests or concerns and try to change

gear and write in a way that might interest children.
I certainly knew that a child must have a story. I have
always felt there was an analogy between writing for
children and writing short stories. You know you have
got to have a story with a child. You have got to grab it
on the first page, and you have got to do that when you
write short stories. But then you can try and do all sorts
of other things as well. For instance, in *The Ghost of
Thomas Kempe* I was very much concerned, and still am,
with thinking about the operation of memory, the way
in which memory works. So, there is a sense in which
the book is about that, but I wouldn't want any child to
come away from it thinking, 'I have read a book about
the operation of memory.' I want it to feel that it has read
a ghost story and so I think what you are trying to do is
write across not down to children.

BIGSBY: Do you get letters from children?
LIVELY: Oh yes, but not so much now, I have to say.
I used to get a lot back then and they were marvellous:
'Dear Penelope Lively, If you are a real person please
would you answer this letter.' 'Dear Penelope Lively, you
are my second-favourite author. I enjoyed your last book
and my mum says it would be all right if you came to tea
but could you make it a Tuesday?'

BIGSBY: I want to read you a couple of sentences from
a short story in your new book: 'I love stories, so much
more satisfying than real life. Real life goes on and on,
plotless and pointless. A story has form and content,
beginning and end.' When you were writing the memoir,
was it so radically different from writing fiction? There is
a narrative to a life, after all.
LIVELY: Of course, but there is this huge sort of
question mark that hangs over a memoir. How truthful is
it? How far is what you remember absolutely accurate?
How far is it contaminated by what people have told you
happened, by photographs you may have seen, all sorts
of things like that, so it is a somewhat treacherous form
I think. I agree, though, that it isn't all that different and
also when you are writing it you are trying to write it so
that it is going to be readable, enjoyable, for other people

in exactly the same way as when you write fiction. You are using the same kind of narrative skills, writerly skills, in exactly the same way, so I agree there is no absolute gulf. It is a difficult form, I think, but it is also a wonderful form and all sorts of people have done it wonderfully. I certainly prefer the non-linear form. I like it to mimic, to mirror, the operation of memory itself, the way in which our own memories are this bundle inside and so the memoir that we actually have is like that.

BIGSBY: There is a moment when you recall something and then you read a diary entry for the same day and they are different.

LIVELY: Yes, I am a diarist. I have kept a diary for about thirty years now and I do find it is quite extraordinary if I go back to some particular event, say a visit to Slovenia for the British Council, and I read in the diary things that I have completely forgotten about but, in my head, there are other things that I never put down in the diary so there seem to be two conflicting things going on. So, which is the more truthful?

BIGSBY: Why did you start writing so comparatively late? You were thirty-seven when you wrote the first children's book, forty-four when you wrote your first adult novel. How come you came to it when you did?

LIVELY: I don't know. I had children quite young and I think I just waited until the youngest had gone to school and then thought, 'What am I going to be doing now?' I had assumed I would get a job of some kind. I think I had probably assumed I would teach. It was the almost automatic progress for a graduate then. You did whatever the teacher-training thing was called and then you started teaching, but instead of that I started writing with no idea of how unwise this was and how unlikely it was to get published. Of course, back in those days there were no creative writing schools up and down the land. Our generation just beavered away on our own, whether for better or worse is not for me to say.

BIGSBY: Was your first published book the first you had written or were there others we have never seen?

LIVELY: No, I wrote a children's book, a very bad one, and amazingly it was accepted by an agent. I had never heard of agents but I found there was this red book called *The Writers and Artists' Yearbook* and I picked an agent more or less with a pin and sent him this children's book and he found a publisher, and so it went. I had no idea how lucky I was. I could very easily have been quenched at the start and this alarms me tremendously. How many people there must be to whom this happens, because I think if I had had a number of rejections I would probably have just folded up and stopped.

BIGSBY: What was the attraction to you of the short story as a form?

LIVELY: A long while ago I was asked to run a workshop on the short story at some literary festival and when I got to it there was a group of mainly middle-aged men and I said, 'Well, perhaps before we do anything else we might talk about what we feel about the short story, talk about short stories we have liked, how different they can be.' And the spokesman said, no, no they didn't want that at all. They knew all that they needed to know about the short story. What they wanted from me was some advice on marketing. So, I said, I was surprised to hear this, and what was it that they knew about the short story that was all they needed to know, and he said, 'The short story is three thousand words long.' What I like about the short story is that it is as long as a piece of string. Mine tend not to be tremendously long but of course, as we know, they can be immense. Alice Munro's are the length of a short novel. Roald Dahl's are the kind with just a sting in the tail. That's the kind I don't like, actually, because it ends up being all about the sting and nothing much else, but one of the attractions, of course, is that they are short. You do get to the end. You finish them. Writing a novel is like hacking at the rock face. The problem with short stories, though, is that I have always found you can never go out and 'get' one. An idea either arrives or it doesn't and the stories in this book have all been written within the last three years or so and I hadn't written any before that for about twenty years. I thought it had left me. I thought the form had left me.

In the interim twenty years, while I was writing novels, I had once or twice thought, 'Why aren't I writing short stories any more?' and the answer seemed to be because I am not getting any ideas. So I was very surprised to find that suddenly ideas came not exactly flooding back, but definitely coming back and once you have got the idea, it is not so much hacking at the rock face as a burrowing away at the idea, seeing what it is all about and then trying to write it.

BIGSBY: One of the things that interests me in the stories is the number of times you have two different timescales operating, and one product of that seems to be melancholy. There are a number of novels in which you do the same thing. Why are you drawn to that?

LIVELY: I think it is to do with my feelings about memory, the feeling that none of us exist in any one time. We exist in all the times that we have already existed, so I don't have great respect for the present. I think that is probably the reason why. It is probably something that I do almost unconsciously. It is a natural reaction to the nature of time itself.

BIGSBY: And in relation to what we were talking about earlier, with age time itself changes. One moment you are thirty and then you are sixty, seventy, eighty and you think, 'What the hell happened to all those other decades that went before?'

LIVELY: Yes, it is an affront. Exactly. We don't think about ageing. When we are young it is never going to happen, so why bother? When we are middle-aged, we see it vaguely looming on the horizon like a hint of bad weather and turn away and get on with doing something else, which is entirely sensible. Suddenly you find yourself this old person always surprised by this face in the mirror, which is not the face that you thought you had. But it is also all those other faces that you were before. It is all the things that you were before. I have got a number of friends who I have known for a very, very long time, one who was at university with me – and I still think of her as nineteen. The fact that we are both in our early eighties didn't change the fact that to me she still seems to be the person she was when we first knew each other at college. So I don't have any faith in people being just as they seem to be now. The young of course have got all the rest of it coming but we do not. We are everything that we have been before as well.

BIGSBY: There is something else about time – the speed of time changes at different ages.
LIVELY: Oh, indeed, yes. There is a very good book by a Dutch psychologist [Douwe Draaisma] about that called *Why Life Speeds up as you Get Older: How Memory Shapes our Past*. There are technical reasons, which I found quite difficult to understand, psychological reasons to do with experience. When you are a child, a day can seem forever and time goes on and on. It is because you are constantly confronted by new experiences. By the time you are old, you are not. You have had so many experiences already that most of the things you have already seen and done and life does indeed speed up as you get older in a most disconcerting way.

BIGSBY: We mentioned memory earlier, and plainly that is at the heart of a memoir. Is a memoir autobiography light, in the sense that an autobiography is researched? You step outside your own memory and have to validate things. Would you ever write an autobiography?
LIVELY: I would not, no. I think they are two very different things. Autobiography seems to me on the whole something that is in the hands of politicians and it is usually to put the records straight before other people get at it. They are written in a slogging, linear way. I was born in such and such and so forth. This is precisely the kind of life writing that I don't very much like. A memoir is much more free floating, it picks and chooses. It probably hasn't got an axe to grind. The ones that I have liked and admired are not linear. They can skip about. They are more like fiction.

BIGSBY: And if we are talking about memory and old age, names have a tendency to disappear into cupboards and when you open the door a name that should be there is not.

LIVELY: I know. It is extraordinary. I got a very long interesting letter from a neurologist because I had asked him why it is that names disappear but language doesn't, unless you have got amnesia, and what he said was that we don't really know but that one colleague of his suggested that it is to do with the fact that a name has no context. A word will have a context but if, for some reason, you are trying to remember the name of the French prime minister and it has dropped out of your head, it is because there is no context to it and that is why later in the day it will come back to you. This seems to be something that taxes people who think about this professionally.

BIGSBY: It is not only names that disappear, people do; the people who corroborate what you were, who were witnesses to your life and surely something of you is diminished by the fact that they disappear, beyond the distress of them going?

LIVELY: Although it can also be a rather strange experience meeting somebody who you haven't seen for a very long time and suddenly they will present you to yourself, as it were, how they saw you then, and that won't be the person you knew at all.

BIGSBY: There is a story in this collection [*The Purple Swamp Hen and Other Stories*] called *A Biography*, in which a biography is being prepared and various people are interviewed about its subject. It turns out, though, that people see that person differently. We don't exist in a vacuum. There is a human context and our own identity is in part a product of the feedback from other people. When they disappear something of ourselves goes with them.

LIVELY: Exactly. There is a sense in which we have a multiple personality. We are all perceived differently by those who have known us, which is a strange feeling. I am one person to somebody but a completely different person to somebody else. That was what I was trying to talk about in that story but also about the problems of biography and the sense in which a biographer cannot tell a single truth.

BIGSBY: Let me just turn to the memoir section of this. As you say, you were born in Egypt and lived there until you were twelve, with a war raging for part of the time. But you were reading books.

LIVELY: We fell back on whatever was on my parents' shelves, middle class reading, though we weren't a particularly reading family. We read a fair amount of Dickens, though, absolutely as literary innocents because Lucy, who was my governess, had never read very much at all. I can remember reading *Nicholas Nickleby* and we were completely absorbed. We were so outraged by what was going on that we would talk about how we would make it all right for Smike. We would find a spare bedroom for him and he would be okay with us.

BIGSBY: And then you came to England.

LIVELY: I came to England. Everybody else was coming home. I came back on a troop ship. It had come from India, up the Suez canal, with seven thousand troops on board and they picked up a hundred British women and children at Ismailia. We were segregated down below, away from the licentious soldiers who were rampaging around upstairs. Everybody in the ship was going home except for me, who was going somewhere I had never been before. I was extremely nervous about the whole thing. I remember we berthed, for some reason, in Glasgow and as we went up the Clyde the seven thousand, as one man, all went to one side of the ship to get their first glimpse of their native land and there were frantic exaltations over the Tannoy for some of them to get back to the other side. I can remember waking up in the morning, when it had berthed, and seeing framed in the porthole an enormous hairy hoof. It was the hoof of a Clydesdale horse. They were being used for haulage on the quayside. Then I remember travelling down to London in a train and looking out into this extraordinary landscape which was green from end to end. I could not understand this. How could it be green from end to end? In Egypt you desperately watered things to make them green.

BIGSBY: And it wasn't a very happy world you arrived in. It was the last year of the war, your parents divorced and you went to a fairly miserable school. When did this country become home, or is it never quite home?

LIVELY: During my teenage years, I suppose. I think it took about five years. It probably wasn't properly home until I was about eighteen or so. I had a complete terror about the class system, as it then was, because I had never experienced it. Those anywhere near my age will remember how much more rigid the class system was back then, in the late 1940s. People were identified by how they spoke and how they dressed but I couldn't see or hear this because I wasn't used to it. So I was always making what was seen as social solecisms. At the boarding school, all the other girls adulated the royal family and fought over newspaper photographs of the royal family and this I couldn't understand. I had barely ever heard of the royal family, rather surprisingly, and certainly hadn't the slightest interest in them. So I was out of kilter, out of step, for many years and I think only really stepped back again by the time I was about eighteen or so.

BIGSBY: You say in your book that, 'we not only contain our own time but we contain the times', what was going on in society. When you look back, how difficult was it to create not just the details of bomb sites and so on but the feel of a time which must be completely alien to the people who read the book?

LIVELY: I think it is not very difficult to recreate it for oneself. You move back into it. You can remember what it felt like, but it is extremely difficult to try to tell somebody else about it. I have got four grown-up grandchildren, particularly two girls in their late twenties who I see a great deal of, and they are mildly curious. I will try to say what it was like for me to be their age but it is difficult. Ultimately, it becomes, I am sorry to say, extremely boring to other people. I think what you have to remember is that reminiscence is only acceptable between consenting octogenarians.

BIGSBY: But change is the default position and the amazing thing is that people do adapt, they do change, although it is more difficult with age. You describe one of your family getting an old portable typewriter and having no idea what to do with the ribbon. So, you could show them that. At the same time if your computer had gone wrong you would be looking around for a twelve-year-old to fix it. You mention some of the changes – the contraceptive pill, attitudes to homosexuality, transformations which are in a way almost unbelievable.

LIVELY: When I try to look back historically it is vastly different than, say, the change between the eighteenth and the nineteenth centuries, not just in terms of technology but in terms of social attitudes. I can remember taking one granddaughter, when she was fifteen, I think, to *The Importance of being Earnest* and she had never heard of Oscar Wilde. So on the bus I told her about Oscar Wilde and T*he Ballad of Reading Gaol*. I told her about the trial and everything and she listened and then she said, 'Granny, I don't believe you. He was sent to prison because he was gay?' I think that to me the social revolution has been the most impressive and the most interesting.

BIGSBY: Two days' time marks the sixtieth anniversary of British troops parachuting on to the canal in Egypt, and that seems to have been the moment when you stepped out from your private world and became aware of the public world you inhabited.

LIVELY: Yes, I do remember 1956 vividly. I was working in Oxford. I had left university about a year or so before and was working for somebody who was a Fellow of St Anthony's, and I was stepping out with Jack, who was going to be my husband…

BIGSBY: Did you say 'stepping out with'?
LIVELY: Yes, I did.

BIGSBY: Right.
LIVELY: Nowadays it would be called 'going out with', which is slightly different, but I remember feeling very involved and very puzzled because here were we,

behaving like this towards what felt to me, in a sense, still my country, Egypt. I think it was the first time, at the age of twenty-two or so, that I felt a grown-up political awareness and involvement. It was certainly a climactic moment for me.

BIGSBY: Could you explain the title of your memoir, *Ammonites and Leaping Fish*?

LIVELY: I had been thinking, looking round my own house, that is absolutely full of things, the accretion of a lifetime, and I picked up six objects that I felt spoke particularly for what I had been thinking about and doing for the last sixty, seventy years or so. There was a fossil, a piece of blue lias with two little curled ammonites on it that I picked up once on the beach at Charmouth and that symbolises a huge interest in deep time. I have always been as interested in palaeontology as in archaeology. The leaping fish are a little pot sherd, of glazed honey colour, with two little leaping black fish on it. It is Islamic pottery. It came from Fustat, which was Old Cairo, destroyed in the 1100s. It was picked up there by a friend of mine who was helping some archaeologists. It is the base of what must have once been a wide shallow dish. I find it very moving because it speaks of a potter who had once seen fish leap in that way and it comes from there and has ended up, out of time and space, on my mantelpiece, so again that speaks of an interest in time and continuity.

BIGSBY: Memory is something that has also been important in your novels. *The Photograph*, for example, plays around with time and your Booker prize-winning novel *Moon Tiger* is concerned with memory, so this has been a rich source for you in terms of your writing. It is not merely that you are now writing about that phenomenon; it has been a part of who you are as a writer.

LIVELY: Yes, it absolutely has and I sometimes wonder if Egypt had anything to do with that. I grew up within that landscape where everything is juxtaposed, everything happens at once, as it were: Pharaonic, Napoleonic, Roman. We used to go to the Pyramids every

Wednesday afternoon for a picnic and I just assumed that everywhere had pyramids but, and rather surprisingly, nobody told me very much about all this. What I can remember vividly is being taken once into the desert. My mother always a had a slight interest in archaeology as well and she had heard of some archaeologists who were excavating what I now know to be pre-Predynastic burial sites somewhere out in the desert. We were shown this little indentation in the sand in which was a curled, barely identifiable skeleton of a person. If it was Pharaonic, it was five or six thousand years at least. I was only about seven or eight at the time and I think somebody explained to me that this had once been a person and because I still remember it, it obviously made a huge impression on me. I never forgot that moment and I think that probably had something to do with the generation of all sorts of future interests and concerns.

DAVID LODGE

David Lodge was born in 1935. He received a First Class degree from University College, London, before serving two years of National Service. He returned to London University and was awarded an MA for a thesis on the Catholic novel. In 1960 he became a lecturer at the University of Birmingham, the same year that his first novel, *The Picturegoers*, was published. Subsequent novels included *Changing Places*, *Small World*, *Nice Work*, *Author, Author*, *Deaf Sentence* and *A Man of Parts*. He has also written for the stage and television as well as publishing a number of academic books and a memoir, *Quite a Good Time to be Born*. Among his many awards are the Hawthornden Prize and the Whitbread Book of the Year, while his television adaptation of *Nice Work* won the Royal Television Society Award for best drama serial.

This interview was recorded at UEA on 5 October, 2016.

BIGSBY: In one of your essays you talk about the novelist and critic, Malcolm Bradbury. It comes as a real shock to me to realise that he died sixteen years ago next year. He was a friend but also important to you in literary terms.

LODGE: Absolutely, yes. I would have had a rather different writing career if he hadn't come to Birmingham University in 1962 when I had been there for a year or two. He joined the English department there and we were the two youngest members of the department, probably the only two under the age of about thirty-five, and we had both published one novel. We both had ambitions to be literary critics and to have an academic career but also to write fiction and other things at the same time. I suppose Malcolm was ahead of me in experience of the literary world. He was about two years older and encouraged me to develop comedy in my work which he saw traces of in my early novels, though they were rather earnest books on the whole. In particular, we collaborated in writing a satirical revue for the Birmingham Rep in 1963, and that was the first time I had tried to make people laugh, to be funny all the time. I found I could do it and it led me later on to write novels, some which are quite comic. So, I really thank Malcolm very much for that.

BIGSBY: One other thing he did, I learned much to my surprise, was to help with the publication of *Changing Places*, one of your best-known novels. I was surprised because it was turned down by three publishers and it was Malcolm who assisted you to get it published, though in response you went up against him in a prize competition, and beat him.

LODGE: Yes, that was potentially quite embarrassing, though Malcolm was very good about it and we joked about it in advance because our publisher was told it wasn't a terribly important prize that we were up for. His book was *The History Man* and mine was *Changing Places*. This was 1975 and the prize was the *Yorkshire Post* Fiction prize, which was only one hundred and fifty pounds, although one hundred and fifty pounds was worth a bit more then. I used the money to buy an automatic dishwasher, which I regarded as buying time for writing, and it shows you the price of appliances then. One hundred and fifty pounds was a huge amount in those days. I went up to Leeds to a literary lunch at which Lord Longford gave the prize and he was of course running a programme against pornography at the time and he read my novel on the way up on the train and was very shocked by it, according to the person who escorted him, so he gave a very ungracious speech. I more or less had to tear the cheque from his fingers. But, as for Malcolm, it was awkward and difficult and it was very lucky that I didn't finish *Small World* in time to come out in the same year as *Rates of Exchange*. Our mutual publisher was very relieved that we wouldn't be competing with each other with that book as well.

BIGSBY: One thing you say in your book of essays is that as you have got older you have got more interested in fact-based writing. Is that as a reader or a writer?
LODGE: I think both, really. I think many people find that fiction doesn't have the allure that it used to have.

BIGSBY: That is a curious thing for a writer of fiction.
LODGE: I don't know if it is simply the sheer labour of constructing a fictional world again every time you open a novel. Having to remember who is married to whom and all the other relationships between the characters, I find that I am more impatient with novels now. They have to be really good if I am going to finish them. The other thing is that, as a novelist, as a writer of fiction, it becomes harder to write fiction as you get older unless you are very exceptional. I think that is because you have used up all the interesting experience in your own life by that time and so the next stage is to write a novel about real people, which is what I did twice.

BIGSBY: Alan Bennett has said that writers hate biographies because they use their own lives in their own work. That is their resource. Whatever is left over is private.
LODGE: I suppose one reason I wrote my memoir covering the first forty years of my life – I am writing a

second volume – is to get my version of it down before anybody else tries to do it. I think many writers do feel that biographies are often intrusive. Sometimes they think the only way to control it is to commission somebody else to do it. Graham Greene is a case in point. Nearly always they regret doing this as they find themselves locked in a relationship with this person who is tracking every move they have made in their lives and I certainly wouldn't do it. Nor would I personally write a biography of a living person. I think there is always tension and difficulty there, but I also think that there is a general cultural trend towards fact-based fiction, fact-based stories, or applying the techniques of fiction to real lives. It is a very common form of novel writing now.

BIGSBY: But in one of your essays you quote Anthony Beevor as being disturbed by fact-based fiction.

LODGE: Yes, that is another side to this interesting subject. Historians and true biographers are very suspicious of the biographical novel, and novelists are very suspicious of biographers and, as you say, I have dealt with this in one of my essays in *Lives in Writing*. I don't think you can deny that this is a significant cultural trend. You just have to live with it and work out a way of treating it fairly from a critical point of view. The biographical novel can take many different forms. In some cases, the author takes tremendous liberties with the facts and invents episodes in the life of his character, his real-life character, that never happened, or two historical individuals who never met but meet in a novel. That is one way of doing it, but it is obviously fictional. I practice a certain kind of biographical novel and I have written two of them, one about Henry James, *Author, Author*, and the other about H. G. Wells, *A Man of Parts*. In both cases I kept to the known facts about their lives and didn't invent anything of consequence in the way I represented them, but I applied the techniques of the novel which essentially show life through the consciousness of one or more characters and to do that in a biographical novel you have to invent, because people don't leave a record of their consciousness behind. They don't leave very much trace of what they said. You get the odd remark, the odd conversation reported, but if you are dealing with a nineteenth century or an early twentieth century figure, like James, then your factual information is very limited. As far as I know, no recordings of his conversation exist and you can't really write a novel without dialogue because dialogue is an essential part of the art of fiction. So, you have to invent it. You steep yourself in the work of that writer, if it is about a writer, as many of these novels I am talking about are, and you try and recreate what it was like from their point of view, to experience the facts that we know about their lives. It seems to me a worthwhile thing to do. You don't pretend that it is a hundred percent truthful.

BIGSBY: But do you think there is any sense in which you can get closer to the truth of a person's life by deploying fiction than you might if you were writing about a biography or historical account?

LODGE: Yes, actually, I think you can, and in my essay on H. G. Wells in *Lives in Writing* I give an example of that. H G Wells was a notorious philanderer. He had many sexual relationships and I tried to get the details of one in particular straight. He had an affair with Rosamond, the daughter of Edith Nesbit, the children's writer, when she was quite young. He tried to take Rosamond to Paris for a weekend and was intercepted by her adopted father Hubert Bland, on Paddington Station. This was a terrific scandal in their set and obviously something I wanted to deal with, but I was relying on a biography of Edith Nesbit which said that this incident at Paddington happened in March-April 1908, a time when Wells was deeply in love with Amber Reeves, a relationship which lasted for a couple of years. Indeed there was an illegitimate child as a result of it. I just couldn't get my head round the idea that even Wells would do a thing like this, would go off for this dirty weekend if he was really in love with Amber. In fact I was unable to proceed with my novel at this point for some time as a result. The biographer placed the episode by referring to a letter from Rosamond, written on 4 March, 1908, to invite Wells and his wife to "our dance," saying Rosamond couldn't have issued the invitation after the scandalous episode at Paddington, so it must have happened before. I agreed with that, but for several reasons it was highly improbable that the Blands would be having dances at their home at that date. I remembered that Rosamond was secretary of the Fabian Society's Nursery, as the young members were called, and it must have been one of their dances Rosamond was referring to. I realised the running off to Paris must have happened *much* earlier and so I felt free to decide when it was likely to have happened and to put Wells in a better light. That is a long-winded explanation but what I am saying is that if I hadn't been looking at the episode as a novelist and trying to get inside Wells' head, I would not have paused and discovered that a mistake had been made. So, yes, it is sometimes possible to get nearer to the truth as a novelist than if you are a historian.

BIGSBY: What made you write a memoir now? Was it a pre-emptive strike against biographers?

LODGE: I always thought that when I couldn't think of another novel to write I would write an autobiography. Writers want to go on writing but, as I say, you use up ideas, you use up your experience, and the older you get the more difficult it becomes to generate it. I didn't want to write a novel just for the sake of it. I had got to be convinced it was worth doing, so then the idea of writing a memoir becomes quite attractive. I wouldn't have written it earlier in life because in some ways it does reveal the sources of my fiction. I don't mind that but I wouldn't wish to do it earlier in my career. When the novels have already been read and consumed then I can give away the sources of them. I don't feel defensive about that.

BIGSBY: You say something intriguing near the beginning of your memoir. You say that you had hoped that you had Jewish forebears. Where does that come from?

LODGE: I have always felt a rapport with Jewish humour, particularly American Jewish humour, and I have sometimes been compared to Woody Allen. I felt quite flattered by that. That is one reason, but there was a rumour in my family that there was a Jewish grandparent on my paternal grandmother's side, and I was trying to work out my genealogy. An ex- student of mine who became quite expert in this field did a lot of research, but couldn't come up with anything. There was no Jewish ancestor, to my regret. I am half English, a quarter Belgian and half English.

BIGSBY: The memoir, it is called *Quite a Good Time to be Born*. Is that the British usage, as in the play was 'quite good.'
LODGE: Quite is a wonderful word isn't it. I am going to write a book about 'quite' one day.

BIGSBY: So, what is the force of the word 'quite' here? Does it mean 'not a very good time'?
LODGE: In my case I thought it was quite good that I was born in 1935 mainly because I was part of the first generation to benefit from the 1944 Education Act. So, I got a free secondary education and free university tuition.

BIGSBY: But before that you had to go through the war?
LODGE: Yes, and one reason I put in 'quite' is that for many people, and in fact almost any young person in Continental Europe, it was a very bad time to be born. If you were Jewish it was a tragic time to be born, so I used 'quite' in order to suggest it wasn't a totally unmitigated blessing. In fact, my school education was rather imperfect because the educational system immediately after the war was short of resources and of course during it there were anxieties, there was disruption. My father was away most of the time during the war, for instance. But I am glad I have the memory of the war. I feel that it gave me an historical sense of the development of Britain in the twentieth century which I could draw on as a novelist.

BIGSBY: There was an incident during the war when you briefly found yourself among strangers while your mother had to go off and do something else. You said that that was possibly the cause of later anxieties. What were the later anxieties?

LODGE: They were just anxieties. I get anxious about everything. For a five-year-old child, who has been somewhat cosseted, to be left in a convent boarding school meant that I just felt totally lost and bewildered and very unhappy. When Mum came back after about ten days or so, she realised that she couldn't leave me there, but it was a fairly traumatic experience.

BIGSBY: You said that you suffer from anxiety occasionally, and you quote Graham Greene as saying that 'writing is therapy.' Have you found that to be true?

LODGE: Yes, I would think so. I think most novelists use it in that way, actually. The great thing about fiction is that it is a way in which you can turn negative experience into something positive. You create something which gives people pleasure, or if it works it does, but you are always examining yourself, filtering your own thoughts, and so it is in some ways related to psychoanalysis I suppose.

BIGSBY: Of course, your memoir is not only a story of your life, it is a story of the times as well.

LODGE: Yes, absolutely.

BIGSBY: How difficult is it not only to recreate that world of the past for the reader but to go back to your own younger self?

LODGE: I have read writers who say they can't remember anything much about their childhood and I find that very strange because my childhood was quite deeply engraved on my memory, maybe because I was an only child, or maybe because of the circumstances of the war. There are gaps of ignorance about the adult world around me. When I sat down to write the memoir I found that although I had been with my mother all through the war while my father was in the air force, and was totally dependent on her, I had no idea what she did or how she managed financially, what she thought, what her feelings were. I never asked her about it. There was a kind of reserve in the family. I think there always is between children and parents. As a writer I very much regret I didn't ask my mother about her life when I was older but I did learn from that regret, in a way, because she died a couple of decades before my father, so I did interview him later. I recorded a long conversation with him relating to his life. His memory was beginning to go but it was immensely valuable to me. I would always advise anybody, if they are ever thinking of writing a memoir, to question parents, to get them to talk about their early life because you can't recover it any other way.

BIGSBY: Your father was a musician but he was also a reader and when you were at school you had one of those teachers who encouraged you to read and ended up in your final year at school determined to be a writer of some sort. Lots of people write in their teens but not that many make that kind of decision.

LODGE: I can't remember a moment when I said, 'yes, I am going to be a writer,' but I was aware that suddenly I had discovered adult literature around about the age of fourteen.

BIGSBY: I think you ought to gloss 'adult' here.

LODGE: Well, not in the sex shop sense of the word but moving on from *Hotspur* and *The Wizard*, Biggles, to adult fiction, partly through the encouragement of this English teacher who as I got a bit older gave me reading lists. I didn't go around saying, 'I am going to be a writer,' but when I was very young I used to say I thought I would be a journalist when I grew up. I was still entertaining that idea until I was fifteen or so but then my father found that if I wanted to be a journalist I should leave school at sixteen and become a 'cub reporter' and the school didn't want me to do that. I didn't either so I took the academic route to university.

BIGSBY: You went on to University College, London, and there are two events in that first year which struck me. One is that it on your first day you met the person you were going to marry.

LODGE: That's right, yes.

BIGSBY: The other thing is that you wrote a novel that didn't work out so well. What was that novel?

LODGE: It was called *The Devil, the World and the Flesh*.

I didn't know anything about any of them actually. I was only eighteen when I wrote it. I wrote it mostly in my first summer vacation and I learned a lot from doing it, but it was unpublishable.

BIGSBY: Does it still exist?

LODGE: It exists in the archive of my work in Birmingham University Research Library. I think my English teacher sent it to the publisher Michael Joseph and they were interested and asked me in to have a talk. They said they would like to see future work but they didn't, in fact, accept *The Picturegoers* which was the first publishable novel I wrote.

BIGSBY: And is it right that your wife, Mary, didn't think that *The Devil, the World and the Flesh* was that great a novel?

LODGE: She was rather shocked by it.

BIGSBY: Does she remain first reader?

LODGE: Yes. I think there was an agreement that she would always be the first reader and if she objected very strongly to something, I would react.

BIGSBY: That raises an interesting question because in the memoir, and in the essay book, you identify autobiographical elements in your work. Do you think that might lead some people to think there are other things in your work that might be autobiographical?

LODGE: That is the risk you take, of course, but if this worried you, you wouldn't go on writing. You just have to be fairly philosophical or thick skinned about it really. I find many people suppose that what I invented actually happened to me.

BIGSBY: Especially the sexual escapades?

LODGE: Yes, exactly, while some of the more improbable things I put into *Small World*, which many people suppose must be wild inventions, actually happened. When I was being interviewed by telephone link on the radio in Australia, for instance, after the interview someone left the line open and I heard them saying disparaging things about me. I used that in *Small World*.

BIGSBY: Did you leave things out of the memoir? Did you censor things, or is this the unvarnished truth?
LODGE: I didn't falsify anything, but I didn't tell everything. One doesn't.

BIGSBY: After university you had two years punched out of your life by National Service.
LODGE: Yes.

BIGSBY: So not a good time to be born. But you did do some writing?
LODGE: I did a lot of writing. Nothing is wasted if you are a novelist. I got a novel out of my army service and I got a knowledge of life that I otherwise wouldn't have had. My main grouse was that it went on far too long and what I learned I could have learned in half the time. We were just being kept as a kind of cheap standing army and it was largely boredom and skiving. It was a very negative experience, except that I was able to find a little place for myself. I had a very spurious security position in a barrack, a little office all to myself to sleep in, and there I read and wrote. I made sure I didn't waste the time.

BIGSBY: There is another dimension to your life which has been important to you, Catholicism. It was to prove a rich vein in terms of your writing but it was also personally constricting because of the attitude of the Catholic church at that time. You are quite frank about this. For a while sex was a cup of cocoa and a cuddle. You took the edicts of the Church entirely seriously and allowed it to constrain your life but at the same time Catholicism mattered to you. How did you square those things?
LODGE: I don't regret having a Catholic background at all. I think it helped me as a novelist. In my early years I identified with the concept of "The Catholic Novel" as represented by Graham Greene or François Mauriac. That was how I developed my interest in writing fiction and was very strong in the first novel. It gave me an edge actually, a certain take on secular liberal society. Catholic

novelists were much more prominent in the English literature of that period than the percentage of Catholics in the country would have led you to expect. Most of them were converts but I was a 'cradle Catholic' and that also gave me a unique selling point, if you like, but that particular kind of Catholic fiction was rather anti-humanist. It was essentially conservative in its view of human life, stressing original sin and the afterlife. What happened to me was that I changed, my Catholicism changed. I became a liberal catholic. I was in favour of Vatican II. I was against the church's teaching on birth control and in various ways campaigned against it, for instance through satire in *The British Museum is Falling Down*. It gave me a subject matter that other people were not writing about. If you read my novels in chronological order you will see a gradual agnosticism getting more and more obvious in terms of the implied author's position. It was a development that was partly personal, partly cultural, partly social, and you draw on this material for your fiction. You find ways of exploring it.

BIGSBY: You say there were two books in particular that were important to you, one was *Ulysses* and the other was *Lucky Jim*. They don't exactly come out of the same box.
LODGE: No, indeed they do not.

BIGSBY: So how did that work itself out in you?
LODGE: Joyce I discovered through my English teacher. He put me onto *A Portrait of the Artist as a Young Man* when I was about sixteen and that made a great impression on me. The thing is that English Catholicism, certainly in those days, was largely an Irish Catholicism and Catholicism hadn't changed very much since Joyce was writing. So, what he was describing I could relate to, but I was also fascinated by his techniques. In every stage in his career he changed his mode of writing and explored new methods. His use of a classic precursor text as the framework for a modern story in *Ulysses* fascinated me, as did his use of the stream of consciousness method. I read that book as an undergraduate preparing for finals and steeped myself in it. It had an enormous effect on me so that books like *Small World* and *Nice Work* make use of

earlier literature, chivalric romance in the case of *Small World*, the industrial novel of the nineteenth century in the case of *Nice Work*. Using those precursor texts creates an inter-textual activity in the novel. I learned that from Joyce, as many other novelists did too.

Kingsley Amis came from quite a different angle. *Lucky Jim* came out 1954, when I was halfway through my undergraduate course, and as an undergraduate I had the usual rebellious feelings about the stuffiness of universities, but although I knew I was going to love reading that book I put off reading it until I had taken my degree. I didn't want to be distracted by it and certainly wouldn't have answered a question on it in finals, though I don't think there were questions on such recent books then. But once I began to read it, Amis's early work became enormously influential. He established a new tone of voice for my generation, as well as his own. I think it was irreverence. It was anti-bourgeois and it perfectly expressed the feelings of someone like myself, our generation, scholarship boys who got into the stream of secondary education which would lead them to university and, if they were bright enough, into professional life and the middle class. We grasped that opportunity but at the same time felt uneasy because we didn't come from that background of public school and Oxbridge, which had traditionally formed the professional middle-class. Amis put his finger on that uneasy feeling of being in an institution which you partly wanted for the knowledge you were getting from it while at the same time you didn't quite feel that you fitted in socially, in terms of manners and so on. But English society was gradually becoming much less class conscious, the divisions between classes much less obvious. Then it was also the way Amis used language, which wasn't poetic, wasn't literary in the usual sense. As a style it was full of repetitions and colloquial constructions, but was quite new. The tone of it just seemed to express the way one felt and that was why he was so important.

BIGSBY: In Penelope Lively's latest book she looks back over her life and raises a question which I suppose is raised by a memoir. When you look back through your life is there a continuous self or do you see a series of different David Lodges at different stages?

LODGE: I think of myself as a continuous self. It is, of course, true that at various points of one's life you come, without knowing it, to a fork in the road and you take one rather than another.

BIGSBY: At University College, if you had turned right instead of left, if you had arrived a week later, your world might have been different because you would not have met your wife?

LODGE: That meeting was obviously a very crucial one, but one is always coming to these forks in the road and you are not conscious at the time that they are. You don't think of it as an alternative. Well, sometimes you do, of course, as you have to make life decisions. You weigh them up. So I think the answer to your question is it depends a bit on the temperament of the person and I would have thought most novelists, by their very profession, are likely to think of life as a narrative. But there are some people who just see it as a random sequence of events.

BIGSBY: A memoir is a narrative. It has a beginning, a middle and not yet an end but it has a narrative structure. On the other hand, if people wrote a biography of you, and there are multiple biographies of individuals all of which are different despite the basic facts remaining the same, they would highlight different aspects of your life. Even when you are writing a memoir the narrative depends on when you write it. If you had written it twenty years earlier it might have been a different narrative. You might have chosen to emphasise different things.

LODGE: I don't think so, though the process of recuperating the past varies as you come closer to your present age or present position. Some people can hardly remember anything of their childhood and you are dependent on the accident of source material being available, photographs, letters. These are invariably much scarcer in your childhood and early years because then you didn't know that one day you were going to want to write an auto-biography, so that is kind of frustrating, though what you do find in the way of that kind of evidence is incredibly precious and you are very glad that it is there. As you get further into life, at least in my life, the data builds up to an almost impossible volume so that it is very difficult to sift out the things that are really useful, but you are able to recapture the past in much more detail.

RUTH RENDELL

Ruth Rendell was born in 1930 and died in 2015. Her first published novel, *From Doom with Death*, appeared in 1964. It featured Inspector Wexford, who would appear in a further twenty-three books, several of which would be adapted for television. In 1986, with *A Dark-Adapted Eye*, she published her first novel under the name Barbara Vine. Alongside novels which appeared with astonishing regularity, she was also the author of three novellas and ten volumes of short stories. She received a cascade of awards and, in 1997, was made a life peer, becoming Baroness Rendell of Babergh in Aldeburgh in Suffolk.

This recording was made at UEA on 20 November, 1996.

RENDELL: Before we have a conversation, I thought I would give you a very long answer to a question I am invariably asked. When I have done a reading, or a talk, and we come to question time, someone will always ask me how I write a book, how I go about it, what happens. So, I thought I would take my time this evening and tell you how I write a book. I am not talking about a formula. I am not talking about a plan. I am talking about a method that is very flexible and changes every time, so I am going to talk to you about the way I wrote my latest published novel, *The Keys to the Street*. I don't go about looking for ideas. I usually have a few ideas floating around and when the time comes to write another book I think of using them, and I also think of my setting.

I have a little mews house in London, to the south of Regent's Park, and when I am staying there I usually walk in the park early in the morning, and one day I was offered a key to some private gardens near the park by the Crown Estate, who administer all the properties in that area, including my house. They offered their residents a key to the private gardens of Park Crescent and Park Square and used to charge thirty pounds a year, but nobody seemed to want them so they have reduced it to ten pounds. I thought that was an offer I couldn't refuse. So, I had my key and I went into this garden and found that between the gardens in the Crescent and the Square there was a tunnel under the Marylebone Road. I found it immediately fascinating that this quite rustic-looking tunnel should pass from these quiet gardens, under one of the busiest thoroughfares in London, and above the Jubilee Line of the Tube, and yet it should look quite rustic, very quiet, Victorian and private. And I thought, I am going to use this as a setting for my next book.

Having thought that, I walked through this tunnel a few times and on one occasion a squirrel came up and sat in the middle of the tunnel and gave me an astonished look, because it was so long since it had seen a human being. Then it rushed away between my legs. I thought, 'No, I will use the whole of Regent's Park as my setting.' I had already done this with one of my Barbara Vine books, *King Solomon's Carpet*, which is both a piece of fiction and a history of the London Underground from its inception in 1863. This time, though, I wouldn't be doing what I did with that book, which was to write the history quite coolly, quite unemotionally, and to italicise the bits which were the history and intersperse them with the novel. This time I would absorb the park into the book. It would almost be a character. So, I had the setting of Regent's Park with the tunnel. I knew I would have to do quite a lot of research because I thought that I would want to mention every landmark and every terrace, let my readers know the history of the park without using a map. I don't like the idea of using a map in fiction, although I have been asked since the book was published why I didn't include one. I think readers can get themselves a London atlas and find out what is going on in the park. I wanted to bring in every monument, every stretch of water – not quite every tree – all the history. So, I did use a researcher who I have used before and who is a wonderful woman who will say to me, 'When I am researching, if I come upon anything that is not exactly in your brief, but something I think you will be interested in, do you want me to let you have it?' In this case that was very valuable. Of course, I did my own research simply by walking around the park whenever I was in London, every morning, starting at about seven o'clock, looking at everything, finding that I really didn't know Regent's Park as I thought I did, noting in my mind that I would know it so well I could find my way around it. I could have drawn a map of it just from memory, which I certainly could do now.

I am often asked whether I start with a character, a place, a situation, a murder, but I never do that. I think the answer is that I start with a character in a situation. So, I had three ideas that I was going to bring together. I wanted to write about the situation of somebody who makes a bone-marrow donation to an unknown recipient, and what would happen when at last these people, donor and recipient, were allowed to meet each other. What would their situation be? How would they feel? I found out that some time would have to elapse before they would be permitted to meet each other, so I wanted to have people in that situation. Also, I am very interested in the street people, the people who sleep on the street in London and other great cities. I have written about them before. Now I wanted to write about somebody who was a middle-class professional person who had had such a great tragedy in his life, so overwhelming, so much greater than most of us will ever know, that he abandons his life because he can't face it and takes to the street without it being so different from anything he has ever known. The third idea was the dog-walker. Watching dog-walkers in the London parks – because I once lived near Kensington Gardens and again near Hyde Park and had seen them in Regent's Park and Central Park in New York – I thought here was a character for me, somebody who makes a living out of collecting people's dogs and taking them for a walk and has perhaps six or even more on a leash. So, I had my three characters in three situations and I saw how I could bring them together in Regent's Park. The bone-marrow donor was going to be a young woman who was going to be, if I had such a thing, my heroine and I suppose the poor man with the tragedy was going to be my hero, but I am not sure that I have characters who could quite come into those categories. If that is so, the dog-walker was certainly going to be my villain.

It is, I must tell you, much easier to write about nasty people or vindictive people, malicious people, criminal people, bad people or untruthful people, than it is to write about good people. I don't know why. Of course, at the beginning of *Anna Karenina* Tolstoy tells us that all happy families are the same, but unhappy families are different. It is very presumptuous of me to argue with Tolstoy but I think he is wrong. The reverse is true, although there is a great diversity in wickedness but not very much in good. That may be the reason, but I did want my bone-marrow donor to be a good, sweet, nice woman. I also wanted Roman, the man who takes to the street, to be nice, but in rather a different way. I think he gave me a little more scope. In this book, though, it is not always so for me. I wanted the murders, because there are several, to be my last consideration. They were going to be there but I was going to do something that I had never done before – and, I think, that no crime writer has ever done before. It was to be a question not of who, or how, or why, which should be unimportant. The significance of the murders was their effect on those other characters of mine, not only the three that I have named to you, but all the others.

I always begin to write before I have done all my research. I like to have an idea but I like to begin to write when the research has only begun. I am not a note-taker and emphatically do not have plans. There are some writers who will have charts on the walls and maps. Of course I use maps, but I don't use charts and I make no notes before I start. The idea of plotting out the chapters, with a synopsis of what the chapters will be in advance, is not only impossible for me, I believe that if I do it the whole thing would fall to pieces. I wouldn't be able to do it. It is as if it will break apart because I am somehow bringing it out into the light of day. I do have a pretty good idea of the beginning, at any rate, and of the first four chapters, in my mind, how it will progress. How it will end, I don't know. I have a theory, not my own, that it is better to let the characters work it out for themselves, interact, that their actions should proceed from what has gone before. So I continued to take my regular walks in the park noticing interesting landmarks and, of course, reading about the park, reading as much as I could, and there was quite a lot of reading to be done because my researcher, who went to many authorities, to the park police for me and quite a lot of archives, also happened to find, among her own father's papers, a Victorian book which dealt very much with the history of Regent's Park from a nineteenth-century viewpoint, which was quite interesting because the things that interested them were not necessarily the things that would interest us today. She photocopied large sections of this book for me and I found a lot with interest in there which I knew I would be able to put into my novel.

When I do my own research, when it is observation, when I did it for *King Solomon's Carpet* and rode around on the London Tube a great deal observing things, I tend not to make notes at the time. I make the notes as soon as I get home and that is what I did in Regent's Park. I would note, for instance, that there is a famous circular rose garden in the inner circle of the park and it was important for me to know the names of some of the roses. I would memorise the names, write them down when I got home and check them out in rose-growers' catalogues to make sure I had got the right names and was spelling them correctly. I then, of course had to choose names for my characters. I think this is very important, and lots of writers don't get it right. Names change so much. I am talking of Christian or first names. With surnames, you are on dangerous ground because it is not a very sensible thing for a writer to consult the telephone directory, which is the obvious thing. I am always of the aware of the possibilities of libel and I would advise any writer to be the same, so I often choose my characters' names from street names. I choose them out of the street directory and I feel that way I am safer, or I choose common names and change the letter. With Christian names, first names, I have three dictionaries, the most conservative, and also perhaps the most interesting, is the *Oxford Dictionary of English Christian Names*. The others I have are perhaps in a way more ambitious as I have taken note of our great influx of immigrants with immigrant names, so one of my dictionaries has a lot of African and Indian names, which can be very useful. My location was, broadly speaking, Regent's Park, but then of course I was also going to have to use the embounds of the park. I was going to have to use those streets which form something like a tangled nest around the park, very much the reverse, in that particular area, of a grid plan. I took my characters up into Primrose Hill and St John's Wood. I took them down to Baker Street and to the east and west of the park, and I became very much aware of Sherlock Holmes being in that vicinity, the museum being at 221B Baker Street, which of course is within sight of the park. I thought that I would have my heroine – my Mary, my donor of her bone marrow – work in, or be part-owner of, a museum in the area that was rather like the Sherlock Holmes museum so I decided to invent a museum in St. John's Wood and call it the Irene Adler Museum because of course Irene Adler was the only woman Sherlock Holmes ever loved. I have since then had several letters from people, I must tell you not from this country, who have told me hotly that Sherlock Holmes was never in love but I reply that love is a matter of opinion and not a matter of fact. So, I invented the Irene Adler Museum. which I placed in Charles Lane, St John's Wood, where in fact it could not be. It is full of Edwardian costumes and facsimiles of the rooms in which Irene Adler may have lived. It also contains the famous photograph which Holmes so much admired and cherished.

The middle of a book is always the hardest bit. The beginning is wonderful. The first page is the bit one enjoys most, I think. Then there is the creation of the characters, the setting up of the characters, the establishing of them with the aim that the reader will know how these people are, what they look like, how they speak and will long to see them on the page again. That is good, that is interesting, but a hard task, a challenge. As to the end, one hopes that one climax will lead to another with a marvellous final one. One hopes for that just as one hopes for a stunning first line. Think of the first lines of some of the novels you have read and what an impact they had. So, I always find that to carry you through the middle I must be sure that my characters have occupations. 'Hobbies' is not a word I like. I think hobbies sounds dreadful. I don't want my characters to have hobbies, I want them to have occupations. I want them to have things that they do and things that interest them when they are not actively taking part in the action on my page. I think that to keep one's characters busy will carry one through that difficult middle part.

Of course, I took my characters into the park constantly. Mary, the donor, had to cross the park, from the house in which she was house-sitting and dog-sitting for an elderly rich couple who had gone on a holiday to Central America, to reach the Irene Adler Museum. Roman, the man who had had the tragedy in his life, spent a great deal of his time in the park, sometimes sleeping there if he was permitted to do so. I, of course, made myself pretty conversant with what the police would permit in the park, along with its opening times and closing times, the rounding-up of people who slept there, the possibilities of escaping the vigilant eye of the police. There was a dog-walker who was in the park every day walking his six dogs, every one of which belonged to somebody who lived in the vicinity. I followed him, not every day but many days, as he did his morning and evening walks. I tried to give those six dogs their own separate doggie characters, so they, too, would be interesting and they, too, would be of importance. And then I had other characters. I had a man who was addicted to almost every drug that would be obtainable in London. I also had the street people who played a very important part in the book. I was interested in them. I wanted to write about them as real people, as human beings, and not a sort of street detritus. They, too, are quite important, how they come into the park, what they do outside it, where they sleep, how they live, what they eat and the attitude of my characters and other people towards them. The title, *The Keys to the Street*, of course means that if you give somebody the keys to the street you are in fact turning them out of your house. You are not giving them the keys to your house or their home, you are giving them, in a sense, the keys to the outside, saying don't come back. Because it was called that, the street had to be very important and also the people who sleep on the streets.

The novel starts in April. I always find dates very difficult. I am quite a numerate person but even so, dates are a problem and the only way to handle them when I am writing is to have a calendar there and to decide before I begin where I am. Am I in a current year or last year? I could even be in next year, although this is a bit dicey because who knows what will happen next year. So, I like to have a calendar near me and note what is happening to my days and not get such a muddle with my days that some poor copy-editor is going to have to sort it all out in the future before the book is in print. So, I began in April with a calendar, watching my days and, since it was in the current year, watching the weather, too. A previous book I had written, which was the second Barbara Vine, called *A Fatal Inversion*, is set in the summer of 1976 which was remarkably hot and I thought I remembered it. Then I asked the meteorological office to supply me with the figures for the temperatures for Suffolk from the middle of June until the end of August and found that they were very different from what I remembered. But to return to the *Street*, I observed the weather myself and referred to my calendar so that I could be sure what I was doing and I knew that I would spread the book over a period of about four months and, of course, I was writing it while I was living it. I was writing it before and I was writing it after but I still had that period of time in which I was watching the seasons and watching events. For instance, while I was writing the book, in comes the fiftieth anniversary celebrations of VJ Day. They were part of the book, something for my characters to see in that area and from the park. So, the seasons changed and the trees came into leaf. The birds hatched out their young and the swans turned from ugly ducklings into swans. The weather changed. It got warmer, the roses came out, and I felt that these things were very important because I was describing that particular area where the weather was of such great significance.

I have a series of violent deaths in the book, all of which are observed by my characters. The victims are all street people against whom this serial killer seems to have a particular vendetta, one of whom was discovered by Roman, the man with the tragedy. Other deaths have a strong impact on the characters. There are other quite decisive events in the plot but all the characters come together, coalesce in a way and fade away until we come to the last chapter in which the killer of these people is discovered and I think that in this discovery, and in what he was and who he was, there is something that I could perhaps describe almost as a negative discovery, something I think has not been done before. I left a somewhat open end as I had often done. Ends were tied but there were also loose ends and I rather like this. I don't want everything to be neatened up. I don't want order to be entirely restored and chaos to disappear. I had no map. The Regent's Park Society have since written to me begging me to have one put into the paperback and also to have a footnote saying who they are, but I don't think we should do that. I think fiction should be fiction and although this book has a lot of facts in it, it remains fiction, and I like to think that when I am writing fiction I can do a great deal of what I like.

BIGSBY: Did you want to resist having a map in *The Keys to the Street* because you have your own mental, fictive map?

RENDELL: No, it is because I have a pure idea of what fiction should be. I don't even like genealogical tables. I don't want a family tree in a book. There was a time in the 1930s when crime fiction – and it is very applicable here – reached such a low that publishers would include artefacts in the book. You would have a lock of hair, a fingerprint and a picture of a magnifying glass, along with maps and plans of houses. I feel that this is so awful. It is something, but it is not fiction, not a novel. It is some sort of *Cluedo* game. I have a map in one book but that was because I didn't know any better. That was a long time ago and I allowed a publisher to force this on me, but I wouldn't do it now. The same with footnotes. It is all right to have an acknowledgement. It is all right to have some sort of disclaimer. For instance, in *King Solomon's Carpet* I do point out, in a disclaimer, that there is no air vent out of a certain part of the London Tube. That was really to stop people trying to put a bomb down it. There is no air vent and I wanted to make that clear. Apart from that, I think the less of that sort of thing, the better. This is fiction.

BIGSBY: What is the line between the literal map of a real place and the fictive elements that you then put into that apparently real place?

RENDELL: I don't know. I know that when I describe a street, if it is a real street, I want to describe what is there, but I will also add something. I would not, though, subtract anything. For instance, if I describe, as I do, the environs of the park, and the place which is called St Andrew's Terrace, I would add another house, or I would add a number, but I would not remove Sir Denys Lasdun's Royal College of Physicians. I think we may add. For instance, say the houses in the street only go up to two hundred, I cannot let a character live at number one hundred and ninety-eight because somebody lives there, but I can make this character live at number two hundred and four.

BIGSBY: I was a bit surprised when you said 'crime novel' because there are crimes in it, there are murders in it, but they take place off stage. You said the characters observed the murders but they observed the consequences of the murders. There are detectives but they hardly make their way in there. Where do we go with this terminology, crime writer, thriller writer, detective story writer? Does it matter what the category is?

RENDELL: No, it doesn't matter to me, but it matters to a lot of people. I don't think it really is a crime novel. More people say that it is than say that it isn't, but I don't care. I just write it. I think readers have to make up their own mind about that.

BIGSBY: Have you always wanted to be a writer?

RENDELL: I don't think so. I wasn't one of those precocious child writers, and I have known a few like that. I think they mostly give up writing when they come into their teens. I did know somebody who came to stay when he was seven and brought me his novel. I read it out and it was very derivative but it was very good and very funny. He was a very intelligent child. He could do all sorts of things. He could draw very well. He was an arithmetical prodigy. Then writing faded away. I have always been a great storyteller. I like doing it. Whether I am a great one is another matter. I told stories to children. I now tell stories to my own grandchildren, which I enjoy very much, but I think in that way I wanted to be a writer without knowing it. I just liked telling stories.

BIGSBY: There was a stage, wasn't there, before you published the first novel, when you had a cupboard full of them?

RENDELL: Oh, yes, probably about six.

BIGSBY: Why do you write about murders?

RENDELL: Oh dear, I am not used to these questions. I will tell you why. I came to this by accident because the first book of mine, which was published thirty-two years ago, happened to be a detective story. I had written other novels but the one that a publisher took was a detective story, the first Wexford book, which I had written for fun. Having done that, I had to do more. I was stuck with it. I thought for a while that perhaps I didn't want this, and I have certainly moved away in all sorts of directions.

But the fact is I am naturally suited to writing suspense and excitement and whatever I wrote would have those elements in it. We write what is in our nature to write.

BIGSBY: Why is that in your nature?
RENDELL: I hoped you wouldn't ask that. You have to admit that there is a great deal in my books that is more about motivation and the surroundings rather than about the actual murder.

BIGSBY: Do you jump into another mindset, another personality, when you write as Barbara Vine?
RENDELL: I don't know that I do. I feel it is the same mind. I am writing a Barbara Vine now and I don't really feel any different.

BIGSBY: Obviously you make a decision to write a novel as Barbara Vine rather than Ruth Rendell, so there must be something that makes it more appropriate to use one sensibility, one name rather than the other.
RENDELL: Yes, there is. The Wexford stories are classic detective stories. The Ruth Rendell books are murder mysteries, even though they don't have any police in them. They may deal very much with motivation and perhaps with a lot of pathology. I think that Barbara Vine's do not. There will perhaps be some violent death but it is peripheral, or distant, or has happened in the past. They are often in the first person. It gives me an opportunity to explore my characters' minds more deeply.

BIGSBY: That is almost a description of *The Keys To the Street*.
RENDELL: I know, but it is the same person you see. I can't help that.

BIGSBY: And why Barbara Vine?
RENDELL: Barbara is my second Christian name and Vine was the maiden name of one of my great grandmothers.

BIGSBY: And Wexford?
RENDELL: Because I had been on holiday in Ireland

a short time before. I might have called him Waterford. I could have called him Cork. I called him Reginald after my favourite uncle. He is still alive and likes to think he is the original Wexford.

BIGSBY: How far do you base your characters on people you know, or observe?

RENDELL: Few of my characters have been directly based on real people. In a book I wrote called *The House of Stairs*, by Barbara Vine, the main female character was based on a cousin of mine, but she had died before I wrote it. I have hardly ever use living people. I don't know where the characters come from. Of course, they must come from life because the alternative is that we get them out of television or other people's books, which of course we would not wish to do. I think they come out of some great pool that a writer of fiction holds inside him or herself somewhere, and they are pulled up like a bucket from a well. Of course, people think that you have based your characters on them and say, 'That's me, isn't it?' and you are absolutely astonished because it is not in the least like them. Many of us of course don't know what we really are like.

BIGSBY: When you wrote that first Wexford book, was that because you were an avid reader of crime fiction at the time?

RENDELL: I don't think I was an avid reader of crime more than any other sort but, yes, of course I read a lot of it. I just thought I would like to see if I could do it. Wexford himself was at that time very much derived from other people's detectives because my other characters were more important. Later on, of course, when I knew that I was going to write more about him, he changed and I developed him. I made him more suited to the sort of person I would want to write about. He became a little bit too literary and liberal and tolerant at one point, so I had to backtrack him, but that was how he came into being.

BIGSBY: There are national differences between the way crime novels are written in this country and, say, Italy. Does it make any sense for there to be national differences? Your books have been translated into twenty-four different languages so are entering cultures which don't have the same kind of tradition that we do, the same literary forms of writing. Does it make any difference when the detective novel moves into different cultures in that way?

RENDELL: It is a very interesting question. I very much like reading novels from other cultures, though I would rather they were written in my own language because I can only read two other languages. For some reason I particularly like crime fiction from, say, Chile or Korea or Namibia. I love American fiction of all kinds because I want to know how people are living in those small towns, what they do, how they speak, what they eat and wear, what their schools are like, what sort of cars they drive and where they go on holiday. When you are speaking of Japan, for instance, or China, anywhere in the Far East, this is a completely different culture. I love to read about them, so I suppose they also love to read about me. I know they do because I sell very well in Japan. I think the mistake is to try and write to accommodate people from another culture, to try to write the sort of thing they are going to read about in San Francisco or Trieste or Istanbul, and, anyway, you can't do it well. We have to write what we can write and what pleases us.

BIGSBY: Can you keep the Wexford in your mind completely separate from the image you see on the television screen?

RENDELL: Not any more. Wexford is described in an early book as an ugly man. He is very big, very tall, and fair haired and George Baker, who plays Wexford on television, is a handsome man and dark, but he is also very big so that is all right. My imagination is not terribly visual when it comes to people's features in that way so I would see George, but it is not very important to me. I have never written a line that I thought would suit George particularly.

KAMILA SHAMSIE

Kamila Shamsie was born in Karachi in 1973. She was educated there and in the United States. Her first novel, *In the City By the Sea*, was published in 1998. Other works include *Kartography*, *Burnt Shadows*, *A God in Every Stone* and *Home Fire*. In 2013 she was included in Granta's list of the twenty best young British writers. Along with awards from her native Pakistan, she is a winner of the Anisfield-Wolf Book Award, which recognises important contributions to the understanding of racism and human diversity. In 2018 she won the Women's Prize for Fiction.

This interview was recorded at UEA on 25 October, 2017.

BIGSBY: Before we talk about your novels, I would like to start with the serious stuff, *Test Match Special*, the BBC radio coverage of cricket test matches. You appeared on that programme. It must have been a very strange experience, because the commentators are largely ex-public-school boys called Aggers, Blowers, CMJ, and that is not your background.

SHAMSIE: I should say that I was nominally a member of the Authors' Cricket Club, the only woman. When I say nominally, what I mean is that when I was asked to join I said, 'but I can't play.' The Authors' Cricket Club, though, has a long and distinguished tradition of writers who can't play. But I had to play a match in order to write about it in a book they put together and to me the most joyous thing that came out of this whole thing was that my team mate, Jon Hotton, looked at me and said, 'You need a cricket nickname, so you are going to have to be Shamso.' So, in fact I am Shamso.

BIGSBY: Is it right you bat at number eleven?
SHAMSIE: No, I bat at number ten. The wonderful Kashmiri novelist Mirza Waheed, who was my coach, said, 'I refuse to let you bat at number eleven. I have coached you.' So, he batted number eleven and insisted I went in at number ten. I was out for a second ball duck. However, I was out to the former captain of the South African International Women's side, so I felt the fact that I survived one ball was an achievement.

BIGSBY: And you live around the corner from Lord's Cricket ground, is that right?
SHAMSIE: I do.

BIGSBY: And you have been to a Wisden Dinner.
SHAMSIE: I was the after-dinner speaker a couple of years ago which is what led to the *Test Match Special*. I am actually doing the *Wisden Cricket Book Of the Year* review, so I have been doing nothing but reading cricket books for the last month.

BIGSBY: When it comes to cricket, the relationship between England and Pakistan has been fraught at times, has it not?

SHAMSIE: It has been fraught. We are doing British understatement here now.

BIGSBY: The other thing to say is that cricket means something very different in Pakistan and India than it does here. Here public-school involvement is not restricted to the people in *Test Match Special*, it plays a different role in the culture.

SHAMSIE: It does, and one of the surprises of moving to England was to discover what it meant to follow cricket here. It did mean the public schoolboy element while the male part was interesting. In Pakistan, it is a game played across class backgrounds. It is played in the street. If people can cobble together enough money to get two bats and one ball in the neighbourhood, that is a cricket match. So, the idea that it was class-related in England was very bizarre and, of course, it is still largely a game played by men, although that is beginning to change. But, in Pakistan, women always watched it as well so it was a shock to me when I went to Lord's. I would have been in my thirties by then. I was standing next to a man and some older English public schoolboy said, 'Are you with him? Is this your first time?' and I thought that in Pakistan you wouldn't say this to a female over the age of twelve if you saw her at a cricket ground.

BIGSBY: I don't invoke cricket entirely arbitrarily because cricket does pop up in your novels.

SHAMSIE: It's like a tick. In every one of my novels there is somewhere some kind of reference to cricket, even if it is the most tangential one, one line. Yes, it is always there.

BIGSBY: You are now a British citizen and have quoted Hisham Matar, who is Libyan, as saying that when you take up citizenship in another country you are betraying your original country and your original country is betraying you in making you choose another country. Was any of that true of you, or is that just Hisham Matar?

SHAMSIE: It was there. It is very odd because largely I don't feel that. Largely, I feel that having more than one citizenship, more than one country to claim, is actually good because there are these two places you have ties to, in different ways. But when I did feel it was the moment of getting citizenship. I went to the citizenship ceremony across the street from the British Library, in Camden Town Hall. I had been spending a lot of time in the British Library researching a novel called *A God In Every Stone*, which is set in the Indian sub-continent during the colonial period. I had been researching a particularly hideous massacre. There were some old pictures of the Union Jack flying above the streets of Peshawar – indeed above the street where later there was a massacre of people calling for independence. So, that was a weird image to have in my head when I walked into the Camden Town Hall. There was a photographer there and, as I walked in, he handed me a Union flag. Of course, you can live in England much of your life without having a Union flag. It is not a flag-waving nation, so to have this thrust at me just when I had been seeing these pictures of the Union flag over the streets of Peshawar in colonial times was very odd. I remembered that both my parents had spent some time in Britain in the 1950s and 1960s and in those days it was quite easy, if you were from a Commonwealth nation, to become a British citizen. Back then, they would just have had to go into the Post Office and fill in a form. They didn't because their feeling, at that point, was, 'we have just got rid of you lot.' So, all these decades later to be someone who was acquiring British citizenship, coming from a nation where anyone who can gets a second passport, it being understood that it is so much easier not to travel on a Pakistani passport, was a very strange moment. I didn't expect to feel any sense of unease because by then I had been living in London for ten years. It is very much home and I was startled by my own response to it. So, for that moment Hisham's line, 'you are betrayer and betrayed both,' made sense. If you are betraying your country of origin, it has betrayed you, and other people of your nation, by making you a national who wants to get a second passport.

BIGSBY: You said this country is very much home but it is not your only home. You haven't relinquished the idea of there being another home, have you?

SHAMSIE: No. I don't know why people have the sense that a relationship with home has to be monogamous. I often think about the identification with cities rather than countries, so Karachi is home, London is home, but they are home in different ways. London is my day-to-day home, but Karachi is home in that it has always been home. You can walk down a particular street, or stand in a particular spot, and remember what it was to be three years old there and what it was to be thirteen and what it was to be twenty-three and thirty-three and forty-three. So, the continuity of your life is in a particular place.

BIGSBY: So, was British citizenship a matter of convenience, in that it made life easier, or did it mean something more than that?

SHAMSIE: It was two things, or convenience in two ways. One was that question of the passport because I travel a fair bit and really you do not want to know what it is like to travel around the world on a Pakistani passport. Let's just say it wasn't fun and there were a lot of times when I simply wouldn't go places I was invited to because I knew what I would have to go through to get the visa and it just wasn't worth it. A lot of times people would invite me six weeks in advance and I would say, 'I need three months to get a visa.' So partly it was that, but more than that it was because I want to live in London and because the rules around visas and residents' permits were changing quite a lot I knew that the only way I would really feel secure that this was where I could stay was if I had citizenship. But an interesting thing happened when I wrote *Home Fire.* I had written novels that touch on Britain before. A previous one, *A God in Every Stone,* has large chunks in London but it is the London of 1915 and 1930, but *Home Fire* is set in contemporary London and writing that did something to my relationship, or my idea of my relationship, to Britain. It felt as though I was writing it from within. I wasn't writing it as a foreigner. I was writing as someone who wants to be part of a conversation about, or an imagining of, the place in which I live.

BIGSBY: You were born in Karachi, into a fairly upper-class family, in a culture where the gap between the rich and the poor is quite wide and there is a caste system. Were you aware of that as you grew up?

SHAMSIE: Well, there isn't definitely a caste system. There is a very deep class system but it is interesting because in many parts of our country people will use the term 'caste' but it doesn't exist in Karachi so it is actually a shock to go from Karachi to Lahore or somewhere and to hear people talk about caste. People in Karachi are more interested in what you have done with your life than anything else, which is one of the wonders of it I think. But yes, it is certainly a city of stratifications and divides which it is impossible not to be aware of.

BIGSBY: Yours is a professional family. It included writers, so the idea of being a writer wasn't quite so alien. On the other hand, was there a Pakistani literary scene, a heritage you could relate to?

SHAMSIE: There wasn't. People say, 'oh well, you came from a family of writers,' which is true and not true. My great aunt Attia Hosain had published a novel and a book of short stories with Chatto in the early 1960s but hadn't published anything post 1965, so by the time I knew her she was someone who had done these two books but nothing after that. My grandmother published her memoirs in her mid-eighties, after I published my first three novels, so she was not a published writer until much later. As to my mother, when I was growing up she was working mainly as a journalist and reviewer. It was probably around the time I published my first novel that she started to do more serious work, editing anthologies and writing larger critical books. So, I grew up in a family where there was writing but not of an ongoing professional kind. It was more that I grew up in a world where books mattered, where people wrote, not necessarily in a career sense, but it was what you did because you loved doing it.

BIGSBY: When you were very young were the books that you were reading Pakistani or were they familiar British children's books?

SHAMSIE: English was my first language so, to go back to the question of heritage, there were no books set in the place I lived. So, I grew up reading Peter Pan, Winnie the Pooh and, like every good ex-colonial, Enid Blyton, but I was always a voracious reader and I would read my way across everything. Then there came a point, when I was probably about thirteen or so, when I began to read Sidney Sheldon and Judith Krantz and Jackie Collins. My mother looked at them and she and my father decided, I think very wisely, that you don't tell anyone what they shouldn't be reading. My parents said that the bookshelves are there and you should find your way through them. So, what my mother did was to start suggesting books for me and among the books she suggested to me were writers such as Salman Rushdie and Bapsi Sidhwa, who was the one Pakistani writer being published. I remember reading *Midnight's Children* for the first time. It was like a miracle that there could be a novel that was coming out of my world, that fiction wasn't something in a very faraway place where I would read about other people's lives in an external sense, but that it could be intimate and familiar to me. When I say intimate and familiar, I mean that Salman Rushdie's relatives were my grandmother's friends so I was recognising people, often in rather tantalising ways, but also that the language he was using, and the history he was referring to, and the political angle, were all astonishingly familiar. At that moment I thought, 'oh, the English language novel can happen here as well.'

BIGSBY: That raises another question, however, and that is Partition. Obviously, you are far too young for that, but your family was divided by Partition. As a result, you have family in India and family in Pakistan.

SHAMSIE: My father was ten and my mother was three then, but, for my grandparents, of course, it was significant. On my mother's side, both her grandmothers stayed in India (her grandfathers had died by then). So, half came over at Partition, but relatives were always coming back and forth, so I was aware of it and, because cricket infuses everything, I think the moment I first realised the deep oddness of it was 1987, when India and Pakistan played a test match against each other. It was the final day of the test match and

Pakistan won. It was the first victory in India against India in a test and my grandmother's brother was in Karachi and he said, 'we must look at the news. I have to see what happened at the Test,' and I said, 'we won,' and he looked at me and his face fell and he said, 'you did?' And I thought 'oh, right.' It was so bizarre. So, I was very aware that, though the Indian relatives did come back and forth, it wasn't always easy and possible. I remember my mother telling me that the first time she saw her mother cry was when my grandmother couldn't get a visa to go to India when her mother was dying. So I was always a bit aware of it.

BIGSBY: You left Pakistan to be educated in the United States. Was that a normal thing to do?
SHAMSIE: For my school. Of ninety of us in my year I think probably about sixty went to America and my sister had been two years before me.

BIGSBY: Why not Britain?
SHAMSIE: Too expensive. If you were an international student, you were being charged that much more whereas a number of American Universities were very generous in giving financial aid to international students, so it was largely a practical financial decision. Also, by that point, in the 1980s, America was seen as the exciting place, whereas in my parents' generation anyone who went abroad would have gone to England.

BIGSBY: You went to Hamilton College and then moved on to the University of Massachusetts where you did an MFA in English and Creative Writing. That was where you wrote your first novel, and that novel was set in Karachi. So, there you were, sitting in America writing about Karachi. Was an element of that home-sickness?
SHAMSIE: It was when I started, although, it should be said, I would spend summers and winters in Karachi, so I was five months of the year in Karachi and seven in America. The book was actually written half here and half there. But, yes, I did start writing about Karachi very much initially as home-sickness and as a way of placing myself within it again while away from it.

BIGSBY: And did you see Karachi differently by virtue of being so many thousand miles away from it?

SHAMSIE: I had to see it as you don't when you are in a thing. And also, because you go to America and people start asking you all these questions about the place you are from, suddenly, at eighteen, you are supposed to be this great expert and answer questions on the political history of Pakistan, and I had to admit that I had no idea. How should I know? I just lived there. And so you start finding it important to answer people's questions or, because they raised questions that hadn't occurred to you, start thinking or learning or discovering. You start noticing things by contrast.

BIGSBY: That novel is set at a time when, back in Pakistan, there was a brutal system operating. There is a young boy at the centre of it who doesn't quite know what to make of what is happening around him. You went through those brutal times. Did you register them at the time?

SHAMSIE: The novel it is about an eleven-year-old whose uncle is a politician under house arrest. I recalled that when I was about five years old military rule had just been imposed the year before. I had an uncle who was under house arrest in the north of Pakistan, in a city called Abbotabad, that, at that point, no-one had much reason to know. Later it was the city where Osama Bin Laden was killed, which put it on the map for everyone. It is a small, very pretty hill station. So, my uncle lived there and was under house arrest. We went to visit him and, in one of my earlier memories, I recall my father explaining to me that we have to get permission from the government to go and visit my uncle, which seemed so bizarre to me. We arrived at his house and there were these two army people checking that our names were on this list. This just to go and see my uncle. When I went in I thought, 'actually, it is not bad at all,' because he had a very nice library and a garden which, to a five-year-old, seemed huge but, by the time I was eleven, I realised it wasn't huge. But what I remember, though we know memory is flawed, was the first moment of empathy of my life happened the following day. My parents and sister and I, my aunt and cousins, were going for a picnic in the hills very near the house. We all got in the car and opened the gate. As we drove out, I turned around and there was my uncle standing in the driveway waving at us. There was just this moment of recognising that he was looking at us drive out, which he couldn't do, and that he didn't know when he would be able to do that again. I was about five then. What I remember most clearly about that visit was the smell of pine cones. So, the novel is about a boy whose uncle is a political prisoner, and the political party he is part of has as its symbol the pinecone. You become aware of the political truths through these very personal, familiar, intimate stories.

BIGSBY: Arthur Miller talked about the relationship between the individual and society. One of his favourite observations was that, 'the fish is in the sea and the sea is in the fish.' You cannot separate them, and that is true of your work because they are individual stories, but they are individual stories intertwined with what is happening in the wider society.

SHAMSIE: Yes, and I suppose it is because of the story I have just told you. It was just how I saw life, or how I experienced life. I suppose if you were growing up in Pakistan in those days it was hard to keep things separate. There were days when there would be violence in the city and school would be closed. I remember a day, when I was six and a friend of my parents, who lived quite near the school, came to pick his son and me up in the middle of the school day to take us home. It was thrilling to be taken out of school and exciting. It was because Zulfikar Ali Bhutto, the former prime minister, had been hanged, killed by the military dictator. I remember that as a thrill – being taken out of school early and then going home full of the excitement of it and my father explaining to me that Bhutto's was a human life and what a terrible thing it is that a man has been hanged and it is irrelevant whether we like this person or not. So, the world of politics, the world of society, the level of military rule, was always finding its way into daily life and disrupting it in various memorable ways. So, if I think about a particular year in Karachi it is quite natural for me to think of the political events taking place then and how they were shaping daily interactions.

BIGSBY: In various of your novels you invoke judicial murders, assassinations, the Islamisation of the culture – is there any resistance to your work in Pakistan?

SHAMSIE: There isn't, partly because I write novels in English. It is really journalists, or writers in other languages, who the State is much more aware of because they have a wider reach. Actually, Pakistan is so used to getting a bad press outside of Pakistan that, if you are a Pakistani who is doing well in the outside world, the primary response is, 'we are so proud you are out there doing well and giving people something other than terrorism to attach to the world of Pakistan.' So, a number of people are proud of me even though they haven't read my novels.

BIGSBY: You write about Pakistan but your audience has turned out to be international.

SHAMSIE: It is true that in Pakistan it is a contained audience but it is still a significant audience for me. So, it is not irrelevant or insignificant, and emotionally the audience in Pakistan matters a lot to me. But it is true that I am read in all kinds of places. It was quite heartening to know *A God In Every Stone* had more readers in India than it did in any other country in the world. It is really interesting the way things in publishing turn. The novel before that, *Burnt Shadows*, for reasons I cannot understand, was on the bestseller list for weeks and weeks and weeks in Norway. I find it wondrous and erratic, but possibly my Norwegian translator is a better writer than I am.

BIGSBY: In *The Buried Giant*, Kazuo Ishiguro considers whether memory is vital to a people or whether it should be suppressed because it opens wounds, whether memory is essential on a private or public level. I just wanted to read a few sentences from your book *Kartography*: 'what happens when you work so hard to forget a horror that you also forget you have forgotten it. It doesn't disappear and it can turn and mutate into something else. We act as though history can be erased. Who could blame us, the cost of remembering may break our wilting spirits, but if we allow for erasure we tell ourselves that things can be forgotten, put in the dustbin. We tell ourselves it is possible to have acts without consequences.' I wonder if that isn't a driving force with you because you go back to painful times, which everyone has a reason to suppress, not just Partition, which you prefer to call 'Independence,' but to Bangladesh, which is probably forgotten in this country and is curiously not a memory to the forefront in Pakistan. So, is that part of your impulse in going back, the belief that memory is important?

SHAMSIE: I think writers are interested in silences because a silence is very often a story waiting to be told, which is a very hard thing to resist. The story that is untold is a source of great interest. Why is it untold? And Pakistan is a nation of storytelling. Why are there some things we will not speak about and what does it mean to not speak about them? I was born two years after East Pakistan became Bangladesh and my parents used to speak about the horror and the trauma all the time, but, at some point I realised that that was unusual. Most people didn't. This thing that had happened two years before my birth and people were acting as though it didn't happen, it didn't mean anything. So, yes, I am interested in going back, unearthing those stories. Why do we work to forget certain things and what is the cost of that?

BIGSBY: In one of your novels, a mother goes missing and there is a sense that letting go may also matter.

SHAMSIE: Yes. My grandparents' generation are quite amazing because they did live through Partition, which, to them, was also independence, but there was also sorrow at the awfulness of the families dividing, even as they had pride in the new, young, country to which they had moved. I never heard my grandmother complain but, every year of her life, starting 1967 and until 2003, when she died, once a week she would sit and write a letter to her sister in India, who would write back to her. Once a week, every week, for forty-six years, these two women did it and they were exceptionally close. There were years when they couldn't see each other and it was a sorrow, but my grandmother was not a sorrowful woman. She was also a woman who very much made a life in the country she went to. She made it a home and I think she was someone who both remembered and moved forward, which I think is an enviable state to be able to manage.

BIGSBY: There is a curious connection between Britain and places like independent Pakistan. There ought to be severe animosities, given the history of the two countries. We were the oppressors, hence your preference for the word independence rather than Partition. It is a strange relationship because there is, surely, a connection.

SHAMSIE: Partly, of course, it comes out of the success of British divide and rule, which means that now Indians and Pakistanis hate each other, and blame each other, and have little time left to do that to Britain. If you look at the way in which independence is taught in those two countries, then the villains are the other side of the border. If you are Pakistani, it is the Indian National Congress, while if you are Indian it is the Muslim League. The animosity between India and Pakistan is still a present thing and so has to be continually re-enacted and re-inscribed, whereas that doesn't apply to the British because that is in the past. It is also because, in the life of Pakistan, America came in as the foreigner very early on and took over part of our imagination. There is this love/hate relationship with America, at the moment much more hate, so in some sense there is not much space left in there for Britain.

BIGSBY: I would like to ask you about *Burnt Shadows*. I think the word that recurs in reviews is 'ambitious.'

SHAMSIE: It is a terrible word, isn't it? It almost says, 'you try well.'

BIGSBY: I think it had more to do with the fact that the novel is set on several continents, at several times. You include traumatic moments, the dropping of the bomb on Nagasaki, Partition, or Independence, 9/11, Afghanistan. That is a lot to swallow. Did you know that when you started out?

SHAMSIE: No, oh God I wouldn't have done it. I didn't have any idea what I was doing. Initially, it was going to be quite a small, contained novel, which was going to be set in Karachi, in the summer of 1998, the summer when India and Pakistan tested their nuclear bombs. There was, of course, much celebration on both sides of the border, which I found a bit deranging. So, I had a notion that I would have a Pakistani character whose grandmother or mother had survived the bomb in Nagasaki and had a real sense of what the bomb meant, who felt himself to be going mad at this moment when everyone was celebrating the very thing which was the cause of the most incredible trauma. So, then I think, who is this grandmother from Nagasaki? How did she end up with a grandson in Karachi? The next thing I knew I was writing a novel that started in Nagasaki in 1945 and then I had to find a way to get her over to Karachi, so I had her leaving Nagasaki after the war, after the bomb, and landing in the subcontinent. But, of course, Partition was about to happen, so I had basically taken her out of Nagasaki into this place where she is going to be hit by Partition. Then I realised that this was going to be a novel in which every section would include some huge event. You can't go from Nagasaki to Partition and then say, 'and then there was this quiet in Karachi twenty years later.' The novel was now about peoples' lives, played out against these huge cataclysmic backdrops. How do they, or don't they, survive them? But as I was writing I did think this is quite probably going to be a disaster.

BIGSBY: Is it right that it took as long to write the first section, the Nagasaki section, as the rest of the book?
SHAMSIE: Yes, maybe a little longer. It ended up being a chapter of twenty-five or thirty pages. Part of it was because I had to be able to see myself into a place I knew nothing of. I had to be able to inhabit a place deeply enough to get to those thirty pages. I went through about seven or eight drafts.

BIGSBY: Did you go to Nagasaki?
SHAMSIE: I didn't, because this was before I had a British passport, and I looked up the visa requirements

for a Pakistani going to Japan as a tourist and it included getting a Japanese sponsor who would fill out long forms about your tax status and things like that. Quite clearly what the application was saying was, 'don't even bother applying.' It was around that time that the writer Andrew Miller, who is a friend of mine, was writing a novel set in Tokyo, in an earlier time period, and he said 'it may not be such a disadvantage to you because I have been to Tokyo recently and I keep having to forget what Tokyo looks like today in order to write.'

BIGSBY: There is something interesting about this tension between the imagined space and what we think of as the real space. In a sense the writer has to take control of that space and make it what they will. Is it also true that, rather more surprisingly, you had to rewrite the Karachi section of the book?

SHAMSIE: It is. I wrote the Nagasaki bit by looking up all kinds of things, like what the weather would have been on a particular day. There was a website where I could see where the foreigners lived. It had a map of every house or building, and who lived there, so if you dropped me in Nagasaki in 1945 I could say where the butcher was and where that temple was, where Mr so-and-so lived. For the 1947 Delhi bit I didn't have to ask much because I had been to Delhi and there was a lot more I knew. My father's family was from Delhi, so didn't have to do the work of figuring out as much, but I still did a lot to immerse myself in Delhi, 1947. Then I came to Karachi and thought, 'I have got this. I grew up here and I know it,' but when I sent it to my editor she said, 'this is very odd. The only place that isn't alive is Karachi.' I had written about Karachi before in all four previous novels but when I sat down to write it for this fifth novel every other place in the novel felt like a place deeply inhabited by the writer while this one section was almost blasé. I thought that somehow any sentence I would write about Karachi would come alive miraculously so I didn't put the necessary work into it, and I had to then go back and bring the place to life again.

BIGSBY: Your new novel, *Home Fire*, is set in the present but you have set novels in the past, going back to 1914, 1915. Beyond the interest in memory, what is the attraction of the past?

SHAMSIE: I think partly it is to do with an idea that we are living in a time that is a consequence of these earlier times but we are not looking at those earlier moments. To properly understand the present, we need to look back to that earlier period and so a lot of it is to do with that. Some of it is that I am interested in history as a subject and ultimately you write about the things that are your own obsessions, what you want to find out more about. I wanted to find out about 1971. I wanted to think about Partition. In order to write *Burnt Shadows* and the nuclear bomb I had to write about Nagasaki, so there is always something in the present that leads me to these moments in the past. When I was writing about 1971, or the war in Pakistan, I was actually interested in how Karachi in the 1990s, which was in a state of near civil war, related to the city I grew up in. So it is always about how something in the present leads your eye back to some other moment in the past.

BIGSBY: *Home Fire* concerns a woman whose father had been a Jihadi and who had died going to Guantanamo. Her brother goes off to join the media unit of ISIS, which was a particularly notorious one. Did you anticipate problems in writing this novel or feel any inhibitions in tackling this area?

SHAMSIE: I felt tremendous inhibitions. There is a bit in the novel when Isma's sister Aneeka is talking to a young man called Eamonn, who is the son of the Home Secretary, the first Muslim Home Secretary in Britain. He tells her to Google something which involves the word 'bomb' and she says, 'yes, that is a good idea to GWM isn't it?' and he says, 'I don't know what that means,' and she says, it is 'Googling While Muslim.' While I was writing the book, I was very aware of Googling While Muslim. My brain was divided, one part saying, 'don't be ridiculous, carry on,' while the other part was thinking, 'but I am looking at all these websites. What will I say if there is a knock on my door and someone wants to know why this Muslim person, who grew up in Pakistan, is so interested in Islamic State and life in Raqqa?

BIGSBY: It is a novel but that is not entirely how it started out, is it?

SHAMSIE: No. I was at that point in a novelist's life when you want to be writing the next thing and you have no idea what the next thing is. So, you are very willing to be distracted and I had an email from a man called Jatinder Verma, who runs the Tara Arts Theatre in London. I didn't know him but he called me over for a coffee and said, 'I really like your novels, the way you do dialogue. Why don't you write a play for me?' and I said, 'Because I don't know how to write a play.' He said, 'I thought you would say that so why not adapt a play. That way, there is already something there. You just have to work off it. The Greeks are speaking to us quite strongly these days it seems. How about something like *Antigone* in a contemporary context, that could work quite well. 'I said, 'Yes, that could work quite well,' thinking 'which one was Antigone?' But I nodded and said, 'I will certainly think about that.' Then I got on the train to go home and literally went onto Wikipedia and went, 'oh, that one,' and very quickly knew the kind of contemporary story I wanted to tell with it. I did try to think of it as a play but, at some point, I had to face the fact that I was a novelist who had got a scent of the next novel. So, I had to write to Jatinder and say, 'thank you very much and I am very sorry.'

BIGSBY: Did you find it liberating to have that structure, or was it a constraint?

SHAMSIE: I am generally a writer who writes without any idea where I am going. Michael Ondaatje, who turns everything elegant, has a great expression for it, 'following the brush,' which is a way of saying that the writing process can be haphazard. With this one, though, I was working from *Antigone*, and, of course, in order for it to work as a contemporary thing, I had to be able to move away from the play. But even so, there was a basis of plot and character there, so part of it was mapped out from the start. On the one hand it made me write faster and know what I was doing, which was a kind of liberation, but, unexpectedly, it was a constraint, though not in the way people often think it was: 'Did you have to really struggle to find a way to make an ancient play fit a contemporary novel?' In fact, that was fun. I enjoyed that part of it, and where it didn't fit I just jettisoned bits of plot from the original. But I realised that, for me, there is almost an adrenalin rush which comes from not knowing, from the point where you have no idea of where your novel is going to go, where your character is going to go, where all these different balls you have thrown up in the air will come down, how it is all going to take place; then there is that moment when you see it is moving in a direction that could be really interesting, the excitement of that, the sense of always scanning ahead for different possibilities. So I did, at points, miss the not-knowing.

JON SNOW

Jon Snow was born in 1947. He spent a year doing Voluntary Service Overseas in Uganda before attending Liverpool University, where he did not complete his degree following his leadership role in an anti-apartheid demonstration. He then worked at the New Horizon Youth Centre. He was involved in the creation of the Prince's Trust. After a time at London's first commercial radio station, LBC, he moved to ITN as a reporter, subsequently, in 1989, transferring to Channel 4 News where he would become its longest-running presenter. He has won several Royal Television Society awards, including Presenter of the Year. He was also awarded a BAFTA Fellowship.

This interview was recorded on
10 November, 2017.

BIGSBY: Before we talk about your involvement in Channel 4 News, I want to ask you about what your background was and how you became a journalist. But first, can you explain how you found yourself naked in a police cell in Switzerland?

SNOW: James Baker, the US Secretary of State of the time, was negotiating with Yasser Arafat in Geneva and we were there to try and cover it. Baker's plane had arrived at Geneva airport and all the hacks gathered on the tarmac to watch him coming down the steps but the Swiss police didn't like it and arrested all of us. We were released in the middle of the night, but at four o'clock in the morning they came and removed me from my room without allowing me to get dressed. They threw a sheet round me and frogmarched me off to the police station. The reason was that I hadn't paid a fine ten years earlier for going through a red traffic light but, worse still, going through it at thirty-two miles an hour. I only managed to get out eventually, after about six hours, by getting the manager of the hotel, who happened to be an Englishman, to come and pay my sixty-five francs fine.

BIGSBY: Let me take you right back, rather further than your time naked in Switzerland. You were born into privilege. Your family had a nanny, a cook, a gardener, a cleaner, though not, I think, a butler.

SNOW: Not a butler, no.

BIGSBY: Your father was a cleric who eventually became a Bishop. He was also headmaster at a public school.

SNOW: A very minor one.

BIGSBY: And while you were at your first school you experienced some sort of sexual assault, although being so young I don't imagine you made any sense of it at the time.

SNOW: I was only six. I was on my tricycle, which was probably rather old to be on a tricycle, but in those days that wasn't so unusual. The school was a very safe place to tricycle about and one of our stopping points was the domestic quarters where they would chat to us and give us sweets. Then one day, instead of being with my two brothers, I was on my own and one of the domestic servants said, 'Come up to my room. I have got some sweets for you.' Neither of my parents had ever talked to me about any of that stuff, and I did. He shut the door, took all his clothes off, took my clothes off, and there we were, he in a very unpleasant condition. At that point a voice shouted from the corridor, 'Jim,' and he said, 'Get under the bed' and threw me under the bed where there was a potty and dust and filth. I was completely naked but he had got his clothes on somehow. He walked out and shut the door. I was lying under the bed. I heard raised voices and when he came back into the room, he said, 'get dressed.' So, I got dressed but couldn't do up my braces and he refused to do them up. I had rather nice little corduroy shorts and braces but I couldn't do the ones at the back and he wouldn't do them. He said, 'get out, get out,' and I got out. So, I wasn't actually attacked but it was a horrible, horrible thing.

BIGSBY: Did that stay with you?
SNOW: Oh, yes. Funnily enough I never really referred to it until I was an adult. I never told anybody. The voice belonged to the Bursar who must surely have told my parents but they never spoke to me about it. Nobody ever spoke to me about it and that is what made it worse in many ways because I felt very guilty when the man was sacked the next day and I thought it was my fault.
I thought what happened was my fault, and I didn't know why. That is a very informing thing as a child, particularly when you are an adult and find yourself reporting and discussing child abuse. But I was very lucky. I was not physically molested. It was merely a horrible situation.

BIGSBY: Because you could sing, you then moved to a cathedral school having won a scholarship.
SNOW: My mother was a concert pianist.

BIGSBY: But she gave that up.
SNOW: She gave it up as all women gave up things to get married. She loved and played a lot of Brahms. I identified with my mother and my two brothers identified with my father, who was always in his workshop making dreadful bodges of things like radiograms, which were very

complex but not very pretty, nor did they function very well. But I was enthralled with what my mother did. She painted water colours, and I still do water colours to this day. I picked out harmonies in what she was playing and used to sing with her. Suddenly she realised that, not only did I sing, but I had perfect pitch as well and said to my father, 'the boy needs to go to a choir school.' So, I was put in for this competition to become a chorister and I got through. It was an absolutely sensational experience being part of Winchester Cathedral, one of the greatest buildings on earth, and with music every day, three to four hours a day.

BIGSBY: Being in the choir, though, meant that, when the vacations came, you were required for services, so I imagine you didn't see much of your parents?
SNOW: No. I basically didn't see them properly until I was about thirteen. Then I went to another boarding school.

BIGSBY: Were you not close to your parents, then?
SNOW: No, I wasn't. I was quite close to my mother. She suffered from Alopecia Totalis, which for a woman in those days was an absolutely diabolical curse. So, she wore a wig, but they didn't tell us until I was… eight, I think it was, when I found out. They had had some sort of a car problem. They turned a car over and it had affected her eyebrows, not that she had any. It meant she couldn't pencil them in. They thought we would realise she had a wig, but we didn't. In any case, my father was driving along in his open top car. She always wore a Jacqmar scarf in case the thing blew off. He turned to the mirror in the car – we were sitting at the back, the three boys in matching cable stitch mummy-made sweaters – and said, 'boys, I have got something I need to tell you. Your mother doesn't have any hair.' It took some time to digest and I burst into tears. My older brother laughed and said, 'I have always known,' but my younger brother didn't know what to make of it. I was eight and was really shocked, but thereafter she sought to confide in me. She would say 'do you think it is powdering?' but of course I didn't really want to talk about it at all in any form.

BIGSBY: You went on to another minor public school where they did what they do to produce the next generation of leaders, that is to say they beat you, and you had a fagging system.
SNOW: All that stuff, yes.

BIGSBY: Was that an unpleasant experience, or did you just adjust?
SNOW: You just take it as it comes. The main problem was I was very thick.

BIGSBY: I was going to mention the fact that, for all your education, you came out with one A level from school.
SNOW: Well, I got a C in English, which I thought was rather fine. But, hang on, I went to a Tech.

BIGSBY: Which didn't exactly burnish your academic credentials. You got two more A levels. Are you going to say what they were?
SNOW: A D and an E.

BIGSBY: With those grades, university would have seemed unlikely and, in fact, you decided to spend time abroad, with VSO (Voluntary Service Overseas).
SNOW: That changed my life and has informed my journalism ever since. I lived on the banks of the Nile in Uganda. I had never been in a plane, never been out of Europe. I had no idea what Africa was about. There were only two white men, me and the Catholic Father who ran the school. For the first month I was very homesick but, by the end of a year, I was trying to do everything possible to stay there for the rest of my life.

BIGSBY: What was it about that experience that has meant so much to you?
SNOW: I think it was the hunger for knowledge. There were terribly few books but they were as bright as hell. They were lovely people and the community was fantastic. It was very isolated. We were in an old cotton shipping station on the Nile which had long since ceased to ship cotton. All the warehouses were classrooms and

I had seventy kids in my class. I remember in my first week I was writing on the blackboard and somebody made a noise, a rude noise, behind my back and I turned around and said, 'who was that?' A girl in the front row said, 'that black boy at the back, sir,' and I said, 'but you are all black.' 'Ah' she said, 'some of us are much blacker than others,' and he was a beautiful blue-black, from the Sudanese border. She was a cappuccino coffee colour from down in the south west. The scales fell from my eyes. They were as diverse a collection of people as you would find in any English schoolroom. We have redheads and blondes and brunettes and they had people of all sorts of different pigmentations.

BIGSBY: That African experience was going to be important to you more than professionally in that you are now married to a woman from Africa.
SNOW: That is true.

BIGSBY: When you returned from Africa, somewhat unbelievably given your grades, you did get into university, Liverpool University.
SNOW: Yes, but the way I got in was the way all those upper middle class and upper-class people do it. My father was on a train and met the professor of law from Liverpool University. He was amazing. He was a Welshman and had inherited Lloyd George's seat. For some reason he said, 'I will take the boy,' and I went. What interested me was that after the first year I was halfway up the order, even though I was obviously the worst A level performer of all time.

BIGSBY: But you were getting ready to sabotage that?
SNOW: Well, yes. It was 1970 and that was a very angry time. We were very resentful of all sorts of things and particularly of apartheid. If you had lived in Africa that would be a very big cause in your heart, so I threw myself headlong into it. I was the first-year rep so I was on the council of the students' union and in the second year we said to the university, 'you have got to stop investing in companies that are doing business in South Africa,' and we had a marvellous cast list, including Tate and Lyle, all

these Liverpool companies which they were invested in. We had a laundry list of offences and they said, 'I'm sorry, but you are here for three years, we are here forever. Get on with it.' And we said, 'No,' so we occupied the administrative block, which must have been an awful pain. We had it for six weeks, until the long vacation dawned, and everybody went home. Of course they picked off the people they knew to be the ringleaders.

BIGSBY: So, you got sent down.
SNOW: Yes. Actually, I was only rusticated.

BIGSBY: So, you could have gone back.
SNOW: I could, but there was no way I was going to.

BIGSBY: What happened next strikes me as another of those experiences which were going to stay with you. You went and worked for an organisation which dealt with homeless teenagers.
SNOW: And still deals with homeless teenagers.

BIGSBY: It was run by Lord Longford, who for a lot of people, for a lot of the time, was a figure of fun. It also involved John Profumo.
SNOW: Correct. John Profumo was on the Board. I knew John Profumo, can anybody say that?! But I didn't know Christine Keeler.

BIGSBY: The impression I get is that, just like your African experience, that has sunk down into you, become part of you.
SNOW: Oh, yes. That absolutely prepared me for life. These were sixteen to twenty-one-year olds who had fallen on very difficult times through family breakdowns at home, drugs, all sorts of things. We were there as a day centre where they would come in. They would want accommodation, all sorts of things, and I threw myself into it in a big way. One of the great moments was when the telephone rang one day and a voice said, 'Mr Snow' and I said 'Yes.' 'My name is Squadron Leader David Checketts. I am the Equerry to HRH,' and I said, 'Yes, and I'm the Pope.' I had no idea what on

earth he was talking about. He said, 'no, I really am. His Royal Highness Prince Charles would very much like you to come and see him.' So I went along, after I had ascertained that I could go on my bicycle. They said that as long as I left it at the tradesmen's entrance that would be fine. A friend and I went to Buckingham Palace and ascended to the White Drawing Room and there was Prince Charles, the Equerry, and a couple of other people. Prince Charles said, 'Mummy is going to live a very long time' – and he wasn't wrong there, that's for sure – 'and I have got to find something that I can do. I want to make a difference.' So we both said, 'If you were prepared to use your name to facilitate the most deprived people in our society and give them a break it would be fantastic. 'Oh,' he said, 'I like the sound of that. We could call it The Prince Charles Trust,' and we said, 'what about the Prince's Trust?' He said, 'Yes, I like that because I can involve other princes. That would be great.' So, there I was in on the ground floor of the Prince's Trust which is an absolutely sensational organisation. It has helped, I would think, a million young people over the years. So, yes, it was a formative experience. I meant to stay there for six months, apply to another university, wreck it, and then go and work but instead I didn't feel I could leave. I was the head of this thing at twenty-three – we had a very small staff – and I stayed for three years.

BIGSBY: You then joined LBC.
SNOW: The first commercial station.

BIGSBY: And this is where your bicycle came in handy, because you were in a city where traffic today moves at the speed that wagons did in the nineteenth century, and that did turn out to be an advantage.
SNOW: It did, because the IRA were bombing their way through the capital and every time a bomb went off there would be an enormous back-up of traffic; Westminster, House of Commons, Old Bailey, wherever it was, and you couldn't move except on a bicycle. The great thing was the police tapes would be across the road for the rest of the people but if you really belted at them on the bike you could get right through and the police were far too busy

doing other things to stop you. We had no mobile phones, but what we did have were enormous Motorola walkie talkies and, as long as we were somewhere within range of the London Weekend Television mast, which was on the other side of the Thames but was quite powerful, you could squeeze the switch, call up and actually get on air from the scene of the crime. So it really was a groundbreaking thing. The BBC would never do it because the quality wasn't good enough, but people just want to hear what the hell is going on.

BIGSBY: How did you get into ITN?
SNOW: I was actually head-hunted, for the first time in my life. The interesting thing is that I said 'no,' because my cousin, Peter Snow, worked there and I didn't want it to be thought that nepotism had prevailed, and I loved radio. It is a fantastic medium, the ultimate medium, no question. You listen to it everywhere you go. Now podcasts have added to it. The whole thing is just magic. I never really wanted to work in television at all. The ITN Editor wrote me a letter saying, 'you just have to sign this paragraph and we will take you,' and so I went to my Editor and said, 'look, I love radio. I want to stay here, but I have been offered this job in television,' and he said, 'go, for God's sake, man. There is no future in radio.' So off I went.

BIGSBY: And once in you were approached by another organisation.
SNOW: MI6, yes. It was very, very interesting. I got very paranoid about it because I thought it was a terribly secret experience I couldn't share with anybody. I had come back from Ireland where I had been at an IRA siege. We had been drinking water from a tap that fed a cow trough and five of us got hepatitis. I was confined to an isolation hospital in north London to recover from this condition and my flat mate would come to see me and came to see me. One day he arrived carrying a brown envelope, which he had clearly opened, which said, 'Strictly Confidential' in red type and, underneath, 'On Her Majesty's Service,' and he said: 'I am afraid I've opened this.' It said: 'Dear Mr Snow, I am doing some work which I think you might be interested in and might be able to help with. If you

are interested would you call the number above. If you are not interested would you please destroy this letter and discuss its contents with no-one.' I thought, fucking hell, that must be The Firm. Anyway, I agreed to go along because, as a journalist, you are intrigued. I was asked to go to Old War Office Buildings, so I cycled the wrong way down one-way streets. I really hid my tracks, and then eventually I got there, but not before I had been to Waterloo Station. I didn't want to photocopy the letter in the office because I thought somebody might get hold of the copy or something. I needed a copy because I knew that, if I went, they would take the letter off me. I was sure that would happen and, indeed, it did, so I went to Waterloo Station where, in those days, there would be a wooden box in the middle of the forecourt area which contained a copier. You put a shilling in, or whatever it was, and then it would release the doors and there would be a printer inside. For some reason when I fed the thing in and pushed the button it went completely berserk and did twenty copies and there was a bit of a wind going and they were blowing everywhere. So, anyway, I gathered them up. I think I got them all, but I don't know. Then I had to find some way of disposing of them. Anyway, I kept one, I am very glad to say, because, sure enough, they took the letter off me but the other one was in my pocket. I went up to see Mr Douglas Stillberry, who had signed the letter. I couldn't believe anybody in Britain would be called Stillberry. It is some kind of a fruit, I think. He was sitting at a desk and I was in one of those then quite modern slump chairs looking up at him. I could see he was Eton and the Guards and very posh. Anyway, he started talking to me about what they did and he asked me a few questions. They had done a lot of research. They knew I had been chucked out of university. What attracted them was that they thought I had been a Communist, which I never was. I was never a member of any party at all. I was just a pinko, a bleeding heart. He said, 'I am not going to take any answer from you now. I want you to go away and think about what I have said.' I said, 'No, I can give you an answer now. I don't think we are on the same side.' I seriously thought he was on the other side, not on the Russian side but on that side, whatever that was. I didn't feel an affinity. I didn't feel I could join the club, in fact I knew I wasn't going to join the club. I just wanted to find out how it worked. I went to see Stillberry again and said, 'I am very sorry but I am not going to do this,' and he said, 'Right. You are not ever to contact us again and we shall never contact you,' but actually, very early on in my journalistic career, they did contact me.

I was in Iran and, driving along the Caspian Sea, I had seen up on a hill tell-tale domes which I knew was the mark of an early warning station. How did I know? Because my father was a Bishop in North Yorkshire and Fylingdales was there so I had seen them and knew what an early warning station was. I thought, 'gosh, let's go up there and see what has happened,' because it was on the day of the revolution. We had left Tehran because it was completely impossible to move. There were millions of people in the streets, so went up there and there were just two lackadaisical sixteen-year-olds seated, with Kalashnikovs across their knees, thrilled to see us, literally thrilled to see us. They welcomed us with open arms, dropping the Kalashnikovs, and we made to go into the domes and my cameraman said, 'Hang on Jon, they are booby-trapped.' 'But how do you know?' 'Well, they might be.' So we started throwing stones into the thing to see if they went off but inside the domes there were still computers, huge boxed computers with great paper spewing out with hieroglyphics because it was watching the Urals where Russia was doing their nuclear tests. There were still pyjamas on the American's beds. There were still cornflakes on the table. They had just left, left everything, it was quite extraordinary. We got back to Tehran having filmed ourselves blue. It was fantastic. It was the stuff of James Bond. After all, who gets to go inside a secret entity like that, but we did and, at four o'clock in the morning, there was a knock on the door. 'Mr Snow.' 'Yes, who is it?' 'Please could you open the door because I need to talk to you.' 'Well, who are you?' 'My name is Major Arthur Blenkinsop.' I don't actually know what his name was but he was a Major, the defence attaché at the British Embassy, and he came in and he said: 'I have got something very serious to say to you. You can't use it.' I said 'Use what? ⊠You have been to somewhere exceptionally secret and it would prejudice the welfare of your own family if you were to discuss what you have seen, let alone show any film of it.' I said: 'I am very sorry but we are not in Britain at the moment and you have no right to stop me doing anything at all.'

The problem was that we didn't really know what we had seen but he did. He wanted us not to show certain things so what I said was, 'look, what we will do is let you see all the footage and anything you think might be just too much we will pull out unless we think it is just what ought to be in there.' As we showed him the footage he started having these terrible seizures. He shouted, 'Oh my God, no, no, you can't possibly show that.' 'Well, will it start a war?' 'It could.' In fact, we had no idea what any of it was and he did remove a few bits and pieces and we then transmitted it on the Iranian satellite and Iran TV asked for the footage and we said, 'Sure, no problem. So, it went absolutely worldwide despite the Major's efforts and in fact the deal was that, if we removed the bits he wanted, we would want something from him. We said, 'just before the Shah fell, America sold Iran jet fighters. Where are they?' He said, 'Oh, my dear chap, you just go down to Shiraz. At the third roundabout, take the second exit, go out along the road about two miles. On the left-hand side, you will see an airfield. There are some bunkers at the end. They are in there.' We got the lot.

BIGSBY: You were with ITN about fifteen years or so and you went all over the world. I have seen photographs of you in shirt sleeves with no flak jacket, no helmet.

SNOW: It is incredible. We were in the Iran-Iraq war where kids were being sent in human waves from the Iranian side. We had no flak jackets, no training, nothing. We were just there and they were frightfully thrilled that we were there but what they would have felt if we had not survived I don't know. It really was a First World War type experience. These days we don't go anywhere without a flak jacket, and they are very heavy.

BIGSBY: And battle training?
SNOW: All that, yes. You have to have it every three

years and there is an awful conspiracy between the insurance company and the people who train you. If you don't get trained by them then the insurance company doesn't insure you.

BIGSBY: Being a reporter you will necessarily have seen some terrible things. Earlier in this festival we had a heart surgeon and he said that it was necessary for him to suppress emotions. He had a professional job to do and it would only interfere if he allowed himself to feel an emotional attachment. But he also confessed that there are moments when he couldn't do that. Did that apply to you?

SNOW: I agree a hundred percent. I don't really even try to suppress it, to be honest. I think it is a good thing to have a cry. At Grenfell, I wept. That it should happen to our people, in our town, in our time; absolutely shattering.

BIGSBY: I watched your coverage of the Grenfell Tower fire and it wasn't just that you offered a *mea culpa* for the media, it seemed like a *mea culpa* from you. I wonder if that didn't go back to your time dealing with those teenagers, being in Africa, and all the rest of it; there was a feeling that you of all people should have been alerted to this, not just the media in general.

SNOW: Yes, I agree. Nobody who reported that incident had ever been up a tower block. Nobody had ever lived in one – a local authority tower block, rather than a posh one. Nobody knew anything about it and I realised in that moment that basically we were of the elite. We don't live in local authority tower blocks. They were run by Tenant Manager Organisations. Local authorities say, 'we don't want to run it, let's pay somebody else to run it.' The utter neglect, yes, reminded me very much of the work I used to do. I did go up a tower block once. When I was at New Horizon Youth Centre one of our clients, who was really a bit of a drug abuser, had a baby and we tended her and got her housed. She was in a tower block and she rang me from a phone box saying that she had left the child aged, what, three months, back in the flat and that she herself was at Piccadilly Circus and I could hear she was very stoned. I set off in my Mini and found the child quite distressed. I took her back to the maternity hospital where she had been born and they said, 'I am very sorry, Mr Snow, children only come in here one way and this isn't it.' Eventually I did manage to get the local authority at Camden to take the child but it reminded me of all that. So, it did equip me, yes. But it doesn't neutralise your emotions. It might even intensify them.

BIGSBY: Just to take you back to the business of reporting for a moment. Technology has changed. For much of the time, you were doing a piece to camera. The camera had film in it and that film had to be processed. Despite the fact that you might be in the middle of God knows where, you then had to get it back to England.

SNOW: If it happened later than four o'clock the chances of getting on *News at Ten* were nil. It had to be two hours in the bath, the chemical bath, and then it had to be edited. It was a very, very crude business. It is now bliss.

BIGSBY: You said you had to get it back to London, and sometimes that meant smuggling film out in a rather intimate way, did it not?

SNOW: In Iran, yes. It was absolutely amazing. That was Desert One where the Americans tried to rescue the US Embassy hostages who had been seized by the angry students. A fleet of eight helicopters had come in from an aircraft carrier. They landed in South Iran and needed refuelling and what we discovered subsequently was that the refueler crashed into one of the helicopters. It hadn't worked out that if you go into reverse thrust to slow this thing down – it had propellers – it kicks up the most amazing dust storm and you can't see the hell where you are so they hit the first one. They were parked too close together because they had to be refuelled quickly and I think three of the six helicopters were burnt to pieces, along with their crews. Anyway, we set off to try and get there. When the incident happened there was a bus of ordinary passengers who had passed through and they had to be taken hostage by the Americans while they tried to rescue themselves so we decided to take the same bus the next night. For two hundred dollars the driver agreed to put us under a tarpaulin at the back. When we arrived, we stepped out of the bus with great authority and they thought we were part of an official delegation so they welcomed us with open arms. CBS did much the same thing but that was all there was, just two channels, and this was a really hot story. We had Ayatollah Khalkhali, Chief Justice of the revolutionary courts, running around in circles waving the thigh bone of an American pilot. It was absolutely awful.

On the way back, we had all the film in round canisters like flat biscuit tins and we had to hide the stuff. The great thing about an observant Islamic entity such as Iran is that they don't go to the nether regions to check you, so we each had a huge roll of film in our underpants, four hundred feet of priceless film. When we got to Tehran the Iranians were hungry for it. It was marvellous propaganda material, so we got our story and they got their propaganda material.

BIGSBY: You had a posting in the United States and my sense is that that is something you really enjoyed. It is a very different society, in some ways more open than ours, although it has other kinds of problems. Why did you take to America in the way you did?

SNOW: I think it is what I thought to be the 'can-do-it-ness.' Now we know it is the 'can't-do-it-ness,' as you wake up to the reality that it is one of the most dysfunctional countries on earth, unbelievably so. The gap between rich and the poor, the very, very rich and really quite poor, is extraordinary. The idea that so clever a country should not have a welfare system, which essentially it doesn't have, is amazing and America has actually not really won a war since the Second World War. Thank God they won that but, if you think of the messes ever since, and Vietnam! I have just been watching a great film, *The Post*, which is about the *Washington Post*, with the great Katharine Graham who is the owner of the *Post*, publishing the Pentagon Papers. So, I could see that it was dysfunctional but I liked the bits to which I had access, Washington DC, New York, the west coast. But, in covering Trump's campaign, I went to the America we never visit and met the Americans who we never know, and they were angry. They know what they haven't got. The digital age has provided them with images and information about what they don't have and have no prospect of ever having. It is not a very mobile society and it is a very, very divided society.

It is deeply dysfunctional and tragic because we have always lionised America for very understandable reasons. It has produced the most dysfunctional leader probably of any country in recent times and it is the curse of all of us because we spend our time wedged between Trump and Brexit and they are both very boring even as, of course, they matter, because one could produce a nuclear war and the other could end everything we love.

BIGSBY: You arrived at Channel 4 in 1989.
SNOW: I did, yes, just before the fall of the Berlin Wall. God I was lucky because Channel 4 can do things at length. I remember standing at the wall and my colleague Nick Garry was on the other side and we were frightfully excited because he had a mobile dish which could send the signal from that side of the wall to our side and then we could send it to London. The only trouble was that he was upside down. The image just simply could not be rectified and we seriously debated whether he should anyway be broadcast upside down, but decided that would be a wall too far.

BIGSBY: You were present, too, when Mandela was released.
SNOW: I was.

BIGSBY: Which posed a particular problem for you because I remember watching and it was a long time before he appeared.
SNOW: Well I burst into tears for a start. I was completely uncontrollable with tears. We didn't know what he looked like. There was not a single image of him except from twenty-seven years earlier as a rather swarthy looking middle weight boxer with a centre parting and very dark hair. So, we had no idea what he looked like but we didn't need to know because when he emerged there was a presence, a sense of aura, and I was live on ITV, but we were live for an hour with nothing.

There was a huge crowd and a shed at the end where he was supposed to emerge from, and I had to talk for an hour. Fortunately, I had read a biography of him on the plane coming down so it all came tipping out. Then there were silly things, like I suddenly realised that we were not allowed to use our crew. We had to speak to South African Broadcasting Pictures which were shot by white men, and I suddenly realised that one of the cameras, the live camera, was showing people's feet. I looked around and the camera man was asleep so the camera had tilted down and was now filming feet. I kicked the guy and we were back in business again, but there was really nothing to talk about. Then, of course, ITV wanted to get off air. They didn't want to carry on with this but just as he came out they agreed to stay on for another ten minutes not realising they were witnessing one of the greatest moments in modern history.

BIGSBY: Can I ask you a basic question? What is 'news'? Presumably, at Channel 4, you have a hand in in deciding what might be covered.

SNOW: Ours is a complete and perfect democracy. Every morning about twenty-five of us, producers, presenters, editors, sit around on extremely uncomfortable sofas and discuss what we should be doing. We have people who have been garnering stuff overnight. There is some preparation that had been done the previous day but, basically, we bounce around what we think is important. It is not how most news programmes work. In most of them, editors come in and say, 'we are going to do this, this, this and this.'

BIGSBY: As a result, BBC and ITN can look exactly the same.

SNOW: They can. It is the same in America with the five networks. The same order, more or less.

BIGSBY: You mention the word 'balanced' just now, but there are certain subjects which don't call for balance. If you get a scientist to talk about global warming, it surely makes no sense to get a former Chancellor of the Exchequer to express a contrary opinion.

SNOW: When three percent of the world's climate scientists think there isn't global warming we were required to balance our reporting, which is just mad, bonkers. Now we have stopped and don't bother to report the denials, except Donald Trump.

BIGSBY: Brexit and Trump dominate the news, they dominate politics as though there is nothing else happening in this country. Do you have any option but to report the latest tweet from Donald Trump?

SNOW: The problem is if he suddenly airs 'Britain First' fascist material, not knowing what it is and not even knowing that it wasn't what it purported to be, you have to kind of report that. The difficulty is that it may not actually mean anything except that it does describe something important about the President of the United States. It is very difficult, but also there is something in each of us that wants to know just how bad he is. 'Good God, he is even worse than I thought,' and so forth.

BIGSBY: We all stand somewhere, as individuals and as groups. The transatlantic connection is a strong one and feeds into news, but there are whole rafts of the world we don't address. You were talking about Grenfell Tower, just down the road, but there are whole areas of the world we don't often see. We see images from Africa when there is a war or a famine, but, after a while, when you have seen one child starving in Somalia and then another child starving somewhere else and then another one somewhere else, and so on, there is surely some sort of fatigue. How do you take that new story and make it feel real and immediate when you have had other such stories in the past?

SNOW: I think the biggest challenge has been the Rohingya because there you are talking about an expulsion, the terrorising of an entire population, vast numbers, seven hundred thousand, eight hundred thousand, maybe a million, which is almost impossible for us to imagine. You just have to slog away and we have. We have had somebody there for months and maybe there is a Rohingya fatigue but you can't allow that to cloud your judgement. It is a very important story and it is an important story because in part it also challenges the question of perfection. We all thought Aung San Suu Kyi was beyond reproach so it is devastating to discover that, good woman though she may have been, she has completely revealed herself as the Burmese nationalist that her father was, and it just tells us that you must never believe in angels.

BIGSBY: One of the things I like about *Channel 4 News* is that, when you get hold of something, you don't move on. For example, you stayed with Sri Lanka for a long time, and nobody else was really doing that.

SNOW: Yes. It is the greatest luxury. Well, the nightly news has twenty-four minutes to play with. Although it looks like half an hour, it has got ads in the middle, ads at the end, and ads at the top. But we have fifty-seven minutes and only one break of maybe forty-five seconds and that means that effectively we have an hour. So if we decide we are going to spend fifteen minutes on something we will. None of what we do report goes out at much less than three or four minutes, whereas on the other channels it may be two minutes. I know that sounds rather ridiculous, but it makes a difference.

BIGSBY: Does the existence of images put that story up the list and, conversely, if you have no images is it more difficult to cover a story?

SNOW: There is no doubt that the visual issue is a very big one but we never allow the fact that we haven't got any images to stop us doing something. But we may do it in terms of a debate or an interview but I don't think the absence of pictures ever puts us off doing it.

BIGSBY: Of course, we now have citizen journalists and, at their best, as in Syria where they are getting places you can't go, they provide both the pictures and the story. People can upload anything from their phones. In fact, all media ask people to upload their images because they are on the spot when you can't get there in time. On the other hand, there is another side to that, isn't there? The younger you are the more likely you are to go to social media for your news and research shows that people read the headlines but don't click to read the rest of the story.

SNOW: But there is a happy underbelly to that. We are now watched by no more than a million people at night, but last year we had 2.3 billion viewings on Facebook. Now you may think 'well, bully for you,' but actually that means that gobbets of news…

BIGSBY: Two or three minutes.

SNOW: Two-and-a-half minutes, three minutes, yes, but it is very professionally produced. It is a cut down of what we have done for Channel 4 and augmented by other material so there is a market for them. The real problem is that Facebook in particular do not pay for content and they advertise a lot off the back of good news provision, so that 2.2 billion viewings are accompanied by plenty of ads that they plough in. We are in a big fight with Facebook. They do want the reach without a doubt but they don't want to pay anything. What has happened is that, in taking all this material, they have bled local news-gathering to death because they have taken all the advertising from local newspapers and many local newspapers have died as a result. Not because people didn't want to read them but because nobody can afford to make them. So, there is no advertising, no paper. At Grenfell Tower there were no local journalists anywhere to be seen. I was searching for them because I needed more information about what I was looking at. There were none to be had because the paper had closed four years previously.

REBECCA STOTT

Rebecca Stott was born in 1964 and raised in a strict religious cult called The Exclusive Brethren. She is a graduate of the University of York, where she also obtained her master's and PhD degrees. After publishing several academic books of literary criticism, she began to publish creative non-fiction books focusing on the natural world and evolution: *Theatres of Glass: The Woman Who Brought the Sea to the City*, *Darwin and the Barnacle*, *Darwin's Ghosts: In Search of the First Evolutionists*. Her historical novels, the bestselling *Ghostwalk* and *The Coral Thief*, have been translated into several languages and published across the world. Most recently, she has published a memoir, *In the Days of Rain*, which won the Costa Prize for biography. She holds a chair in literature and creative writing at UEA.

This interview was recorded at UEA on 18 October, 2017.

BIGSBY: How did you come to write *In the Days of Rain*?

STOTT: My father was writing a memoir when he died ten years ago and was struggling to finish it because it was so painful and difficult. On his deathbed I pretty much promised I would take it forward but, of course, I realised that I couldn't tell his story without telling mine at the same time because they overlapped. So, I had to figure out a way of writing two memoirs together, which was not easy, but they interlaced. As he lay dying, in a remote eighteenth-century drainage mill on the Fens, he was struggling to remember the terrible things that had happened in the 1960s when we were all of us, as a family, in this cult called The Exclusive Brethren. I tried to interview him, and we both knew we were running out of time, but he died before I could get very much information from him. But after his death I gathered up six boxes of papers from a very chaotic study, diaries and documents and letters, and it was really at that point that I knew that this task was going to be complicated. It was going to take me back into a history that I hadn't fully understood myself and it was going to be a painful task.

BIGSBY: There are moments in your book which are really frightening. Your great-grandmother was put away for forty years because she was wilful. If you committed an offence within the family you could be isolated.

STOTT: The Brethren were formed in the 1830s, so by the time I was growing up in the 1960s it was very well established and had become in many ways vicious and controlling. In the 1960s they developed this new form of punishment whereby if you were deemed to be non-compliant in whatever way, not quite toeing the party line, not quite doing what you were told, you could be withdrawn from. It is an interesting phrase, 'withdrawn from', because effectively you were expelled at that point, except you weren't allowed to leave your home or your house. You would be isolated within your own house, in your own room, and your family couldn't have any contact with you. That would go on sometimes for weeks, and the Brethren Elders, the Ministering Brothers – which included, of course, my father and grandfather – would come and visit several times a week and you wouldn't be released until you were deemed to be right with the Lord and that, as I say, sometimes took weeks. There were suicides as a result of it. I am sorry, this is a very shocking story, but there is one case involving a man called Roger Panes, who was friends with my parents. He was shut up, or withdrawn from, for weeks and weeks, possibly months, and he became so convinced that Satan had got hold of him and his family that in the middle of the night, he went to the shed, got an axe, axed his wife and children to death and then hanged himself. That is a very extreme and terribly tragic story but there were many, many suicides and breakdowns. This was happening in the suburbs, in British towns all through the 1960s.

BIGSBY: You were born into this, and children just accept as normal what they encounter. When did you first realise what you were in?

STOTT: Probably going to school, because we had to wear headscarves and at that point all women and girls had to have their hair down and I had a lot of hair. Sometimes I had it in plaits but we wore these little headscarves to have our heads covered. Also, we weren't allowed to go to many of the lessons. We looked so different from the other children. We were normal to ourselves but the other children spoke completely differently from us and they had a completely different culture. They would be talking about what they were watching on television and about Brighton and Hove Albion, who were called the Seagulls. I was growing up in Hove and didn't even know what the Seagulls were. We had no cinema, no television, no radio, no newspapers. We had almost no contact with the outside world except at school, so I think it was at school where it first occurred to me that there were so many people outside and they all seemed very nice. My brothers were there as well and we were given worksheets so we would have a lot of time in the corridor of this school, a lovely old Victorian school, where we would see each other up and down the corridor. That was when I first had a sense of being different. Up until that point we were just like any of the other Brethren children, and there were a lot of us.

BIGSBY: As in so many other religions, women had a very subordinate role. How subordinate? What could women not do?

STOTT: The Brethren increasingly focused their doctrine on just a handful of verses from Paul's letters, which we heard day in day out, and they justified their decisions and their rules based on that. So, they believed that women should not express opinions, should be completely subordinate, had to have their heads covered. Women were always silent in meetings, never spoke, were not allowed to. They had to sit on the outside ring of the meeting with the children, and were completely subordinate in their own homes. I saw a lot of very bullying behaviour from my grandfather, from my father, from every household we went into. We had no way of questioning that, or its normality. Since this book came out I have had nearly two hundred letters from Brethren who lived through this same period and left. Some of them have asked to see me. I had lunch with a ninety-one-year-old woman last week but many of them just write letters describing how it was. It is interesting to me that when I meet very elderly couples, the men do all the talking and the women are still very reticent. It is not that they don't feel they can speak, but somehow the trauma is very differently experienced by the women. They don't feel as easy talking about it.

BIGSBY: For someone who was going to be a writer, what access did you have to books?

STOTT: Almost none. We had a set of encyclopaedias in the house and transcripts of all the sermons and ministries that their famous Ministering Brothers had given, so there were loads and loads of those. Brethren had to have those in the house. Even encyclopaedias were censored. As a small child I was always really curious about loads of things, so the encyclopaedia was my favourite place to spend time. But on one occasion I went looking for Charles Darwin. We were told he was a mouthpiece of Satan. Satan was in cinemas and radios and TV sets and Satan was especially good in the mouth of Charles Darwin. Charles Darwin had been sent to lead men astray. They talked about him as 'the monkey man'. So, I went looking for Charles Darwin in the encyclopaedia. I think I was five or six. I went looking for Darwin when my parents weren't around and I found the page. I remember really clearly the sense of danger. But when I got to the page where Darwin should have been it had been razored out. There were two pages missing, so there was just a sharp stub of paper. My father told me later that when the encyclopaedia arrived in the 1950s, when he was a child, my grandfather had assembled the entire family. 'I will not have any wickedness in this house,' he said, as he took a razor to the Darwin page. I had access to books at school but fiction was disapproved of so we couldn't bring books home. We weren't supposed to go into the school library, but I did and I have had a wonderful frisson about books, particularly fiction, and school libraries, ever since.

BIGSBY: It was also difficult because you were looking for the Rapture, when the worthy were going to go up while people like you, who read books, were presumably not.
STOTT: Yes.

BIGSBY: Is that how you felt as a child?
STOTT: Yes. There were times when I thought I might go in the Rapture. If I concentrated hard enough and worked really hard I would probably get to lunchtime and think, 'I might do it. I have been good enough today,' but then I would do something and I knew I'd blown it and would have to start again the next day. But generally, I think most of us knew. I certainly knew my brothers weren't going, no chance. So, the assumption was that any day all the grown-ups were going to disappear in the Rapture and we would be left behind to manage. Of course, the terrifying thing about that, and the terrible cruelty of that, I think, for Brethren children, is that you had been taught that everyone on the earth is worldly, Satan's people, bad people, and those people are going to come for you when all the good people go. So there was a no-win situation and I spent a lot of time as a small child – I am embarrassed to say this now – just preparing for that day when I knew I would have to hide my brothers.

I knew that they would be rubbish in that emergency and that they wouldn't have thought about where they were going to hide or where we were going to get food. So, I figured out that my grandparents' garage was the best place for us to go because it had food in it. I knew where the key was and taught myself how to open tins because I knew that there were a lot of tins and fizzy drinks in my grandparents' garage. There was a lot of very imaginative survivalist play going on in my head.

BIGSBY: I feel you need a hug at this stage. It is quite terrifying.

STOTT: I think it is very funny. My brothers were not anxious in the way that I was but I discovered later that my father had exactly the same fears when I read through his manuscript draft of a memoir. He came home from school one day at the age of seven and his mother and sister were out and they hadn't told him they were going to be out. He told me there'd been a lurid sunset and he collapsed on the front doorstep because he thought they had all gone. He didn't know what to do, whether or not to run.

BIGSBY: You need two hugs.
STOTT: One for him as well.

BIGSBY: Unbelievably, It got more and more restrictive. I am really struck by the fact that members were not allowed to join associations. Doctors were in associations, lawyers were. They had to leave their jobs and abandon them.

STOTT: Yes. In the 1960s a new leader took over. He was called JT Junior. He was the one who brought in all of these really punitive new rules, so although the Brethren had always tried to live separately from the rest of the world, to keep themselves clean and pure ready for the Rapture, he decided that they weren't clean enough and that they had to absolutely separate. Up until that point you couldn't be a member of a union but the doctors and the lawyers and the architects were all members of professional associations and he said, 'Enough is enough. We can't have that any more.' So, no universities or professional associations, no contact with non-Brethren. There is a line in the Bible which is, 'Be ye not equally yoked with unbelievers' and that was the mantra. We couldn't be equally yoked. We couldn't have any contact with people who were worldly, so loads and loads of people lost their jobs overnight because they couldn't practice anymore as solicitors.

BIGSBY: A lot of those American groups ended in a particular way. Evangelists would be found in a motel room with an underage girl and it was actually that, or something similar to that which fractured the movement, and it and was something like that which made your father withdrew. How did he and your family get out of it, and why?

STOTT: My father, when he was dying, was obsessed with trying to understand how he could have been compliant, how could he have been so stupid to have stayed in, so that was the question I was pursuing as well. Through the 1960s, as the rules were stepped up, people left in droves and the ones who were still standing somehow were really invested in staying. JT Junior would say, 'This is what the Lord wants you to do. You have got to suffer. Suffering is the way.' Then, suddenly, he flew to Britain, in 1970, to give his usual three-day meetings across Britain. He had been acting strangely for a while. He was in his seventies by this point and was giving increasingly unpredictable preaching. During the course of his visit there was what we have always known as 'the Aberdeen incident'. He stayed in a bungalow in Aberdeen with lots of other Brethren and it became clear that one of the young wives was spending a lot of time in his room, actually overnight. She was being taken to his bedroom by her husband, day after day, evening after evening, and he was also preaching the most extraordinary sermons full of expletives and sexualised ramblings. He was also drinking really heavily. He was by this point a very ill alcoholic. He was found in bed with the young woman. She had no clothes on, or very few clothes on. He had very few clothes on and he claimed there was nothing impure going on. And, of course word got out very quickly. And because my father and grandfather were in the network of people who had been staying in that bungalow they got first hand news very quickly and decided they couldn't stay any longer. Of course, once JT Junior had been flown back to America the spin began. He told everyone that the Lord had told him to do it in order to test who was true and who was not true. My father and grandfather just said, no, we are leaving, and so with four hundred others, in Brighton and Hove they left. NO one knew how to live in the outside world, though, none of us did.

BIGSBY: And you became a wild child and your father ended up in prison?
STOTT: Yes.

BIGSBY: Because you had been under this pressure and once it was released you went somewhat berserk?
STOTT: Yes. Well, I didn't go 'berserk' immediately. My father did. I became extremely puritanical for a while because I couldn't figure out, at the age of seven, eight, nine, why we suddenly had a TV set in our house and why my father was taking us to the cinema to see films like *Gone with the Wind*. It was terrifying because of course we had been so brainwashed by that point that cinema and radio and television were where Satan was, so I became very puritanical for a while. I started going to a scripture school called The Crusaders.

BIGSBY: I was in The Crusaders.
STOTT: Were you?

BIGSBY: Yes, and so was David Hare. Incidentally, Garrison Keillor was in The Brethren.
STOTT: Yes, I think I knew that. So, within two years, my father changed. It was a very exciting time I have to say because he had never heard popular music. He was a really charismatic man, six feet four, huge and hungry for literature, for music, and he couldn't catch up fast enough. His friends were making him tapes of The Beatles and The Hollies and all this amazing music. He had never heard of The Beatles. He joined a theatre group and was acting all the time, but very quickly he also became addicted to gambling – roulette, seriously

addicted to roulette – so it took only a few years before everything collapsed. He decided he had a system. While I was a teenager he would be talking about gambling all the time, as well as music and literature and Shakespeare. He had these little books, beautiful notebooks with columns of numbers with circles around them because he was absolutely convinced he had cracked the system.

BIGSBY: And he embezzled to pay for his debts.
STOTT: Yes, and ended up going to prison.

BIGSBY: How did you end up stealing books?
STOTT: Talking to lots of ex-Brethren it is amazing the range of peculiar behaviours that emerged in the wake of it. Yes, I was a shoplifter, a book thief in my teens. I didn't need to be. I was working in a sweet shop and so I could just about afford books. I think it was some kind of forbidden secret thing, a thrill.

BIGSBY: Were you caught?
STOTT: Yes, on one occasion I was, but not generally. I wonder now whether it was to do with the prohibition of books when I was a small child but it is interesting how many ex-Brethren I have met who became addicted gamblers who stole. The easy answer is we had such a controlled moral framework and when you take that away people don't know how to adjust. I think it is more complicated than that. The Brethren taught how pretty much anything you did to the 'worldlies' was okay. It was called 'stealing from the Egyptians'. If you wanted something it wasn't corrupt or immoral. That is not to say that I absorbed that but it was a very strange moral code they taught.

BIGSBY: It strikes me that almost everything you subsequently did could be seen as a reaction against your upbringing. You were not allowed to go to university, so you went to university; you were in a subordinate position as a woman so you become a feminist; you were banned from reading literature so you became a writer. But let me move on to that career. You began with academic books. You wrote, for example, on Tennyson but then moved on to write about evolution and even a book called *Oyster*.

STOTT: I was commissioned to write *Oyster* because I had written *Darwin and the Barnacle*, which was a book about Darwin's barnacle obsession and my first non-academic book.

BIGSBY: They thought you were a mollusc person.

STOTT: They did. Apparently, the word was, 'No one can do *Oyster* because we can't find any shellfish specialist.' Then someone said 'You should talk to Rebecca, she knows a lot.' I was such a geek about barnacles by this point.

BIGSBY: I will come on to barnacles in a minute, because it is the lead into your interest in Darwin, but there is another book, *Theatres of Glass*, which I suspect was your idea.

STOTT: I went to talk to Faber about writing a big book about water in the nineteenth century, which I had been planning for years and they said, 'it is not really our kind of book. It is too big. It is too broad. It is too academic, but this story that you tell in your proposal about Darwin's obsession with barnacles is fantastic.' So they said, 'Can you write us a whole book about that?' To start with I said, 'Absolutely no. There isn't a story.' Then I began to think about it. I could do what I wanted to do with the nineteenth century but through the tiny lens of a man's obsession with barnacles. But of course what that meant was that in the two or three years of its writing, when I sat in the university library, read all of Darwin's letters, read all the books that he was reading during that time, I discovered all sorts of amazing things. I think you know if you choose the right hole to go down you can come up with all sorts of extraordinary stories. In writing *Oyster* I discovered this woman, Anna Thynne, who lived in Westminster Abbey. She had gone to the seaside and was obsessed with madrepores, a kind of sea anemone. She read very widely in marine zoology. She was the wife of the under-dean of Westminster Abbey, so she lived in Westminster Abbey, and she had to try and figure out how to get these sea anemones back to Westminster Abbey because she wanted to watch them, to figure out how they bred. So, she had people make her huge glass tanks and had her maids aerate the water by hand. Eventually, she had hundreds of these things in Westminster Abbey and wrote about them, observing them closely. Of course, she doesn't appear in any of the publications because you couldn't as a woman, but effectively she invented the aquarium. There are several historians of science who claim that it was a man who invented the aquarium but, as far as I can figure, she did it by a whisker, so I decided I had to write her story. She was a bit of an off-cut, if you like, from *Darwin and the Barnacle*, but such a bizarre and eccentric and wonderful woman.

BIGSBY: *Darwin and the Barnacle* is interesting not least because Darwin set aside what would become *On the Origin of Species* in order to work on barnacles, something he had picked up on a beach while on the *Beagle* voyage. So, there was this major work sitting there while he was working on barnacles. Why did they so fascinate him?

STOTT: He brought back thousands of specimens – marine invertebrates, mammals, birds, insects – from his journeys in South America. When he got back he sent them to various people for their collections. But there was one aberrant barnacle which he had found in a conch shell on a beach in southern Chile that vexed him. It was so tiny you couldn't see it with the naked eye but he'd pulled it out of the conch shell and popped it into wine and spirits and called it Mr Arthrobalanus because of its weird shape. Then, I think six or seven years later, it was the last thing on his shelf. He could see it was a barnacle in terms of the body structures of the sub-species but it was a seriously aberrant one, so he decided he'd try to figure out how that weird creature had evolved that way rather than the usual ways of barnacles. Of course, he thought it was going to take him a month. It was eight years before he had figured it out and even at the end of that time, when he had become a world expert on all the living barnacles and fossils he could get his hands on, and written these four volumes of books which are still used today, he still hadn't nailed Mr Arthrobalanus.

It is such a great story. He tried to crack the riddle of this deviant, or unusual form, and couldn't do it but ultimately what that meant was that by the time he had done it he was well respected by his peers for spending all this time looking down microscopes at these bizarre creatures. When I was researching the book, I was taken into what is called 'the spirit store' in Cambridge Zoology Museum. It is down below stairs so the curator took me down stairs and into this little room and opened up the doors of a beautiful oak cabinet. He put it on the table and pulled the drawers out and said, 'Do you recognise it?' And, of course, when I looked closely I could see that these were Darwin's barnacle slides, little glass slides with tiny barnacle parts, hundreds and hundreds of them. I think I was probably one of the only people on the planet who would recognise that but also because some of those barnacle slides had been sealed with bitumen and others with gold size [a thick glue] I could date exactly the day on which he decided bitumen wasn't any good any more and he was going to use gold size. I remember that sense of excitement that I could identify that. Oh dear, I can really become a geek about something very inconsequential.

BIGSBY: As a result of deferring his major work, he was nearly pipped to the post and his failure adequately to acknowledge the work of others left him with a sense of guilt which is, in part, what *Darwin's Ghosts* is about because it is about the need to acknowledge that in science you are always building on other people's work. You have traced back some of those who might have a claim to be his forebears.

STOTT: Yes, when I was working on Darwin I was struck by two pages at the beginning of *The Origin of the Species* in which he tries to acknowledge his predecessors, his intellectual predecessors, the people who had tried to prove natural selection before him, or tried to find a mechanism for evolution before him. That list was so revealing to me because you could feel his anxiety about his predecessors and I had come across some of them myself. One of them, of course, was his grandfather, Erasmus Darwin, and I thought I really want to go all the way back to Aristotle and come forward to Darwin and try and do what Darwin couldn't do, use my skills as a historian, and as a researcher, not only to find out who these people were but to try to see the world through their eyes. I knew Darwin couldn't do that. I wanted to reconstruct what it would be like, for instance, to be writing a book on animals in ninth-century Baghdad, as one of my subjects was doing. What was your world view at that point? How did you make sense of how animals had come to be? So, I suppose by that point what I was trying to do was use my skills as a novelist, and also as a researcher and historian of science, not just to tell a history but to try and take readers back into that human being in a particular time and place. To try to tell a story covering two thousand two hundred years but to do it through these little keyholes, if you like, where we jump from one person to another. The other thing that really struck me from talking to scientists is that increasingly people are very specialised in science. They don't read very widely. Most of them are not polymaths. All of the people in this book, all of these incredible thinkers and groundbreaking non-conformist heretics, if you like, were incredibly widely read. They were reading literature and poetry and philosophy as well as doing their narrow scientific research. And that meant that their vision was perhaps more creative in some ways. They could imagine possibilities and so I think *Darwin's Ghosts* is very much about how these early brilliant natural philosophers, who wouldn't have called themselves scientists at that point, were polymaths and polyglots. They were reading really widely. They were speaking lots of languages. Most of them lived in port cities of various kinds. They all had access to huge libraries and had encyclopaedic knowledge which helped them to jump from one thing to another, and they all had patrons who didn't control what they did.

BIGSBY: There is something wonderful about the little girl who went to the encyclopaedia and found Darwin cut out growing up to write about Darwin. Let me, though, move on to your novels. You have said that you got the whole idea for *Ghostwalk* in a fifty-minute taxi ride. How does that work?

STOTT: Yes, the book just came to me. I hadn't written a novel before, or I had written a novel but not a complete one. After I had written *Darwin and the Barnacle* I was beginning to read about Newton. I was curious to see whether Darwin's early years had any similar pattern to Newton's. I was reading about Newton because I had come across a footnote in this wonderful biography of Newton in which the biographer says Newton was lucky because he got a Fellowship at Trinity [Cambridge] when he was in his early twenties and that enabled him to do his amazing work. He was a very strange man and he really needed this institutional environment to work in. And I thought 'in what way was he lucky?' Go down to the bottom, to the footnote, and it says, 'Newton was especially lucky because that year there were more vacancies than usual in terms of fellowships in the college because several academics had fallen down staircases to their deaths, apparently drunk.' For someone interested in stories, this was intriguing. I remember putting three asterisks in the margin. I had a pen with me, and though I hate writing on books I put asterisks by that footnote and then a great big circle round it and then an exclamation mark. It was the following week, when I was flying to Spain very early in the morning, that I ended up in a taxi to get from Cambridge station to Stansted. There was a meteor storm going on that night. I didn't see it but, in the middle of an amazing conversation with a man who was sharing my taxi, a complete stranger who turned out to be a meteorologist, and who was telling me about what we would see if we could see this meteor storm, we fell silent. There was another thirty minutes of the taxi journey through the dawn and the fog, and by the time I got to the airport the whole plot had unfolded in my head. I remember rushing to get a notebook as quickly as I could, afraid that it would disappear. I think there is something about the human mind at dawn. I do a lot of my conjuring of plots and making of scenes just as I wake up. So I always try to have a notebook to hand just in case that happens. I think there is something about the human mind that is especially creative in these in-between states between dreaming and waking.

BIGSBY: *Ghostwalk* begins in East Anglia and I felt I could follow it on a map because you are very precise in the locations you use. It takes place in two timescales but it is also a mixture of the rational and the irrational, that is to say there is a detective element to it and there is a gothic element. It is called *Ghostwalk* for a reason and that kind of tension is part of what drives the reader through this book because there is a mystery to be solved and yet there is a mystery that can't be solved because it is beyond the rational. But let me move on to *The Coral Thief*. It takes place in 1815. Napoleon has fallen. A young medical student goes from this country to Paris and 1815, as you point out, was a period of enormous ferment because Napoleon had fallen. But to me the most interesting character is a woman, the coral thief. The young student takes coral with him to Paris and it is stolen, and we are into another detective story in some ways, a subterranean world in a metaphorical sense but also in a completely literal sense.

STOTT: Yes. When I was working on *Darwin's Ghosts*, which took a really long time because it covers such a long span of time, I was frustrated as an intellectual historian, I suppose, that there weren't women who I could include. Or rather there were women everywhere in *Darwin's Ghosts* but they weren't evolutionists who were publishing evolutionary ideas. I was about halfway through the book and sitting in the library one day just daydreaming – this is by way of explanation for this woman and where she came from. I was wondering if there was a woman in this history of mine and if so where would she emerge, because women were really restricted in terms of the clubs they could join, the books that they could read, access to specialist knowledge, microscopes, all of that stuff. It occurred to me that if there was to be such a woman she would almost certainly be French because the French had some of the most radical ideas around this time to do with evolution. She would probably have lived through the revolution. She would probably have been raised an aristocrat to have access to a sophisticated education and a particular kind of library. She would probably have come to Paris in her twenties, probably traumatised from having lived through those terrible years, and she would have had a collection of some kind. She would be a geek of some kind, obsessed about one thing, and she came with a name, Lucienne Bernard. In my novel she cross dresses in order to pass, in order to get into the various groups of scientists that she needs to learn from and, indeed, the people who she needs to steal from because her precious coral collection has been taken from her by Napoleon and she is gradually collecting them again by stealing them back. So, yes, my young man meets her, a complicated older woman, and her group of thieves and then gets drawn into her world. But he is also educated by her in terms of her evolutionary sensibility. So, it is a love story, but it is also a story about coming to see the world through evolutionary eyes, coming to see the world as in a state of beautiful flux.

BIGSBY: I mention subterranean, and this is literal because the climactic scene takes place underground, in the quarries and catacombs under Paris, and there is a detective who could have come out of *Les Misérables*, Javert.
STOTT: Yes, he was based on Javert.

BIGSBY: Was there such a person?
STOTT: A real figure turned into a fictional one. He is based on a real figure but I try not to write too much in my historical prose about figures who we know a lot about because I usually try and keep them on the side-lines.

BIGSBY: How much research did you do for *The Coral Thief*?
STOTT: A lot. There was a wonderful moment when I discovered that there was a guidebook to Paris in 1815. It had a fold-out map. It was like a guidebook. It told you where the British visitor could buy pigs or ribbons for hats or particular kinds of glasses, so I could gradually reconstruct the shop fronts of the streets my characters were going to inhabit. But, also, I needed to map the city underneath as well because so much of it takes place underground. So I found another map that told me where all the entry points to the quarries were. I work a lot with maps and at that point I think I had seven or eight maps

of the city up on the wall. You can't hold all of that in your head but you can at least double-check. All of that really matters but at some point I just let all of that drop away. You just get to a point where you know enough, you feel confident enough about being able to walk through Paris. Actually, going to Paris was no good for me because Paris has been extensively reconstructed since 1815.

BIGSBY: Also, the imagined world has an integrity of its own.
STOTT: Yes, it does. One of the things I do at UEA is I teach a course on writing historical fiction and we talk a lot about these things. The constant question is how much do I need to know? How much do I need to research? I think there is a point where you can just swamp yourself in a really dangerous way. There is a point when you just need to let it go. On the other hand, I think visiting places has been really important for me. Sometimes, as in the Paris example, you think, 'Oh no, I am in the wrong place. This isn't right. This isn't giving me anything,' but there are other times when with particular sounds or smells you begin to inhabit your imaginary city.

BIGSBY: You are writing a new novel, set far further in the past: fifth-century Britain.
STOTT: Yes.

BIGSBY: Is there a problem with language setting a book back there?
STOTT: I haven't figured it out quite yet because it is still very early days but, yes, it is going to be a real challenge. I want to create a Saxon and Romano-British mindset, a way of seeing, but I think for this book my characters will talk in quite a modern way because it is going to be that kind of book. I don't have a rule of thumb about this. I think you have to make it work for whatever book you are writing, or whatever world you are recreating, but what is fascinating to me about the fifth century is that there is almost nothing known about it because written history came later.

BIGSBY: It is partly a world of myth.

STOTT: Yes. I am interested in the pre-Christian communities that lived after the Romans left. The Romans left in AD410. They bailed out of this huge city they had built and left it derelict and empty, so a lot of my novel will be set in the city itself. At the moment I am doing research and am increasingly confident about not just reading for my research but going to people who know and explaining what I am trying to do because what I find over and over is a) that people are really generous and b) if you ask a really good question, that is informed by what you have already read, people can't help but want to answer it. So, I am going to linguists, archaeologists, anthropologists. I am interviewing retired people, sometimes by email, sometimes by going to visit them in order to try get to the heart of the mystery, but what everyone tells me is, 'We simply don't know.' That's a great place to be. There will be two books, a short book of non-fiction about the process of reconstructing, and there will also be a novel.

D J TAYLOR

D[avid] J[ohn] Taylor was born in 1960 in Norwich and studied history at St. John's College, Oxford. He is a novelist, short story writer, a biographer, journalist and reviewer. Following a biography of Thackeray, his study of George Orwell won the Whitbread Biography Award. His novels include *Trespass, Kept: A Victorian Mystery, Derby Day* and *The Windsor Faction*. He is the author of several volumes of literary and cultural history, including *After the War: The Novel and England Since 1945, A Vain Conceit: British Fiction in the 1980s Bright Young People: The Rise and Fall of a Generation* and *The Prose Factory: Literary Life in England Since 1918*.

This interview was recorded at the King's Lynn Literary Festival in March, 2017.

BIGSBY: You publish as D. J. Taylor. Why?

TAYLOR: Because when I started writing seriously, about thirty years ago, the place was packed with David Taylors. The editor of *Punch* was called David Taylor. There was a BBC zoo vet. There were two BBC producers. When it was finally brought home to me that D.J. Taylor was the right moniker was when, in the late 1980s, I went to interview J. L. Carr, author of *A Month in the Country*. I got off the train at Kettering Station to meet him. Mr Carr was a small doughty Yorkshireman and he looked at me and said, 'See that Datsun over there. That has done fifty-nine thousand miles, that has.' I went, 'that's great' and we went off to his house to do the interview and all the way through lunch he kept on referring to cars. At one point I said to him, 'I don't drive a car. Why are you asking me these questions?' and he gave me a rather puzzled look and at the very end, when we had finished the interview, on the doorstep he turned to me and he said, 'ah, you are not the motoring correspondent of the *Daily Telegraph,* are you?' and that cemented my view that initials give you gravitas. They make you sound professorial.

BIGSBY: You were born in Norwich.
TAYLOR: Born and bred, yes.

BIGSBY: Raised in Norwich, educated in Norwich, and your family worked for the Norwich Union, as it then was?
TAYLOR: Yes, apart from a period from 1981 to 1984 my family has been continuously employed by what was the Norwich Union Insurance Society since 1920.

BIGSBY: Did they expect you to follow in their footsteps?
TAYLOR: Oh, no. My father hated the Norwich Union. It bored him sick. He spent forty-three-and-a-half-years there, rising to a modest middle management post, but he was never so happy as when he could leave the Norwich Union at the age of sixty and start a new career as a broadcaster on BBC Radio Norfolk. He never looked back.

BIGSBY: I was struck by the fact that when you were a teenager you sent material to a publisher.

TAYLOR: I'll tell you exactly how it went. No disparagement of my parents, but I did not come from what I would call a bookish household. Neither of my parents had studied English beyond the age of sixteen. There were a very few books of a not very prepossessing nature which I sometimes read. From the age of about eleven onwards I had a massive Tolkien fixation, like many adolescent, pre-adolescent, children and in my early teens I wrote two semi-Tolkien novels. One of these, with the glorious insouciance of youth, at aged about thirteen, I sent to Tolkien's publisher because they obviously published the kind of books in which I was interested. I got a very nice polite letter back from a director of Allen and Unwin saying that they thought it was very well written but that Professor Tolkien was well established in his field.

BIGSBY: Did they know you were thirteen?

TAYLOR: Oh, yes. This Tolkien fixation lasted and I remember that at the end of the Christmas term in the first year 6th when I should have been out partying and chasing the chicks, or whatever you were supposed to do, I spent three weeks writing a political novel, a dystopian fantasy where the Conservative government wasn't able to govern because of the trade unions. I sent that off to Secker and Warburg who, of course, very properly rejected it.

BIGSBY: I am guessing your family were Conservative.

TAYLOR: My father was a working-class Conservative.

BIGSBY: Did you put the stickers on the windows as I did, to my shame?

TAYLOR: I did. I seem to remember having the poster up in the window in 1975 and it read Radical Youth for Europe. My father was intensely Conservative and his family is a very interesting example of the fact that there is no such thing, and never was, as working-class solidarity. It was not in the least homogenous. My father used to say that his parents ought to have been classic

Labour voters, living on the Earlham Estate in Norwich in the 1930s, but my grandmother was a Conservative because Mr Baldwin had said, 'a fair day's work for a fair day's wage' which struck her as acceptable. My grandfather was an Asquithian Liberal who regarded the Labour party and the trade unions as a lot of riff-raff. So that is where it all came from.

BIGSBY: You went to Oxford, but not to read English.
TAYLOR: No. I read history.

BIGSBY: Given aspects of your later career has that turned out to be useful?
TAYLOR: Yes and no. I did history because I was taught modern history at Norwich School by an extraordinary gentleman called Richard Harries, R. H. Harries, known inevitably as Tweedy, Tweedy Harries, as in Harris tweed. He was extraordinary. I thought my father was right wing, but Mr Harries was a complete old school Conservative. I remember him once saying about another member of the common room at school, 'Mr Wills describes himself as a progressive Conservative,' pause, 'which is no doubt a very excellent thing to be.' When I was about thirteen or fourteen Mr Harries decided that I would do history at Oxford and ensured that this happened, and I was immensely grateful because at that age you like being a protege, having big serious grown-up people thinking, 'this boy can do something.' His attitude to literature was respectful but he used to say, 'English literature is something an educated gentleman does in his spare time.' It was rather like the trouble they had introducing English to Oxford and Cambridge. It was assumed that you picked up the classics of English literature in the same way that you ordered up your evening suit. You suddenly knew about Milton. So I did history without a second thought and in fact my chief interest, when I was in my late teens, and I know this will sound absurd, was in Anglo-Saxon field settlement and church dedications.

BIGSBY: You were living in the right part of the country.

TAYLOR: Yes, exactly. 'Why is that church called St Botolphs?' that sort of thing, and I hit mid-degree at university before I suddenly thought, 'I am not really as interested in this as I thought I was. I should have done English.'

BIGSBY: It didn't exactly prepare you for the career you then entered.
TAYLOR: I worked in the marketing department of an accountancy firm.

BIGSBY: Was that corporate communications?
TAYLOR: Yes. This was around the time, in the mid-1980s, when what was called 'the big bang' happened in the City of London. This was about deregulation, and all the American firms, all the accountancy firms, could suddenly do more things than they had. They could advertise. They could promote their services, and there was a sudden demand for literate young men who could write press releases and chairman's speeches, so I ended up doing this and I was as bored doing it as my father was working for the Norwich Union but I made a foolish mistake because I thought that however stultifyingly unedifying it was it would give me copy. I thought there would be books lurking in the City, but in fact there weren't. There was half of one novel. That's all I got out of that ten or eleven years in the City.

BIGSBY: But during those years you were writing.
TAYLOR: I was writing, yes. I was always writing.

BIGSBY: Writing a novel. You were also reviewing. How did you get into that?
TAYLOR: That is an interesting question. The first book review I ever wrote, that I got paid money for, was the week after I came down from college. But those were difficult times. This was the early 1980s, before the newspaper revolution of the mid-1980s when there were suddenly more papers and more space was available for slightly farouche young men and women. So, it was a bit difficult to get yourself established. But come the mid-1980s, Rupert Murdock appeared and, whatever

equivocal views of him we might have, he broke the print union power, ensuring there were more newspapers with bigger arts sections and more jobs for people like me. By the late 1980s there were five quality Sunday newspapers, and if you could hold a pen, and if you were reasonably good at cutting up people like Kingsley Amis and Margaret Drabble, the phone would ring. There was one extraordinary week in, I think, 1987, when three people rang me up – I was about twenty-six – and said, 'will you review the new Gabriel Garcia Marquez?' and I thought wow, because he was a big, serious, Nobel-winning Colombian novelist and three people want me to review his books.

BIGSBY: You said something interesting just then about cutting up. There is a model of the young reviewer who attacks established writers
TAYLOR: Biting the hand that feeds you. It is the only way.

BIGSBY: In your early book, *A Vain Conceit*, you did hack away at Margaret Drabble and Kingsley Amis. Even Ian McEwan gets a back-hander from you.
TAYLOR: I was an enormous fan of his early work, but he went off.

BIGSBY: There is often a certain truculence in the new young reviewer, surely.
TAYLOR: Absolutely.

BIGSBY: You have to stake out your territory and be noticed?
TAYLOR: Oh, you do. New kids on the block. That book, though, was written in a fortnight. It had to be. It was the only time I could get off work you see. You do try and annoy people, I think. The thing is, too, that when you are starting out doing this the problem is that the people you read when you were younger inevitably you are not going to like as much when they start writing books in their maturity. The thing about Margaret Drabble and Ian McEwan was that I loved their early books when I read them in my late teens. I worshipped Ian McEwan.

BIGSBY: But you didn't like *The Child in Time*?

TAYLOR: No. It all gets tedious because he starts trying to write about politics and he doesn't know anything about it. The last time I was talking to Ian McEwan about his early work he more or less repudiated it, those wonderful early short stories, those macabre short stories.

BIGSBY: At the same time as you were establishing yourself as a reviewer you were also writing a novel. Indeed you wrote a series of novels which came out very quickly. There is sometimes suspicion in this country of those who work in several different areas, as there is of someone who is prolific, a word which is sometimes used as a reproach.

TAYLOR: Craig Raine once said to me 'of course you write for money, don't you?' to which I said, 'yes. I don't have a soft college job like you,' and we left it at that. And, yes, you are supposed to do one thing, to plough one line.

BIGSBY: You once said something rather strange: 'my first five novels were all essentially the same'.

TAYLOR: Yes. I didn't notice this until I re-read them subsequently. Between 1986 and the early 2000s I wrote five novels and although they have a wide variety of scene and setting and characters they were all essentially about the same thing. They were about a young man who grows up in a relatively small place and then goes to a big place because the big place is the only place where he can do the work that he wants to do. He then grows disillusioned with the big place and goes back to the smaller place but realises that he doesn't belong in either of them. So, he is spiritually adrift and all of those first five novels are about that theme, and I only realised, when I went back and read them some years later, that they are also all about fathers and sons, all about the male parent child relationship.

BIGSBY: There was a change of direction, though, when you started setting your novels in the Victorian period. Of course you are not the only person to do that.

TAYLOR: It is called neo-Victorian literature.

BIGSBY: What do you find back there that makes you embrace that period?

TAYLOR: I have always been fascinated by the Victorian era, and I had always wanted to write about it. I had written five novels and it was the mid-2000s and I had just published the Orwell biography. My publishers were fairly interested in what I was going to write and I remember saying to my editor at Chatto and Windus, 'I am going to write another novel. I can either write another one of those deracinated provincial things or I could write the Victorian one,' and the words 'write the Victorian one' came out before I had even finished the sentence. That was a novel called *Kept*, which came out in 2006. It is set in the 1860s and is about the first great train robbery and other things. I had always wanted to write a critical book about the Victorian novel, which I had loved and wanted to analyse in greater depth. In some sense those two novels, *Kept* and *Derby Day*, are works of literary criticism because they are teasing away, I hope, at the conventions, the tropes, the way in which Victorian novels work. They are trying to have little jokes about the way the dialogue works, the philosophical throat-clearing that starts Victorian novels. *Kept* starts with a description of the Scottish Highlands in just the way a certain kind of Victorian novelist starts his or her book. The idea was to try and write a novel which would say something about the way in which Victorian novels are written on the grounds that I couldn't write a book of literary criticism because I wouldn't earn enough money to pay my children's school fees by doing that.

BIGSBY: You are interested in pastiche. Certainly, there are echoes of Victorian writers.

TAYLOR: Absolutely, deliberately. *Kept* is a series of pastiches. The idea in *Derby Day*, though, was to create a lost Victorian style where the reader would think, 'yes, this is a Victorian style but I don't think it's like any particular Victorian novelist that I can instantly identify.' The idea was to create a found text with its own authenticity.

BIGSBY: With a more recent novel, *The Windsor Faction*, you deal in what, in a Trump world, would be called alternative facts.

TAYLOR: Yes, alternate history.

BIGSBY: In fact, you won a rather strangely named award?

TAYLOR: The Sidewise Award, yes. Isn't that weird. They give it at the Sci-Fi Convention and it is for 'what if history,' or subjunctive history, I call it. What if the world had happened in this way rather than in that? I couldn't go unfortunately but a friend of mine went to get the award and she said it was completely weird. You looked at the audience and they were all dressed up as Star Wars characters and that kind of thing.

BIGSBY: In the novel Edward VIII did not abdicate and they are working for a relationship with Hitler, which is not entirely implausible.

TAYLOR: They were real people in it and were doing what I say that they were doing, yes.

BIGSBY: In fact, at the end you say that because they are real people a moral question floats into your mind. Can you use people in a fictive way?

TAYLOR: I think that is a central question for modern fiction because you can either put unreal, made-up people in a real world or you can put real people in a fictional world. The real people who are walking around in *The Windsor Faction* include a maniac right-wing Tory MP, called Captain Ramsay, who started an organisation called the Right Club, which was very anti-Semitic, and a rather flibbertigibbet journalist called Beverley Nichols who writes a diary, which is part of the novel. I did think a bit about whether I was traducing them but when you read some of Captain Ramsay's utterances it would be impossible to traduce him. I think it is actually rather a favourable portrait because I present him as a patriot. If you had said to him, 'you, sir, are a traitor. You are trying to sell us down the river to Nazi Germany,' he wouldn't have known what you meant. He had a son fighting in the Norway campaign and was absolutely outraged when he was interned and had to spend three years in Brixton. The moment he came out of Brixton he resumed his place in the House of Commons and started asking incredibly awful questions about how many Jews were serving in the armed forces and the front line, but he would have thought himself an English patriot.

BIGSBY: The British have always had a fascination with the Second World War and, of course, it could have gone the other way because there were enough members of the aristocracy who were flirting with appeasement.

TAYLOR: I remember my father telling me about this because he was in the RAF in the Second World War and was in Occupied Europe in 1945. There was a small but significant body of opinion that said that when the Allied Forces reached Berlin they should ally with the residue of the German army and head east because that was where the real enemy lay. Captain Ramsay's argument was that we were fighting the wrong dictator. He said that Russia was much more of a threat to us than Nazi Germany.

BIGSBY: You mentioned biography. Your first was on Thackeray. What got you into that?

TAYLOR: It was simply fervour. I said to my publisher, many years ago, that I wanted to write a critical book explaining why Thackeray is the greatest English novelist there ever was, how much I love him and why we underestimate his importance.' And the publisher said, 'that will sell about six copies. Why don't you write a biography?' So I said, 'okay, I will if that is what it takes'.

BIGSBY: Both your biographies are of people who said they did not want a biography. That is just a stimulus is it?

TAYLOR: That is just a stimulus. You can't say that. You can't live your life in the public world and say you don't want to be written about.

BIGSBY: Thackeray's life is almost a Victorian novel in its own right, isn't it?

TAYLOR: Oh, it is, absolutely.

BIGSBY: Poverty, mad wife…
TAYLOR: You have a fortune, you lose the fortune. It is an absolutely circular tour. His father left him twenty thousand pounds in Indian banking funds. They collapsed. He spent the rest of his life working to support his mad wife and his daughters and he left twenty thousand pounds. The whole thing comes full circle. He laboured to get back to the place where he had begun his life.

BIGSBY: You said that your aim was to demonstrate that he was the greatest English writer of the nineteenth century.
TAYLOR: Absolutely, yes.

BIGSBY: Defend, discuss?
TAYLOR: Well, certainly the greatest Victorian novelist because he is a realist whereas Dickens was a sentimentalist.

BIGSBY: The greatest English writer of all time?
TAYLOR: Absolutely, but the thing you must understand about me is that I was never taught English literature properly. I never went to University to study it. With no disrespect to the people who taught me English at school, I am self-taught when it comes to literature and I have read modestly of the canon. I am not especially interested in it because I read the books that I want to read.

BIGSBY: Well at least it doesn't inhibit you from saying he is the greatest writer.
TAYLOR: Why not? As my old Oxford history tutor used to say, 'value judgements? We are here to make them.' When I started reading the books that I really began to appreciate and like, Thackeray was the writer who meant the most to me. He seemed to me to get to the heart of a particular kind of human psychology. His readings of character and motivation, even though he was writing about the 1840s and 1850s, were truer to observable life than anyone else I came across. You don't read people sometimes because you want them to be true to observable life but it seemed to me that this was, and especially to someone who was then studying history.

His discriminating eye seemed to me to be truer to the circumstances he was writing about than anybody else.

BIGSBY: But while you make a case for him as a writer, it is not primarily as a novelist.

TAYLOR: Thackeray's great work is his sketches and journalism, some of which is hardly in print. In fact, I remember in the early 1990's editing a selection of Thackeray's occasional journalism for Everyman because I thought that they should be in print.

BIGSBY: You then wrote a biography of George Orwell who, in the age of Trump, has suddenly come back into prominence. Penguin has just ordered a seventy-five thousand print run of *1984* for which there has been here a nine hundred and fifty percent increase in the sales.

TAYLOR: On a daily basis I was getting emails mostly from American radio shows saying, 'could you come on?' What was quite worrying was that I was approached by one of those alt-right websites in the States that supply stuff to Fox News saying, 'could you write a piece saying isn't this all a bit farfetched and that in fact Orwell wasn't really predicting trouble?' I just said no, although the money was tempting.

BIGSBY: A question about biography. I think people are sometimes perplexed that you can have multiple biographies of the same person. After all, the subjects only lived one life. There have been several Orwell biographies.

TAYLOR: Five or six.

BIGSBY: Yet publishers like to claim that there is the definitive biography. Plainly there is no such thing.

TAYLOR: If you read a novel different people interpret different characters differently. There is that aspect to biography, but there is also generational change. Different generations look for different things in the people they interpret. For example, in the interwar period Dickens was reinterpreted as almost a Catholic by G K Chesterton, as almost a Marxist by a Marxist critic called T. A. Jackson. Then people began to be interested in the social aspects of his work. The other thing, of course, is the emergence of new material. The great thing about Orwell is that there are at least two vital manuscript sources that no Orwell scholar can get at for various reasons. When they are got at there will be another Orwell book which will reinterpret serious parts of his life. I know where they are but I can't get to them. So, I can't do it myself. When I was finishing Orwell, in fact when it was being printed, I got friendly with a woman who I interviewed and kept on asking, 'have you got anything else upstairs in the cupboard?' Then Orwell's list of the Soviet fellow travellers was released to the newspapers two weeks after the book was published. What are you supposed to do? This always happens. Some Orwell papers were stolen from Orwell's hotel room by the NKVD [the Peoples Commissariat for Internal Affairs] in Barcelona in 1937. They are in the NKVD archive, in the closed section, and you can't get at them. I know of someone who saw them but when he came back the next day he was told to go away.

BIGSBY: A couple of times you have mentioned money, and your book *The Prose Factory* is about the business of being a writer. I suspect people don't realise that the average income of a novelist today is eleven thousand pounds. You stepped out of your job in the City after thirteen years. That must have been a nervous moment.

TAYLOR: It was a terrifying moment. Even Evelyn Waugh's elder brother, Alec, said that that is the defining moment of a writer's career when he decides, 'I have got to make a living out of this.' It is increasingly difficult to do. When *The Windsor Faction* came out I was interviewed by *The Guardian* and I made what I think was an unexceptionable point. I said that there are probably a dozen 'serious' novelists in this country who can actually survive on their literary earnings. Two or three days later, at a party, I met a stratospherically distinguished novelist, a Booker prize winner, and he said to me, 'I liked what you said in *The Guardian* but who are these people?' and I said, 'I thought you were one of them?' and he said, 'oh no, I make my money out of films'.

BIGSBY: Your new work is *The New Book of Snobs*. The Society of Authors has just conducted a poll of two thousand people and asked them to identify the most frequently named living writers of literature? Number one was J K Rowling, number two Stephen King, number three Dan Brown, number four James Patterson, five Lee Child, six Danielle Steel, seven Jeffrey Archer, eight Jacqueline Wilson, nine Patricia Cornwell, tying with Wilbur Smith. I feel snobbish about Jeffrey Archer but have never read a word of his so what right do I have to feel snobbish about Jeffrey Archer?

TAYLOR: That is an interesting point, because it is the sixtieth anniversary of Richard Hoggart's *The Uses of Literacy*, that famous investigation into what people read in the past and the influences to which they were susceptible in a debased modern era. He is very honest because, in the 1950s, he buys a pile of dreadful American magazines which featured blood and guts, people being beaten to death, women being molested. He describes the style as debased Hemingway but is honest enough to admit that it is actually rather a decent style. There is an excitement to them. The moral message that you get from these books, 'stomp on his head before he stomps on yours,' might not be agreeable but he thought that they were actually quite well written. You should know that to my mind one of the greatest historical novelists, as good as Stevenson, is George MacDonald Fraser with his *Flashman* novels. He seemed to me to be a genuine literary artist and I would sooner read him than most literary novels.

BIGSBY: How far is snobbery, in its various guises, like the animal that pisses to mark out his territory, to exclude other people. We have our own values. Other people might want to intrude but they have no right to do so. They don't have the education. Look at our our attitude to those who voted for Trump and for Brexit. In both cases the less educated you were the more likely you were to vote for them. Democracy is all very good until people perversely vote the wrong way.

TAYLOR: Absolutely right. I picked up my copy of the *London Review of Books,* that highly sagacious and elevated literary publication, the week after the Brexit vote and the headline across the front was, 'What Have We Done?' and I thought to myself, this is seriously wrong because what you really mean is 'what have they done?' or 'what have you done?' The opinion of the *London Review of Books* was obvious. They were simply being snooty about the *hoi polloi* who had voted to leave Europe.

BIGSBY: And *hoi polloi* is one aspect of snobbery.
TAYLOR: Yes, and I have just used a Greek phrase. I am really sorry and if anyone said to me, 'are you a member of the *hoi polio*?' I would say 'you don't use the definite article because *hoi* is that in Greek'. Which is awful. I should say I had great fun writing *The New Book of Snobs* which is an updated version of Thackeray's *The Book of Snobs*. The point I make, which I think is an accurate one, is that we are all snobs. Every echelon of British society is snobbish. It has been rightly pointed out there is really no such thing as the middle class anymore. There are about fifteen different gradations of the middle class and the more fragmented society becomes, the more technologically obsessed it becomes, the more snobbish we are becoming. What could be more snobbish than technology? You know you either have the latest whizzy gadget, so extraordinarily detailed and obscure that you barely know how to operate it, or you are like my mother who won't have anything to do with this email business, which to me is a snobbish attitude although I would not ever say that to her. To a certain degree *The New Book of Snobs* is about my own family history, going back to my father on the Earlham estate. He maintained that Hodgson Road, Norwich, in the 1930s, which had sixteen council houses, eight on each side of the road, was the most snobbish place in Christendom and that some of the housewives who lived there were far more snobbish than the Duchess of Devonshire. My grandmother, who died before I was born, pined for what was called a double bay front. There were three council houses on the Earlham estate which had double bay windows and they were absolutely prized. When, finally, two years before the poor woman died, she moved into a private house

with my father he said that one of the proudest moments of her life was to read the lease and to discover that you were forbidden to hang out washing to dry on Sundays. My grandmother thought she had arrived. Or again, take my father, the proud possessor of a privately-owned residential dwelling. On one occasion, in the 1980s, a jobbing plumber moved into the house next door and parked his van – K. Temple, Plumber – in the drive and my father was incandescent. I said, 'what is the matter?' and he said, 'that man is an artisan. This is a respectable residential area. It has been going downhill ever since I moved here.' So, I said, 'are those facts possibly not unconnected?' and he was even more furious. I suppose the other thing I should say is that I think there are good things about being a snob as well as bad things because one of the things that snobbishness does, in a perverted a way, but which is very important for a lot of people in the shifting sands of twenty-first century society, is to give us a sense of identity. It helps us to work out who we are. Now what we are may not, in the end, be terribly wonderful but it is very important to know the kind of person you are in society.

BIGSBY: You also point out that there is regional snobbery. Norfolk, for example, is a victim of other people's perception?

TAYLOR: When, as children, we were driving across the Norfolk/Suffolk border and got to Beccles my father would say, 'right, last clean breath of air boys' as we went off into Suffolk. It is just like the rivalry between Norwich and Ipswich at football. A Norwich City employee lost his job once for flashing up on the scoreboard, 'Blackburn 1, Scum 0.' Twenty thousand people shrieked with laughter and he got sacked.

ROSE TREMAIN

Rose Tremain was born in 1943. A graduate of UEA, she went on to teach creative writing there and, in 2013, became the university's chancellor. Her first novel, *Sadler's Birthday*, was published in 1976. Since then she has published a series of prize-winning novels including *Restoration, Sacred Country, Music and Silence, The Colour, The Road Home, Merivel* and *The Gustav Sonata.* Her awards include the Orange Prize for Fiction, the Whitbread Novel Award, the James Tait Black Memorial Prize (for Fiction), and the Prix Femina Étranger. She is also the author of five volumes of short stories and a memoir, *Rosie: Scenes from a Vanished Life*.

This interview was recorded at UEA on 23 November, 2016.

BIGSBY: You have won an impressive array of prizes for your work. Is there one that was particularly important to you?

TREMAIN: I think the Booker is still the bump in the road that you can't quite get around. After a forty-year writing career, I shouldn't care at all about prizes, but there are just so many books published and they have a very short life. When I first started writing, books could be around in the shops for a long time. Now, if a book doesn't do something in the first month of its life, it tends to disappear. What a prize listing can do – certainly a prize win – is to bring a book back, so although we shouldn't care about these things, it is the crowded arena that makes us care. I was shortlisted for the Booker (for *Restoration*) but won the Orange Prize for *The Road Home*, which *was* wonderful. I know this is a prize which excludes one half of humanity, so it is not really a fair test of literary quality, but it was a great night to win.

BIGSBY: Besides novels, short stories, radio plays, you have also written screenplays. Christopher Hampton has made quite a good living out of writing screenplays that were never made, and that is often their fate. Has that been true of you?

TREMAIN: Oh yes, absolutely. I think I have done something like fifteen that have never been made. I believe the average ratio of things that are written to things that are made is ten to one. I have a couple of projects at the moment which might or might not happen, but the thing is that they could suddenly be revived even if you think they have gone. Another company could take them on. What I feel is that it is that screenwriting constitutes a very good workout for the novelist. You haven't got character interiority in a screenplay. You have just got what you see and what people say and you have to work with those two quite limiting things. In my novels I would say that often emotion is action, so I am very interested in what people are thinking and feeling, what they don't say in between the lines. However, I don't think that the skills that one needs as a novelist feed into screenwriting tremendously well. Very few writers manage to do both and my success rate in screenwriting is fairly low, but I keep doing it because it's a huge cultural challenge.

BIGSBY: What is the rhythm of your writing? Do you have to have finished a novel in order to write short stories or screenplays? Can you interrupt a novel?

TREMAIN: Sometimes. It depends on the book. I wrote *The Gustav Sonata* fairly fast and, as I recall, I may have written a couple of short stories because short story ideas are like dreamlets, odds and ends that come to the writer's mind and, for me, it is quite important to seize them fairly rapidly. Otherwise they have a terrible habit of vanishing. So, I may have interrupted that book with a couple of stories but mainly I wrote *The Gustav Sonata* with a feeling of the need to press on with it, even though the story is told in a very elliptical way. It was important to write it like that, but some of my much bigger novels are more discursive, baggier, more multi-stranded, so that I could have been meandering through other work at the same time. In fact, sometimes I think that is quite a wise thing to do, to give your mind a rest from the main work in hand. It is interesting how in a writer's life, a lot of things come to you when you are not consciously thinking about them, sometimes even in dreams or late at night or early in the morning, ideas which you didn't know you had there. So, I think pauses are quite good. I am always very impressed by writers who say they put themselves in a little shack somewhere and write a novel in six weeks. I just can't imagine that that kind of intensity would be any good for me. You would get so tired and so bored with your own self in your shack that the act of writing would be no joy, and I think that the key to having kept going for forty years is my joy in the day-to-day act of writing. That is not to say I don't have bad days, bad weeks, but it is an activity that I have always just loved, and that love hasn't really gone away.

BIGSBY: On the whole, writers don't retire.

TREMAIN: I think if you are in any creative endeavour retirement is like a death sentence. It seems that way to me, anyway, but maybe in five years' time, when I am really old, the ideas will have gone away. I don't think that is something that one can necessarily force but I don't see myself giving up. Maybe it will just give up on me, in which case I would just have to accept it.

BIGSBY: I mentioned short stories. Do you ever feel them pressing against the margins of their own defined limits?

TREMAIN: Yes. I have described short stories as a petulant form. I think the short story is a difficult form to master and they do a strange thing to readers which writers have to take into consideration. They turn readers into critics. When they get involved in a novel, most readers relinquish that side of themselves. They surrender to the story, or the unfolding ideas. In the short story, readers remain outside it and judge it in a critical way, so that it has to be written with a huge attention to technique and form. With the novel you also pay a lot of attention to technique and form and but it goes on less consciously. You surrender to your characters and your ideas. In the short story it doesn't go away in the same way. When I was teaching I used to say to the students that they needed to understand how hard the short-story form is. A lot of writers start with short stories because they are short but I had a huge body of bad short stories when I was in my twenties, none of which found any outlet, so that I decided I would have to pluck up the courage to begin a novel. It was only much later, after I had published a couple of not-too-bad novels, that I came back to the short story and thought, 'I have got to try and master this now.'

When I did a semester at Vanderbilt University in Nashville, Tennessee, I thought I was going there to teach creative writing but on the first weekend – I got there on a Friday and my class was starting on the Monday – the dean said to me, 'You are running a course on the American short story.' I thought, 'Right, well I have got Saturday and Sunday to master some of the greatest writing that has ever been done.' So I owe a fantastic debt to Professor A Walton Litz of Princeton, who had compiled – especially for me, I think – this amazing anthology of the greatest American writing, from Herman Melville right through to Joyce Carol Oates, and I said to my class, 'I am going to learn with you about the great American short story because it includes all the great American writers that have ever lived.' I think in that term I learned more about how to construct a short story – what works, what doesn't, all the different voices you can use, the tenses, all the technical stuff about the story – thanks to Professor Litz's marvellous anthology.

BIGSBY: I read an article you wrote for the Royal Society of Literature in which you said, 'Truth is all.' What is the nature of truth in fiction?

TREMAIN: It has to seem real. I don't mean that I am drawing more and more on actuality, or the back story of my own life. I don't mean that at all. I mean emotional, intellectual truth so that everything that the reader is taken to has particularity and believability in it and that when I lead the reader to the end, that end has to seem earned and right, in other words it has to follow what would psychologically, reasonably, happen. It is those kinds of truths that I mean. I think we all read novels where you think, 'Well, I am quite interested in this little story but actually I don't really believe in the emotional truth of these characters. I don't believe that these things would be said and done by them.' So, it is that kind of truth I am talking about: the feeling of being real.

BIGSBY: So, it is integrity, in other words.

TREMAIN: Yes, absolutely, but the integrity of the characters can change. Our late friend Malcolm Bradbury used to plan his novels from beginning to end, and the writing of them was just a sort of complex infill, but mine are very unplanned. When I have got a certain way into the book, maybe thirty or forty pages, it is only then that things start to become clear. It is like getting to know somebody in the real world. Only then do I really understand where this character is going. I will give you an example of that. When I wrote *Restoration*, the central character, Robert Merivel, is torn all the way through his life between the idea of going back to the thing that he starts off with, which is medicine, and relinquishing that to be seduced by the trappings of luxury offered by the King. He is caught between these two opposing modes.

My plan for the book was that by the end of it he would have renounced all the sweet delights of the court. He would have become less fat, less greedy, less venal – in every sense – and he would, in due time, as urged by his Quaker friend, return to medicine. But when I was about forty pages in I thought, no, I don't think he can accomplish this. I think I have created somebody who is going to try, try incredibly hard, and we are going to be witness to these struggles, but in the end, he won't quite pull it off. And I was thrilled with that discovery because I thought, 'This humanises him.' It makes him funnier and it makes him more interesting, and I realised that I had by that time created a character who had a certain integrity, and the only truthful path for him was to fail.

BIGSBY: That is interesting because, also in that article, you look back at your very early novels and accuse yourself on occasion of contrivance but, then, a novel surely is a contrivance?
TREMAIN: Yes, but it has to be a very clever one. If the reader has an abiding sense of inhabiting a contrived world, then the book will fail.

BIGSBY: *Restoration* became an important book to you.
TREMAIN: It was my expansion moment. Until then, I had written closely constrained domestic dramas, although one of them was set in France and actually took my character beyond our shores, but they were quite small in scope and in emotional reach. Then, suddenly, in *Restoration* I found myself landing on this enormous canvas. Obviously, the preparation for writing that book was much longer than the preparation for writing any of the others, but I was so thrilled to find myself in this very noisy, highly coloured, vibrant world, even as I wasn't absolutely sure whether I could inhabit it wittily enough to do it justice. I think I owe a fantastic debt to *The Diary of Samuel Pepys,* which is the research I started with. Sometimes the book, or books, you read very early on in a research path turn out to be the ones that help you most. I am sure that many people are familiar with the diaries. They are so funny and clever and there are almost no strata of society that Pepys doesn't visit, from the Navy Office

to the river, to the theatres, to the court. He is everywhere and he was Everyman for me, my guide and my redeemer.

BIGSBY: I am interested that you used the words 'highly coloured' because in a previous conversation I said that I thought your books fell into two parts, tuppence-coloured and penny plain, and you looked at me oddly. What I meant by tuppence-coloured was precisely *Restoration* and *Merivel*, both full of life, energy, drive, exuberance, the very thing you were talking about, and then there are the others which are drained of colour. Strangely, and despite its title, your novel *The Colour* would be an example of that in which people lived constrained lives. They are denied that very expansiveness. Are you still looking at me disapprovingly or do you recognise it?

TREMAIN: No, no, I do absolutely. I would just say that obviously the mode has to fit the subject and the mode and the subject come together. I can usually see, even though my subject may be a bit half-formed, what mode the book has to take, and when we come on to talk about *The Gustav Sonata*, this is penny plain, the most penny plain of them all I think because I wanted it to be very short and to say a lot in a very economical way. The metaphor I came up with – and which is appropriate to Switzerland, where it is set – was the Swiss watch, which has a very plain, maybe rather beautiful, face on it and fantastical, clever workings within but which the reader doesn't see. I wanted it to be a tightly withheld book. The thing I feel about readers is that a lot of novelists underestimate them and tell them far too much. I believe that readers love to work. There are a lot of moments in this book which are not filled in and the readers have to work out what happened in those intervening, elliptical moments, but I think readers who read fiction like this are very astute. What did you call the other ones, tuppence-coloured? I'd prefer a slightly higher denomination(!) but I think in those perhaps the readers don't need to work quite so hard.

BIGSBY: Also in that article you talked about the centrality of voice. I take it that you meant by that the narrative voice, as opposed to the voices which proliferate in the novel. Why is that central? Do you have that voice before you type the first word or do you begin to hear it as you type?

TREMAIN: I have it before, but sometimes I get it wrong. With *Restoration* I wrote the first fifty pages as a third-person narrative. Then I had an accident with it in an aeroplane travelling back from Sicily. I had packed this manuscript in a bag with some olive oil and the olive oil broke. In those days I wrote in pencil – this is pre-computer with no backup – and the olive oil soaked into the fifty pages and made them absolutely translucent so I couldn't read them properly. I thought, well, instead of being dismayed by this, perhaps it is telling me what I already knew, which was that there was something wrong with this narrative and the thing that was wrong was the voice. I had launched myself into a third-person narration and actually the voice somehow smothered the colourfulness and the intrigue and humour and singularity of the character. I thought I have really got to take the bull by the horns and go into a first-person narration. I took a few goes at finding Merivel's voice, and again I probably owe a debt to Pepys, but once found, it felt completely right. And that is the key question, whether the narrative voice is appropriate to the story you are telling, because sometimes you want a voice to yield up a lot to the readers and sometimes you want the voice to be very withheld. But that choice has to be made even before the first words are found.

BIGSBY: Last week, as you know, I was talking to Richard Holmes, your partner, and I wanted to put a couple of things to you that emerged from that. When he is writing a biography, he wants to go to the places his subjects went to. He can't breathe the same air but he can look through the same window. He can stand in the same place in the countryside. Does this apply when you are writing fiction, or do you prefer an imagined landscape?

TREMAIN: I think both apply. The thing about Richard is he has to go there for rather a long time. Biographers and the historians have to gather more material than us fly-by-night fictionistas. We are just like the dog that goes flying along the hedgerows snaffling things that it feels are attractive, then retreating to gnaw on them. For my novel *Music and Silence*, which is a very big novel, I did go to Denmark, and in fact the whole idea of that novel came from a trip to Denmark. The legend of the musicians in the cellar was told to me by some Danish friends and then later, when I started to think about it as a novel, I did go back there and I am glad I did, but I went for a scandalously short time. People say to me, 'Oh, you must have spent months in Denmark,' but I didn't actually. Richard couldn't come with me for some reason, so I went with Penny, my editor, and we were there for about six days. The lovely thing about Denmark is that a lot of my novel is set in Copenhagen and the buildings that were made by King Christian IV, who appears in my novel set in the 1630s, are still there and have been restored. So, you can get the feeling of this very small city in a very short amount of time. Then we went up to Jutland for two or three days. Knowing what landscapes actually look like and how they smell and feel is important. I had imagined Jutland as being steep and forested and it isn't like that at all.

With *The Colour*, the idea came to me when Richard and I were in New Zealand. It came in a gifted way, a rush of an idea that just fell into my lap, but I did think later on, when I was about a third of the way through it, that I must go back, even though I had done a heck of a lot of reading about New Zealand at that time: the 1860s, the gold rush, the landscape and farming, all those things that come into that book. I thought I must go back and make sure of these facts that are the groundwork of this novel. But then I choked on that idea. It was the imaginative world that was real to me by that time and I thought that going back and trying to verify things on the ground risked disturbing everything that already had imaginative life. However, I would have been very thrown if I had got things wrong. I think we are back to truth here. If a place has an absolute integrity in my head, and is based, in so far as possible, on the truth of a landscape, or the truth of where a road along a map leads, that should be enough. I don't have to keep going back. But this is just my anxiety. If you talk to other writers, who are as heavily involved in research for books as I am, they would say, 'Oh no, I have to spend months there.' Some novelists love this kind of searching and I like it to a certain extent but my heart opens when I can start writing, so I keep longing to get to that moment. That is when I start feeling joy.

BIGSBY: I asked Richard whether there was a value to him, as a biographer, to be living with a novelist. What about the other way around? Is there a professional advantage as a novelist in living with a biographer?

TREMAIN: I think straightaway we would both agree that it is good that we are not involved in exactly the same mode of writing but then I think, well, there is a fantastic advantage, just for a start, in living with another writer. I am, incidentally, in awe of how much more work Richard does than me. He is much more studious and double-checks and triple-checks and re-writes far more than I do.

BIGSBY: In one of Richard's books he says there was an occasion when you asked him how he found his subjects and he said, 'Why are you asking that?' You replied, 'Because that is what I am always asked, so I am going to ask you.' Isn't there a sense with you that there is serendipity to it? Often, as you were saying, there are chance encounters which spark a story.

TREMAIN: I think that is probably true for every writer, because we don't walk through life deaf and dumb. As Keats said, you are not irritably reaching and searching after fact but you are alert, you are waiting in tranquillity for things to offer themselves to you. Your mind is tuned up so that when the thing comes along, or passes, or just visits you in a dream, you are immediately aware of it and can seize it at that moment. I think maybe one goes in and out of that state of alertness. As I get older, my absolute preferred mode of existence is attending on ideas and then starting on them in tranquillity, at home, not flying around the globe in the way that I used to long to do.

BIGSBY: Turning to *The Gustav Sonata*, there is a figure based on an actual person. Was that the trigger for the book?

TREMAIN: No, it wasn't, Although it now has an

amazing centrality and grip. It comes in the middle section of the book, which perversely takes you back in time. We have been in 1947 and then, suddenly, in section two, we are in 1937 but there is a reason for this. In the first section I am establishing Gustav as a little boy, and the mother, Emilie, who doesn't love him, and I think the only question that the reader is asking, when he or she gets to the end of the first section, is why doesn't this mother love this rather sweet little child? Therefore, I felt that that before I could move Gustav's story on we had to understand why Emilie is the way she is – which is why I go back to section two.

The real person you mention is the person who I have fictionalised as Emilie's husband, who was an assistant police chief in my story. It is set in Switzerland, in a little town, originally Saint Gallen, near the border with Germany. My town is actually in Mittelland, which is further in the interior of Switzerland. I found that this very heroic man, who is called Paul Grueninger, had been a police chief at Saint Gallen. Switzerland had hoped, at that time and then during the war, to hang on to its neutrality and that its refusal to take either side would be respected. It was a safe haven for Jews coming across from France on one side, and from Germany and Austria on the other. Then this edict came down from Bern, dictated by the Germans of course, saying that no more Jews were going to be allowed in after a certain date, which I think was August 1938. This man, Paul Grueninger, defied it. He decided to falsify dates of entry for the Jews. He knew, or suspected, that after a while this falsification would be discovered. He didn't know what the consequences of that would be but he could have anticipated they would be very bad, as indeed they were. So I thought that was just such a fantastic story, a man who acts with great courage and great integrity and is later punished for his moral strength.

BIGSBY: You said it is a great story and it is because what happened subsequently, outside of your book, is that, decades later, the Swiss government apologised and today his name is in Yad Vashem, the Holocaust memorial in Israel, as one of the righteous. In fact, he saved three times as many people as Schindler and about a third of the number that Nicholas Winton did on the Kindertransport. Were you ever tempted to make him the story?

TREMAIN: I found this out very late, not too late in terms of the writing of the book but quite late in my researches, so I didn't start with it. The day that I found it I thought that alters what I am able to do with that middle section. Occasionally this happens in writing fiction: things you have been driving towards are suddenly given a blessing by something that you find.

BIGSBY: His actions, of course, tie in with a concern of the novel, the Holocaust, though it is approached mostly obliquely. Gustav's friend is Jewish and his parents are quite well off. Everything seems secure except that his mother is frightened of trains. Nothing is made of that, nothing is said about it, but for a Jew trains had a special significance. Then the two boys go off and find a ruined sanatorium and begin to play a game. In this game they divide the imaginary patients, some of whom will live, some die. Finally, at the end of the game, they decide that one of the 'patients' has to be cremated. All of this is logical in terms of the characters and their relationship. They are doing no more than play a game, except that something else is surely going on at the back of your reader's mind.

TREMAIN: In a way you have said everything that I would need to say about it. The Holocaust is there as a shadow across this book but I don't need to retell any of the stories. We all know them. We all know the imagery, and you can find that imagery in the book, as when Gustav and Anton go to the sanatorium. It is there if you hear those echoes. I always try not to be too prescriptive to readers. They may discover things in a book, patterns, historical echoes, or these may pass them by. Here, the story of Gustav, his becoming a man and his relationship with Anton, is central to the book and you could go through it almost not noticing the Holocaust. I think maybe some readers have. Indeed, it was very interesting, when the reviews came out, that not many reviewers picked up on this at all and I didn't know whether to feel pleased by that or a bit miffed that my subtleties had been so subtle they weren't noticed at all.

BIGSBY: One thing that is central to the book is love: love denied, offered, and not recognised, love subsumed, suppressed and so on, in different kinds of relationships. Gustav loves his mother but his mother does not love him, as her mother did not love her. There is this kind of void in their lives. In some ways they live temporary existences There are emotional disconnects, breakages.

TREMAIN: Yes, I think that is right and the thing that enables Gustav to survive that is precisely the rather harsh training that he receives from his mother, who says that he has to learn what she calls 'self-mastery', what we would perhaps call 'self-control' though I think self-mastery is a more elegant term, very Swiss. At one point he is given the image of a coconut, which stands for Switzerland – girt by mountains but protecting a valuable but fragile world within – but also for himself as he is told by a teacher that he has to be hard on the outside like his country, not to reveal his feelings, not to give in to despair, not give in to the sorrows of being not loved. He must not faint and fade but stay strong, and he takes this deeply to heart, which is what enables him to have a life because, as we all know, if you really are not loved in the way that he is not loved as a child, it is very difficult to have a proper and meaningful life with any kind of relationship with another human being later on. In his adult life, in particular, he finds a lot of displacement activities, which is I think how people who have not been loved probably have to cope. Gustav runs a hotel and although he is tempted at moments to think of himself as a very mediocre person, because that is all he is, he has got his little hotel and runs it in a way that feels important to him. He wants it to be very homely and comfortable because he understands that, as one gets older, it is the small things in life that enable one to bear life's brevity: the open fire, the warm bed, the good food, the fresh air, the walks, the garden. All those things that he tries to contrive for his guests are small but he sees them as absolutely fundamental, while all the time neglecting his own deep feelings. And why does he do this? Because he has to, because the feelings threaten to overwhelm him.

BIGSBY: And there comes a moment when he says now we must live the life we should have lived. In other words, life has gone by without him ever really grasping it. And this applies to his closest relationship, with Anton, his friend, but the nature of that relationship is another one of those understated areas as, for much of the novel, we are never entirely sure what the nature of that relationship is and what direction it is going to go in.

TREMAIN: That was what I started with, the difference between love and friendship. So much is written about romantic love and I thought that, actually, friendship is a wonderful subject. I have written about it before. In a sense *Restoration* is about friendship, friendship between men. But here I was interested in how these two boys, who have come to know each other from when they were very little, define what they feel. They both feel something very strong and Gustav understands that what he feels for Anton is love, something Anton doesn't admit or choose to see until very late. And that seemed to me to be how friendship and love often goes: one of you understands the nature of the thing and the other one doesn't, and then you both suffer.

BIGSBY: It is set in the past, in the 1930s and 1940s, and leaps forward to the end of the 1990s. It is surely hard not to feel the pressure of now in this book because it is about people who are suffering, immigrants who are not allowed to cross the border or are there illegally. In *The Road Home* you wrote about an immigrant moving from eastern Europe. How far was that in your mind as you were writing this? Although set in the past, did you see it as speaking to something that is going on now?

TREMAIN: I don't think it was there right at the beginning. In the early chapters it is very focused on what Gustav's childhood was like, and the questions of love and friendship, but it certainly crept in. But again it is something that the readers can take from it or perhaps fail to see. There are parallels. I don't make any great claims to that but it is just quietly laid in.

BIGSBY: It is set in Switzerland, as you have said, but that is not just a setting, it is virtually a character. It is a place that has always tried to immure itself, cut itself off from history. It wants to feel that it is secure within its own boundaries, controlled, and the characters reflect that sensibility.

TREMAIN: I think only Gustav does, really, or possibly the father to some extent, but Gustav does, yes, absolutely. He is a walking Switzerland, with this self-mastery, attention to rule, to what is right, what is clean, what is honest. That is absolutely in him and it never leaves him. That really interested me, to take this idea of a kind of neutral but very clean, orderly and self-mastered place, and to create a character who was like that. The question that I suppose you are asking is, towards the end of the book, has neutrality turned into a kind of neutering. Has Gustav become a hollow person, unable to feel, unable to be creative, unable to do anything in a very bold way. Again, those questions are not exactly answered in a definitive way.

BIGSBY: It is called *The Gustav Sonata*. Why sonata? Is it a structural device to you as well as relating to a character?

TREMAIN: Well, again, you don't have to notice this. In fact, you could sleepwalk through this book not noticing a whole lot of things that are actually in there. People can feel free not to notice it but, yes, it was helpful to me to conceive of it in three movements: exposition, development and then recapitulation. The fact that the development goes backwards risks being probably extremely irritating to the reader, but it does develop in the sense that your store of information, your store of understanding, is being filled up so your ability to engage with the book is developing in that middle, backward-looking section. Then, in the third act, Anton and Gustav are in their main lives and Anton is wrestling with this talent, which is severely compromised because he doesn't have the physical or the mental temperament for it so he gets sick with nerves. This dilemma is set up in the first part so there is a reasonably neat recapitulation in the last movement of things that I set out in the first, but then take ultimately to an earned ending. Also, sonata is a beautiful word.

STEPHEN WESTABY

Stephen Westaby was born in the same year the NHS was created: 1948. He was raised on a council estate in Scunthorpe and went on to train as a doctor at Charing Cross Hospital. He became a heart surgeon with a reputation for adopting and developing new technologies. He conducted some twelve thousand operations for the NHS in the course of his career, finally being forced to retire when his hands were no longer fully functional. In 2017, he published *Fragile Lives: A Heart Surgeon's Stories of Life and Death on the Operating Table*.

This interview was recorded at UEA on 15 November, 2017.

BIGSBY: Since you are a heart surgeon let me ask, if I were to have a heart attack, what would my chances be and what would improve those chances?

WESTABY: The last person you need is a heart surgeon at that point but I'll tell you what you will get. You will get bystander cardiopulmonary resuscitation. If they are not very good at it you will barely feel it. If they are good at it they will break your ribs and you will definitely feel it. Then when you pass out in a heap somebody will fetch the defibrillator, paid for by the local charities, and they will give you a zap and hopefully bring you round. Then, instead of getting you straight to hospital, where you belong, they will probably faff around for half an hour trying to find a vein to put a drip in and then they will give you cold, clear, fluid which will do you absolutely no good at all. I have a bee in my bonnet about this. So, if you have your heart attack and come around with electric paddles across your chest and burns on either side, say, 'Get me to hospital now, please. Let's not sit here for a long time.'

BIGSBY: How long would I have? Presumably it is time-critical.

WESTABY: Yes, time is absolutely critical. In my other life I wrote a couple of textbooks on trauma surgery and I used to love flying around North London, and out to Harefield and places like that, to operate on major injuries after road traffic accidents. The reason I have a bee in my bonnet about this is that I used to operate on a fair number of people who had been stabbed in the heart. What happens when you are stabbed in the heart is that you lose a bit of blood, but then your blood pressure falls and you become stable. Then you are in a fine balance and if somebody tries to resuscitate you with lots of fluid they tip that balance and make everything worse. I have had to stand there at an operating table, with a chest open and a heart in front of me, and put a pair of forceps through a stab wound and let out a full litre of dilute blood which won't clot, because it is full of cold, clear fluid, before I could put the patient back together again. So pre-hospital care worries me an awful lot.

One of the reasons I have got a bee in my bonnet is that when Princess Diana crashed in Paris it took a hundred and ten minutes to get her from that tunnel into the cardiothoracic centre that she went to. Christiaan Barnard, who knew her, rang me when he heard that she had died, in a hell of a state, to say, 'What on earth was going on? What went wrong? Why was she out in the tunnel for a hundred and ten minutes when she should have been in the hospital with surgeons operating on her?' That is because if you have got a hole in a blood vessel – and, in cardiac surgical terms, she only had a trivial injury – then you should get the hole repaired.

BIGSBY: You had a very unlikely beginning for someone who was going to be a major surgeon. You were born on a council estate.
WESTABY: On the back streets of Scunthorpe.

BIGSBY: With an outside toilet.
WESTABY: And an air-raid shelter full of asbestos.

BIGSBY: Yet at the age of seven instead of wanting to be an astronaut, or own a sweet shop, you wanted to be a surgeon. How did that come about?
WESTABY: In the back streets of a northern steel town families lived quite close together so I lived with my parents. My dad left school at sixteen to fight the Germans while my mother ran the Trustee Savings Bank on the High Street in Scunthorpe while the men were away. My grandfather, who lived across the road, was the air-raid warden and had one of those air-raid shelters which, when I was a boy, was full of chickens and geese. As I was growing up he taught me to draw and paint and saw that I was ambidextrous. I wish I had carried on but we used to walk his dog and the only place to walk the dog was round the slag heaps which were covered in grass by then. One day I was out walking with him and he suddenly clutched his chest. He was only fifty-nine at the time, and he sunk to his knees and I could see he was as white as a sheet and of course was having a heart attack. I was only about five or six, so I just stayed with him. I didn't know whether to run and get somebody else or stay with him, so I stayed with him and eventually we got home. That happened six or seven more times.

Then he developed severe heart failure and with severe heart failure he couldn't walk across the room, couldn't go out to the outside toilet. It was too cold. He couldn't put on shoes because his ankles were so swollen, couldn't lie flat in a bed because when you lie down and you have heart failure you get very breathless.

Eventually, I came home from school one day and the black Austin Healey of the very fine local GP was there, just five years after the NHS was born, and I looked through the curtains and could see my grandfather dying, with froth coming out of his nose and mouth. That was death from heart failure and I was profoundly affected by that and said, 'We have got to be able to do something about this.' There was no heart surgery of any significance at the time. Interestingly, in the maternity bed next to my mother's when I was born, in Scunthorpe War Memorial Hospital, a blue baby came back with its mother in the bed next door and one of my earliest recollections is of my mother telling me that she used to visit that mother every year on my birthday because she had lost her baby. So I was brought up with this and, at the age of seven, saw a programme on television called *Your Life in Their Hands*. It came from the Hammersmith Hospital in London and the doctors all wore starched white coats down to their ankles and the nurses were all matronly with nice belt buckles and smart hats and looked like 'proper nurses'. The patients sat up to attention in their beds in those days and all the talk was about how the Americans were trying to develop a heart-lung machine so that it would be possible to open a heart and repair it for the first time. That happened in 1953. The man who developed the heart-lung machine did five operations with it. Only one of those survived. They were all young people with holes in their hearts and he did not have the character to go on and be a heart surgeon. He gave up and nobody would have known about the heart-lung machine had somebody not asked him to go to a surgical meeting and tell them about it. Then some very good American surgeons, with whom I trained, eventually made a success out of the heart-lung machine.

BIGSBY: You were a beneficiary of the 1944 Education Act and went to a grammar school. And while you were there, at the age of sixteen, you had a part-time job as a porter in a hospital. And it wasn't just a case of pushing beds around or cleaning up. You actually went into the mortuary.

WESTABY: Yes. I forced my way into places that other people didn't want to go. I wanted to be an operating-theatre porter because I never wavered from that desire to be a heart surgeon. I never wanted to be a proper doctor, a GP like the nice old boy who saw my grandfather off. I decided I was going to be a heart surgeon and actually to get to that from the back streets of Scunthorpe was not that easy, but I did, and actually when it came to going to interviews for medical school I had spent so much time in operating theatres and autopsies, and had already seen so much death and destruction, that I knew anatomy. I went to Cambridge for an interview but never saw myself as being a Cambridge student.

BIGSBY: Is that because of your Scunthorpe background?

WESTABY: My horizon was smoke and steel. There were no golden sunsets in Scunthorpe but when the blast furnaces opened up at night the whole sky was red. Now I went to Cambridge and it was totally beautiful – as was Oxford, where I ended up – and strangely enough eventually trained in surgery in Cambridge, but I went to my first interview and was looking for the college so I asked a nurse from Addenbrooke's Hospital and she said, 'I'll take you there. It is on my way home.' So I chatted to this very nice nurse, in her smart uniform, and she said, 'Where are you from?' and I daren't even admit I was from Scunthorpe. I said 'Lincoln' and she said, 'Oh, that's funny. I live in a place called Brigg, just outside Scunthorpe,' and I felt an absolute prat before I had even started.

In my Cambridge interview there were two Cambridge dons and it was very smart, with old leather armchairs and one of them said, 'Can you think of any diseases that the soldiers might be worried about in Vietnam?' I couldn't remember whether there was malaria out in

Vietnam so I said 'syphilis' and they looked at me long and hard and I knew I had to say something else so I said maybe the bombs and the bullets and the napalm were more to worry about than syphilis.

BIGSBY: You ended up by going to Charing Cross Hospital, where you were interviewed by somebody who was known for a rather strange reason.
WESTABY: Yes, he was the anatomy professor and the model for Sir Lancelot Spratt in *Doctor in the House* and, my name beginning with W, they were all bored stupid by the time they got around to me. It was about five o'clock, the end of the day, and there was the dean, Sir Lancelot, a very fine surgeon, in his morning suit, pinstripe trousers. I had waited an hour to go in and a very nice matron had given me tea and chatted to me to keep me calm. She told me all about the hospital during the war and where the bombs landed and how many people they saved, and so on. The first question they asked me in the interview was, 'What you know about the hospital?' I just reproduced everything the matron had said. There was only one more question. They asked me about cricket, because I had been a county cricketer in Lincolnshire, and then they said, 'Can you play rugby?' So I said, 'I am going to learn how to play rugby,' because in London medical schools in the 1960s that was all that mattered.

BIGSBY: You, eighteen, and one of the things you did, entirely unofficially, was to go across the road to see an operation.
WESTABY: I had seen hearts in a mortuary, and I had dissected animal hearts at school. Now I got to go to the dissecting room that everybody worries about – but not me, because I had seen so much death and destruction in Scunthorpe – so I said, 'I want to see a heart operation' to the hospital porter, and he said, 'You can't. You are not a clinical student,' but I persuaded him that I was going to find the operating theatre whether he told me where it was or not and he pointed me in the direction of an operating theatre gallery which was known as 'the Ether Dome,' a glass dome where you could look down into the operating theatre and watch them operate. So I found

myself in the Ether Dome late in the afternoon when the heart operation had already gone on for an awful long time. The patient died. She was in her early twenties and she had just had a baby and had no husband. I think she had been a prostitute in the East End. The baby was on the ward. There were no grandparents. They had been killed in the Blitz, so my first heart operation saw a twenty-two-year-old go down the drain with what these days is a very simple and straightforward operation and a baby was made an orphan.

BIGSBY: And your own first operation was not an unalloyed success, was it?

WESTABY: As a determined young man I applied for a job that I was not qualified for in any way. I applied for a resident surgical officer's post at the Royal Brompton Hospital, which was a pure cardiac centre, and I talked my way into that job. There was a reason by then that I could talk my way into anything. I came from Scunthorpe very shy and retiring but I did play rugby and one day, when I was on a rugby tour in Cornwall, I had a very bad head injury with a fractured skull down the front and I was left face down in a puddle of water on the pitch while the game went on because medical students are very caring people, as you know. When I eventually came around in the changing room, instead of taking me to hospital, they took me to the bar, which made the brain oedema even worse. So that changed my whole life because thereafter I became uninhibited and psychopathic and fit to be a surgeon. It was by talking my way into the Brompton that I got a start and you are right, I had a six-foot-six German boss who was an irascible guy and we were late to start an operating list. He was in the out-patients seeing private patients and he said, 'Westaby, it is time you got started. Go down and open the chest.' I had never done any surgery of any sort, except a couple of appendix operations when I was a student, but I was the sort of character that is not going to say 'No' to that, and I had found, in a dusty old cupboard in the surgeons' changing room, the old white wellington boots that surgeons wore and down the back was 'Brock' – that was Lord Brock, the man who had started heart surgery for the UK. So I purloined Lord Brock's now-discarded white operating boots, put them on and I strolled into the operating theatre. The nurses were very irascible because we were very late and they wanted to get on with it. The anaesthetist was playing chess with the profusionist [in charge of the bypass machine]. They were totally bored until I made the incision up the front of the little old lady's chest which was fine, the knife down onto the breastbone, blood trickling down the edges, no problem. I take the cautery and open through the fat. The smoke rises – absolutely fine. But then, it came to running the saw up the breastbone. Now what Panith had not told me, because I suspect he forgot, was that she had had an operation before but the incision was round the side. It was one of those 'poke your fingers in the heart and open up the rheumatic valve', but I couldn't see the scar because she was already covered up. Anyway, to cut a long story short, the saw goes straight into the front of the heart and, before I had got the breastbone open, blood comes through the sternum and the very experienced scrub nurse opposite me just said, 'Press on it. We'll send for Mr Paneth.' Pressing on it didn't do the job. The blood kept pouring out, so we changed positions and she went into the first assistant's position and I just opened the chest and found the hole in the heart and stitched it up. I had just stitched it up and was totally soaking with perspiration when Paneth walks into the operating theatre in his pinstriped suit, no mask, no nothing, looks over the top and says, 'What have you done now, Westaby?' and I said, 'I had a small misadventure, Mr Paneth, but I seem to have been able to sort it out.' So, he said, 'Fine, I'll go for a cup of tea. Don't do anything else stupid,' and that is how my career in heart surgery actually started.

I can't move on, though, without the next Lord Brock story. It was just a couple of weeks later, coming up to Christmas. At the Brompton, the junior doctors were served dinner in the board room, with wine and they didn't have emergencies at night. There was no accident department, so we used to go to the pub on Fulham Road. We had a couple of glasses of wine and a few pints. Then, on Saturday night, at ten o'clock, there was a call from the switchboard. 'There is an Air Force jet coming in from Iceland with a young man with a ruptured aorta and Mr Paneth is coming in to operate on him.' We knew Paneth was coming in from a Christmas party himself so I knew that I was in dead trouble. My career had just started quite successfully, but now I was in trouble and the reason I was in trouble was because I was fluid-overloaded. I thought, 'I have got to get myself out of this', and I thought about putting a urinary catheter in. I had had one before when I had had the head injury but I didn't want to put a catheter on myself. Then I remembered that there is something called Paul's tubing up on the wards for incontinent males, so I went up to the ward and got some of this long rubber tubing and I cut it to the length of my inside leg and attached it to my person, so to speak. I let it down the inside of my operating theatre's trousers into Lord Brock's right boot. I then went to theatre full of confidence, whereas the senior registrar hadn't been quite as astute. He stood opposite Paneth while I was nextdoor cutting the stitches. Then the senior registrar starts to get restless, moving from foot to foot. Eventually, he has to say, 'Mr Paneth, I need to go out for a minute.' So, he goes out and he comes back. Then, half an hour later, when the operation is getting tense because we weren't doing terribly well with this young lad, he has to go out again, at which Paneth turned around to me and said, 'Westaby, what's wrong with Reece? He has been drinking, hasn't he?' and I said, 'Well, Mr Paneth, I really couldn't tell you because I have been sitting in the library working all week.' And he said, 'Very fine. You come into the first assistant's position and take over. We don't need Reece back.'

BIGSBY: You have a reputation for being fascinated by new technology, new devices. There is even one which carries your name.

WESTABY: The Westaby tube. I did a lot of chest surgery out at Harefield Hospital and the Westaby tube came about because we had another patient shipped in from abroad. Harefield is part of the Brompton and this patient had been in an explosion in Saudi Arabia and it burned out his windpipe and his larynx while his face was badly burned. His airways were just filling with what we call 'granulation tissue and secretions'. We had to keep hoovering him out with what we call a 'rigid bronchoscope', a brass tube that you look down with a light in the end, sucking out secretions. He was in his thirties and it was quite clear he was going to die. I finally said to my boss, 'Either we do something different or he is going to die.' There was no tube you could put in down the trachea and the bronchi and everybody said it wouldn't work at all. If you did it would just fill with secretions, but I designed a tube, and my boss got it made by a company in America. They sent it back and I worked out a way of getting it into this guy. We saved him with it and then I went to South Africa for the twenty-fifth anniversary of the first heart transplant with Chris Barnard and they showed me a case of a township boy who had also been badly burned in an explosion but the tube was too big. There was no way I could get this into a child conventionally, so I came back to England and thought about it, then wrote back to the paediatric surgeon there and said, 'I have got a way of dealing with this.' I went back to Cape Town and the first thing I saw was a hoarding saying, 'UK Doc flies in to Save Township Boy.' So, there was a bit of a build-up for this. I put him on a heart-lung machine, so I could stop his breathing and take all the tubes out, and literally filleted his airways. I put this tube in and reconstructed the front of his airways with the material that is in the sac around the heart. Yes, innovation was one of my things.

BIGSBY: You mentioned Saudi Arabia and that puts another thought in my mind. You have talked, in your book, of the need for a surgeon to be objective, not to empathise too much, not to be too involved emotionally, but there are occasions when that didn't apply to you. I wonder if the Saudi Arabian incident wasn't one of them, which again involved a young boy.

WESTABY: Yes, in 1986 I was appointed to build a new heart unit essentially in Oxford and the way I was, with my megalomania psychopathy and lack of inhibitions, I had spent the whole year's money in three months and Oxford just closed me down. They said, 'We can't afford you. You are going to have to stop operating now,' because I was a prolific operator. I used to do six hundred cases a year. Anyway, the day before they closed me down I had a request from Saudi Arabia because their children's heart surgeon needed back surgery and they were looking for somebody to fill in. In Saudi Arabia they used to take complex congenital heart problems from all over the Arab world, so when they said, 'We are closing you down', I said, 'Fine, I am off to Saudi Arabia and I'll come back with a goldmine.' I wasn't interested in the money. I was interested in the experience and, as a result of the experience in Saudi Arabia, I set up a children's heart surgery unit in Oxford. However, when I was there in Saudi Arabia a cardiologist from the Mayo Clinic came along to see me and said, 'I have got a case that I don't think you will be interested in but I feel sure I have to put it past you.' This was a child with dextrocardia, the heart round the wrong way, with a tumour in the heart. The kid was emaciated and dying. There were two reasons for that: firstly, the heart was killing him but, secondly, his mother had been kidnapped from Somalia and this woman was totally stunning but again emaciated. She had walked out of Yemen having been kidnapped by Yemeni pirates and because she knew her kid was dying she just set off and walked until she got to Oman. She was picked up, almost dying, on the border. They passed the kid straight on to the big hospital I was at in Riyadh. So I was presented with this child, and I never said 'no' to anything, so I said, 'I'll find a way of doing it', but I couldn't work out how I was going to get to this tumour because the heart was back to front. Then, one night they took me out in the desert, because all there is to do in Riyadh is to go out in the desert with a load of booze that nobody can see you with and look at the stars. And out in the desert that night a camel train came past, with a load of Bedouin, all with Kalashnikovs. It was a very scary experience, but they just drifted past in the moonlight and as they were drifting past I had a Eureka moment, which I didn't tell anybody about until I was actually in the theatre. My Eureka moment was, 'You know how to do a heart transplant. You have been working with transplants. Take the child's heart out and operate on it on the bench because then you can twist and turn it and define the anatomy,' and that is what I ended up doing. I thought I had done a good job. I took the child's heart out, put it in a dish of ice, dissected out the tumour while the kid was on a heart-lung machine, transplanted it back into the child and thought that was great, and it was for a while. I had more children to operate on the following morning, but when the child was in the ICU he had what we call 'temporary heart block'. I had put pacing wires in and they turned the child over in the ICU and the pacing wires disconnected so they couldn't pace the child and the child went down like a stone and died in the middle of the night. I didn't know that the child had died. They didn't want to disturb me for somebody that was already dead so I found out the next morning and I asked, 'What's happened to his poor mother? The child was all the mother had in the world. You need to look after her.' And they said, 'We put her in a room and brought the child to her, with the drips and drains still there because they have to be left for the autopsy, and she has disappeared. She has taken the baby off.' And I just thought, 'Oh God, help us.' I went to theatre the following morning and very soon somebody said, 'Did you know about your patient's mother?' and I said, 'No, tell me about the patient's mother?' and they had found the mother at the bottom of a tower block. She had taken the dead baby, gone to the top of the tower and jumped. So that was two hundred percent mortality for me. That was a miserable, miserable experience, and of course in my career I have had many, many, many miserable experiences.

BIGSBY: There was another twist to that though, wasn't there, because when you talked to the mother you couldn't get anything out of her. Whatever you said, she didn't reply.
WESTABY: That's right.

BIGSBY: And only subsequently did you find out why?
WESTABY: Yes, she was dumb.

BIGSBY: Let me take you back to the machines. You didn't actually create them but you were a first user, a very fast adopter. If you had to choose from the various technologies which you have introduced, which do you think was the most important of them?

WESTABY: I started pioneering American artificial heart technology because when I was training in America I went into rounds at five am one morning and the residents were all excited because Dr Cooley in Houston had put in a total artificial heart. This was 1981 and I was so excited about it that I actually left Birmingham, Alabama, that evening (a Friday evening) and flew to Houston to meet Dr Cooley and see the artificial heart, which I did. I then had a career-long association with Texas and Cooley and they gave me an award for pioneering new technology.

Everybody thought that artificial hearts had to replicate what the normal human heart does and, of course, what the human heart does is it fills and then it contracts and empties. It pumps blood round the body and then fills and empties, and that produces a pulse. I tried various American pulsatile devices that were very large. They were all the size of a melon but I used them as permanent rather temporary artificial hearts. The Americans couldn't use them as permanent artificial hearts. If you got one of these devices you had to have a heart transplant. The two were linked. But there are so few heart transplants. At least fifteen thousand people under the age of sixty-five die from heart failure but there are only one hundred and fifty or fewer heart transplants a year. So heart transplants only apply to less than one percent of the people that need them, so my quest was to find a replacement for the heart that was realistic. The total artificial heart that I saw Cooley with was not realistic in any way. It was attached to something outside the body the size of a fridge/freezer and the idea that you could put one of those in patients and that they could have a reasonable quality of life was nonsense. Now I saw a thumb-size high-speed axial flow pump that somebody was developing as a substitute for the left ventricle. He was a famous artificial heart engineer called Robert Jarvik and I met him by accident. I was asked to comment about another of his inventions but after we had decided that that was no good he said, 'Come up to my room.

I have got something very interesting to show you.' I went and he put this device in a bucket of water and switched it on and it went whoosh. It pumped five litres per minute and I said, 'That's a great pump for water but, if you put it in blood, which contains a lot of delicate cells, it is going to chew the cells up and haemolyse the blood and it won't work but, nevertheless, I would love to be able to test it for you.' He said, 'Come to Houston and see it in the calves because the pump was working in the calves and the calves looked quite cheerful to me.' So I came back and I set up a lab in Oxford. Animal work is very distasteful and it was distasteful for me. I've got dogs, I've got llamas on the paddock. I have got chickens running all round the garden and my family are very much animal lovers, but nobody was going to let me implant a revolutionary new artificial heart without testing it in animals. What I did was I actually rescued old lady Welsh mule sheep from the slaughterhouse so my conscience was clear in that they were going to be killed anyway. I implanted this device into them, a device that took away all pulse because it pumped continuously at high speed. So there was no pulse pressure at all and my sheep were perfectly content. Their organ function was normal with no pulse at all in their circulation, which was a massive revelation. Nobody believed it was possible. As a result of that I said to the Department of Health, 'I have a revolutionary new way of treating heart failure so you had bloody well better let me get on and do it', and eventually, after a lot of haggling, they said, 'Okay, fine, but as long as a team of very eminent heart failure cardiologists select a patient who they are sure is going to die within six weeks.' The trouble is that patients in heart failure, in that category, are essentially not fit for a haircut. They are not fit for anaesthesia. They are not fit for anything, so I had the challenge of being able to do this but only in a patient that I was likely to lose.

 Eventually I met that patient and he was a great character and very religious. He had had the last rites and his nose was blue and he couldn't walk into the office. He was in a wheelchair but was too proud to come through the threshold in a wheelchair so he got up and staggered into my office. His ankles were like tree trunks and he had ulcerated legs and was absolutely at the end but he was amazing. He had been turned down for a transplant twice because the thing about heart transplants is that if you have got any of the complications of heart failure, you are not fit for a transplant. Anyway, we accepted him and the Americans came across and we did this jointly. We got him through and he lived for eight years and became a very famous character. He travelled to America a lot to persuade the FDA that this was good. My pulseless man had a plug in his head because we came up with a new way of putting power into the body. With the American electric devices, a big power cable came out the belly and when a rigid cable comes out the belly it moves in relation to the skin and the fat and they all eventually broke down and got infected. Then the patients were given antibiotics and the bacteria disappeared but fungus came in and infected them. Anyway, to get over that, Jarvik and I came up with the idea of screwing a plug into the patient's head because there is no fat in the scalp and if you rigidly screw a titanium plug to the skull it doesn't move in relation to the skin. We literally had a plug coming out of the head that connected to the artificial heart within the chest and the external power cable leading to the batteries and controller was plugged into the head. It was very difficult and the Americans never ever used it because it was too intimidating. These patients literally had life on a battery. They had to change the batteries twice a day and plug into the mains overnight. A plug in the head made me the first real Doctor Frankenstein.

Once, my patient was out in Birmingham shopping, because he was totally transformed by the technology, and somebody thought the bag containing his controller and batteries was a camera bag with an expensive camera so the lad snatched his bag and ran away with it. Of course, the cable was connected to the plug in his head that the lad couldn't see because the patient's hair had grown back, so the cable pinged out of his head and the alarm went off to say, 'Power disconnected.' The lad dropped the bag, thinking he had been rumbled, and ran off and a little old lady picked it up and brought it back to the patient, plugged it back into his head, and the pump started again.

BIGSBY: In another case a man died because he didn't have a spare battery with him.
WESTABY: Yes.

BIGSBY: You seem to have repeatedly come up against administrators because you didn't always push things past them or the ethics committee.
WESTABY: I never did.

BIGSBY: But you did use a system which had already killed three people in America.
WESTABY: It had killed three people in America but the young woman that I put it into in the middle of the night, only three days after it had arrived, was dying of viral myocarditis and I put this temporary device in at two o'clock in the morning. We had to rescue her on the heart-lung machine and I put in the new device, a temporary device, and tided her over. But what we showed with that case was that if you have a viral infection of the heart – and people remarkably didn't know that in 1997 it was a virus, like influenza – it gets better. So, I supported the girl on the temporary artificial heart for a week and then her heart started to improve and we took the device out. But as happened on numerous occasions, with the mad, bad operations I used to do that nobody else had ever done before, I came out of the operating theatre first thing in the morning and had a message to go see the medical director and was threatened with the sack. Two weeks later I did it again with a different pump and, when I was threatened with the sack, that time I said, 'Look, I am telling you one thing. I am here to save people's lives. I will use the technology available to me and if you are not interested in me doing it here I will go back to the United States.'

BIGSBY: You have a particular animus about the publication of the death rates of surgeons, which you think has had a damaging effect on the profession.
WESTABY: We have proof that it has absolutely decimated the profession. This came after the Bristol children's heart scandal, which was a terrible business, and the surgeons in Bristol got struck off but they

weren't bad people. They just did not have insight and were attacked to make an example out of the medical profession and, in particular, arrogant surgeons who were not answerable to other people and were totally autonomous and crazy – as I have always been. So Bristol was a disaster, and then one of the ministers of health in the Labour government went to New York City and saw that in New York state they publish surgeons' death rates. That wasn't deliberate. A newspaper found that the information was being collected within the society. We have always collected outcome data but the minister of health decided, 'Let's do that with the surgeons in Britain.' Now, ask yourself who has the highest mortality rate? Good surgeons or bad surgeons? The answer is if you are the sort of surgeon that gets people better, accepts stuff from all over the country, accepts patients from abroad, does all the difficult stuff, you are going to have a substantial attrition rate because if you do all the difficult stuff then, by definition, they are the patients that don't make it. All the publishing of death rates did was make people defensive. Surgeons started to care about themselves and their reputations and their private practices, rather than the patients.

BIGSBY: And what has happened about the number of people therefore wanting to enter this specialism?
WESTABY: They have disappeared. Last year they could not fill the training slots, even with overseas trainees. If you look at the heart surgeons that do children's heart surgery in the UK now, only forty percent of them trained in a British university and that proportion is going down rapidly. The same is happening with adult heart surgery. I have trained surgeons from all over the world and am very proud of that. I have no racial biases at all. I have looked after everybody, but it is very difficult to find a heart surgeon in the UK now with an Anglo-Saxon name. There are an awful lot of Italians because Italy has got too many heart surgeons.

This is one area where we are going to have to hold on to the Europeans, I am afraid, because general medicine as a profession now is far less popular than it was and one reason for that is the old-fashioned respect for doctors disappeared. It started to disappear after the Bristol affair. One thing that I discovered was that risk aversion, preserving your reputation, means avoiding high-risk patients. Risk aversion is not a voluntary thing. A professor of heart surgery used to talk to me about it and she said, 'Nowadays, for the young guys, every time they go to an operating theatre it is as though they are defusing a bomb in Afghanistan,' and that's right. They have made surgery tense. What stress does is put up cortisol levels and high cortisol levels make you risk-averse. Cambridge University did a fantastic study of financial traders during times of market volatility. They found that in times of market volatility, when they wanted their financial traders to take risks, they wouldn't do it with high levels of cortisol. Then they infused cortisol into volunteers and got them to do tests on computers and proved that stress makes people risk-averse. So, it is not a voluntary thing. The [Royal] College of Surgeons tick-boxed the whole thing and said, 'anybody who has demonstrated that he or she is risk-averse should be referred to the GMC.' They haven't got a bloody clue and, of course, I let them know about that on more than one occasion.

BIGSBY: Thanks to the rugby accident. You fly everywhere, travel everywhere. You get speeding tickets as you rush to hospitals. That must have put an enormous stress on private life, but you did find love in an operating theatre over the open chest of a patient, did you not?
WESTABY: I did, yes.

BIGSBY: So the heart is connected to love after all?
WESTABY: This was in my total disinhibited madness when I was actually married at the time, which was very disgraceful, but I have been married to a very nice lady for well over thirty years and she was a sister in the accident department in Addenbrooke's and I was working with the famous Professor Calne. We were doing liver transplants and they were just starting heart transplants up the road in Papworth. It was an exciting time and I was one of those who spent all day, every day, and most nights, in the hospital because anything I could get to operate

on, I would operate on. I never left the hospital in case I missed something. I got to know a lot of the nurses in that hospital pretty damn well, but this particular nurse, who I married, was just an apparition. She was so drop-dead gorgeous. Her dad was a Battle of Britain Spitfire pilot. She had been brought up in Kenya and was a free spirit and she was a girl who stitched my head up on numerous occasions when I came in from the rugby matches on Saturday. But there was this time when I had played rugby on a Saturday, again coming up to Christmas, and I had made a lousy tackle and got a very bad fracture across my jaw. I knew that the surgeons would want to wire me up just before Christmas and I didn't want wiring up so I went to the bar with my fractured jaw and had a couple of pints. Then I went to A and E in my rugby kit and sat there and my future wife was the sister in charge. I had sat there for about twenty minutes and she rushed out and said, 'Look, we have just taken in a road traffic accident. A young man came off a motorbike and he is bleeding into his left chest, but all the chest surgeons are miles away in Papworth. We know you have done chest surgery at the Brompton. Can you do anything for him?' So I gowned and gloved on top of my rugby kit, with mud all over my knees, and I opened this guy's chest, spitting my own blood into the sink beside me. That kind of made me a legend in Cambridge coming up to Christmas but, yes, I fell for the very gorgeous accident and emergency sister, I am afraid.

WRITERS IN CONVERSATION
WITH CHRISTOPHER BIGSBY
VOLUME VII

International © 2018 retained by
individual authors.
Selection copyright © Christopher Bigsby.

This book is sold subject to the condition
that it shall not, by way of trade or otherwise,
be lent, resold, hired out, stored in a retrieval
system, or otherwise circulated without
the publisher's prior consent in any form of
binding or cover other than that in which it
is published and without a similar condition
including this condition being imposed on
the subsequent purchaser.

A CIP record for this book is available from
the British Library.

Writers in Conversation is typeset
in Haarlemmer.

Printed and bound in the UK
by Imprint Digital.
Proofread by Imogen Lees.
Typeset by Emily Benton.

Distributed by NBN International,
10 Thornbury Road Plymouth PL6 7PP
t. +44 (0)1752 2023102
e. cservs@nbninternational.com

ISBN: 978-1-911343-52-3

BOILER HOUSE PRESS

ISBN 978-1-911343-52-3